Teach Yourself VISUALLY™

PowerPoint® 2013

Visual

by William Wood

WILEY

John Wiley & Sons, Inc.

Teach Yourself VISUALLY™ PowerPoint® 2013

Published by
John Wiley & Sons, Inc.
10475 Crosspoint Boulevard
Indianapolis, IN 46256

www.wiley.com

Published simultaneously in Canada

Library of Congress Control Number: 2012956412

ISBN: 978-1-118-51042-1

Manufactured in the United States of America

10 9 8 7 6 5 4 3 2 1

Trademark Acknowledgments

Contact Us

For general information on our other products and services please contact our Customer Care Department within the U.S. at 877-762-2974, outside the U.S. at 317-572-3993 or fax 317-572-4002.

For technical support please visit www.wiley.com/techsupport.

WILEY **Sales** | Contact Wiley at (877) 762-2974 or fax (317) 572-4002.

Credits

Acquisitions Editor
Aaron Black

Project Editor
Jade L. Williams

Technical Editor
Vince Averello

Copy Editor
Marylouise Wiack

Editorial Director
Robyn Siesky

Business Manager
Amy Knies

Senior Marketing Manager
Sandy Smith

**Vice President and Executive
Group Publisher**
Richard Swadley

**Vice President and Executive
Publisher**
Barry Pruett

Project Coordinator
Patrick Redmond

Graphics and Production Specialists
Ana Carrillo
Andrea Hornberger
Jennifer Mayberry
Corrie Niehaus

Quality Control Technicians
John Greenough
Lauren Mandelbaum
Susan Moritz

Proofreading
Shannon Ramsey

Indexing
Potomac Indexing, LLC

About the Author

William (Bill) Wood is a consultant who teaches the Microsoft Office Suite and develops programs with the VBA language. As a part-time writer, he has written books and classroom workbooks about Microsoft Access, Excel, and PowerPoint. He has a formal education as a Biomedical Engineer, a field in which he has worked for many years. He also continues his education in graduate studies at Milwaukee School of Engineering and Medical College of Wisconsin in the field of Medical Informatics. Bill also works as a volunteer member of the National Ski Patrol.

Author's Acknowledgments

Thank you to the entire Wiley team for helping me complete another book — you are all very friendly and helpful. Special thanks go to Aaron Black and Jade Williams, who gave me their undivided attention when I needed it.

Thank you to Technical Editor Vince Averello for doing a thorough and detailed job. Thanks to Copy Editor Marylouise Wiack for being thorough. I write like an engineer and Marylouise gave my writing eloquence with her recommendations.

Special thanks to my sweetheart and wife, Shane, who kept things together while I took the time to write this book — it would have been difficult to do it without her help and support.

These people had a direct influence on this book, but thank you also to my friends who took an interest in this book and listened to me talk about it while I wrote it.

How to Use This Book

Who This Book Is For

This book is for the reader who has never used this particular technology or software application. It is also for readers who want to expand their knowledge.

The Conventions in This Book

① Steps

This book uses a step-by-step format to guide you easily through each task. **Numbered steps** are actions you must do; **bulleted steps** clarify a point, step, or optional feature; and **indented steps** give you the result.

② Notes

Notes give additional information — special conditions that may occur during an operation, a situation that you want to avoid, or a cross-reference to a related area of the book.

③ Icons and Buttons

Icons and buttons show you exactly what you need to click to perform a step.

④ Tips

Tips offer additional information, including warnings and shortcuts.

⑤ Bold

Bold type shows command names or options that you must click or text or numbers you must type.

⑥ Italics

Italic type introduces and defines a new term.

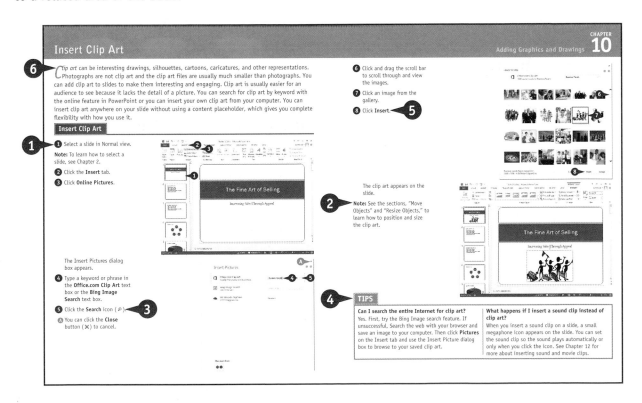

Table of Contents

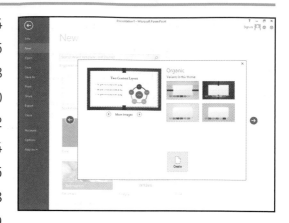

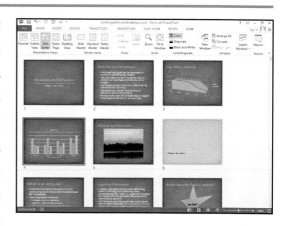

Chapter 3 — Changing PowerPoint Options

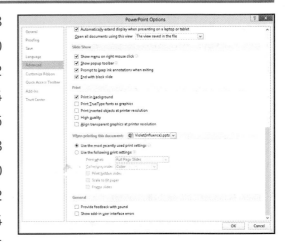

Chapter 4 — Writing and Formatting Text

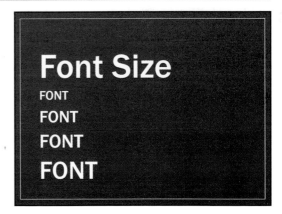

Table of Contents

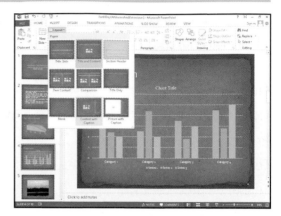

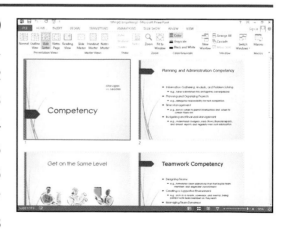

Chapter 7 Working with Outlines

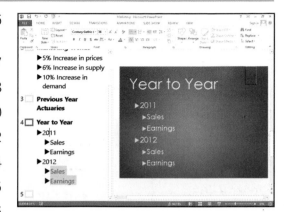

Chapter 8 Using Themes

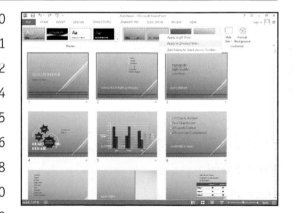

Table of Contents

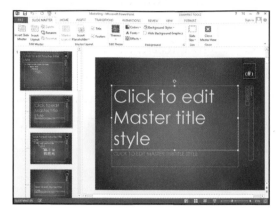

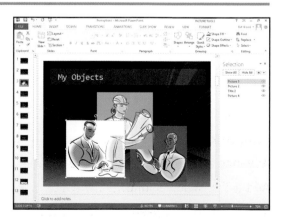

Chapter 11 Enhancing Slides with Action

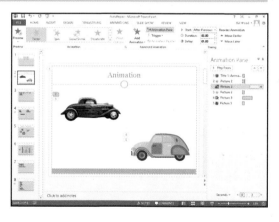

Table of Contents

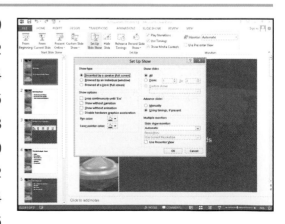

Chapter 14 — Printing Presentations

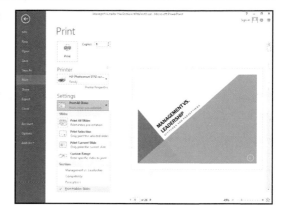

Chapter 15 — Presenting a Slide Show

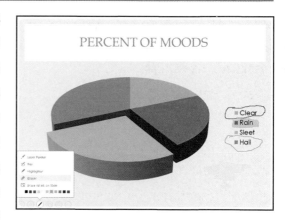

Table of Contents

Chapter 16   Publishing a Presentation

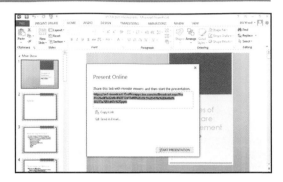

CHAPTER 1

Starting with PowerPoint Basics

Discover PowerPoint basics such as creating, saving, and closing a presentation. Each presentation you build exists in its own separate PowerPoint file. After showing you how to create a new presentation, this chapter teaches you how to find and open existing presentation files.

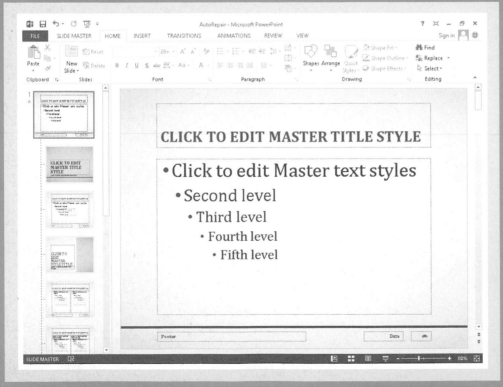

Introducing PowerPoint

With PowerPoint, you can create a professional-looking slide show. The PowerPoint program provides tools you can use to build presentations that include graphics, media, animations, and an assortment of ways to transition from slide to slide. It provides various views and user interfaces to suit your particular needs. These PowerPoint tools enable you to design and build a quality presentation. Many tasks start in Backstage view. To access this view, click the File tab on the ribbon.

Build an Outline

You can type text in outline form to build slides for your presentation. In the Outline view, an icon represents each slide, and each slide contains a slide title next to the icon. Second-level lines of text on the outline appear as bullet points on the slide. These bullets convey the main points you want to make about each topic.

5 **BUSINESS REVENUE**

6 **QUARTERLY SALES**
- 10 Clients Added
- 2 Clients Lost
- 20 Leads Called
- 5 Proposals Completed

Choose a Slide Design and Layout

A slide design applies preset design elements such as colors, background graphics, and text styles to a slide. A particular slide layout applied to a slide determines what type of information that slide includes. For example, a Title Slide layout has a title and subtitle. A Title and Content layout includes a title, plus a placeholder that holds a list of bullet points, a table, or other graphic elements.

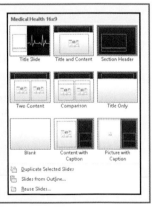

Add Content

You can add content such as text, charts, and pictures to the slide in the Slide pane of Normal view. You can also insert text boxes that enable you to add slide text that does not appear in the presentation outline.

Work with Masters

A set of slide designs and a slide theme combine to create a set of master slides. Masters enable you to add content that you want to appear in a particular location on slides. This saves you from having to add repeating content, such as your company logo, to each slide. For example, you can set up the master so an identical footer appears on every slide.

Organize Slides

After creating several slides, you may need to reorganize them to create the proper sequence for your presentation. You can reorder slides in Slide Sorter view. This view shows slide thumbnails that you can move, delete, duplicate, or hide. You can also perform these actions on the Slides Thumbnail pane in Normal view.

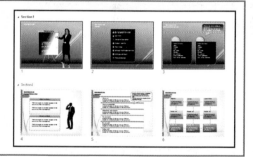

Set Up Your Show

You can add narration, animations, and transitions to your slides. You can record a narration that plays when you give your presentation. Use animation to move an element on-screen, such as a ball bouncing onto the screen. Transitions control how a new slide appears on-screen — for example, a slide can fade in over the previous slide.

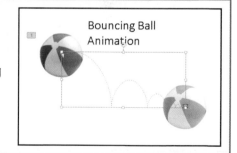

Run a Slide Show

After you add the content, choose slide designs, and add special effects, you are ready to run your slide show presentation. Tools appear on-screen during the slide show — they help you control your presentation and even enable you to make annotations on your slides as you present them. Presenter view shows your notes and provides a timer to ensure that your presentation is flawless.

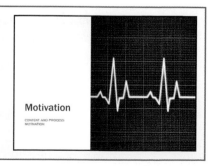

Start PowerPoint and Explore the Start Screen

You can start PowerPoint from the new Windows 8 Start screen so you can begin designing a presentation. When you open PowerPoint 2013, the redesigned start screen appears automatically. From the start screen, you can start a new presentation or open an existing one. The start screen lists recently opened presentations and allows you to create a presentation from templates on your computer, or search for PowerPoint templates on the Internet.

Start PowerPoint and Explore the Start Screen

1 Turn on your computer.

2 Press ⊞.

The Start screen appears.

3 Right-click the background on the Start screen.

The All apps button appears.

4 Click the **All apps** button.

6

All applications appear on the Start screen.

5 Position the mouse pointer (🔓) at the bottom of the Start screen.

Ⓐ A scroll bar appears.

6 Scroll across to find the PowerPoint 2013 icon.

7 Click the **PowerPoint 2013** icon.

PowerPoint opens and displays the start screen.

Ⓑ You can open a recently opened presentation.

Ⓒ You can open a file from your computer.

Ⓓ You can create a new presentation by clicking a template.

Ⓔ You can search for a template on the Internet.

TIP

Is there a quicker way to open PowerPoint?

1 Repeat Steps **1** to **6**.

2 Right-click **PowerPoint 2013**.

3 Click **Open file location**.

4 Click the **Home** tab.

5 Click **Copy** and the shortcut appears on your desktop.

Start a New Presentation

You can create a new presentation from the start screen when you start PowerPoint, or from the File tab on the ribbon *(also known as Backstage View)*. You can create a new presentation from scratch or by using a template. Creating a presentation from scratch allows you to design freely without preconceived notions, while working from a template saves time and promotes ideas by starting you off with a certain look and theme. You can find templates on your computer, as well as on the Internet for free or for a fee. Your computer needs an Internet connection to download online templates.

Start a New Presentation

1 Click the **File** tab to show Backstage view.

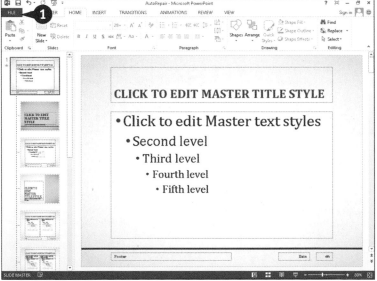

2 Click **New**.

Templates available on your computer appear.

Ⓐ You can choose a blank presentation.

Ⓑ You can click the **Pushpin** button (📌) to pin a template to this list (📌 changes to 📌).

3 Click the presentation template of your choice.

This example uses Organics.

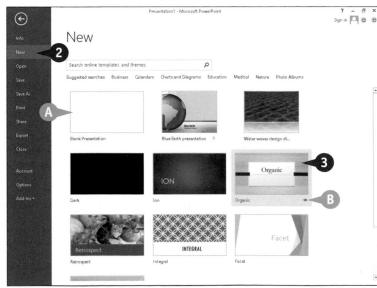

A dialog box appears, showing a preview of the template.

Ⓒ You can click the **Close** button (✖) to cancel.

Ⓓ You can click **Back** (◉) or **Forward** (◉) to view other slides from this template.

Ⓔ You can click **Back** (◉) or **Forward** (◉) to view other templates from the list.

④ Click a color scheme.

The preview changes to reflect your preferences.

⑤ Click **Create**.

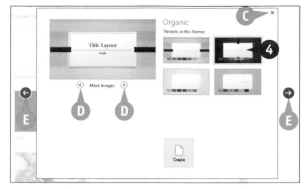

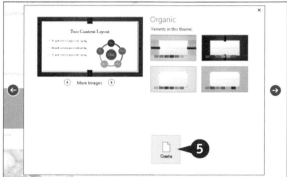

PowerPoint creates a presentation from the template.

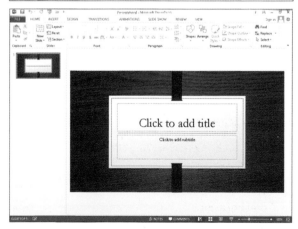

TIPS

Is there another way to create a blank presentation?

Yes. When you launch PowerPoint from the Windows 8 Start screen, the start screen has an option to create a blank template. Simply click the **Blank Presentation** option.

Can I get templates from the Internet?

Yes. You can find many templates online, a lot of them free. Click the **File** tab, and then click **New**. At the top of the screen, click the **Search online templates and themes** text box to start the process. A dialog box appears that allows you to search online.

Search for Templates Online

The larger your choice of PowerPoint templates, the greater the chance you will find one that suits your needs. Fortunately, there are literally thousands of PowerPoint templates available online. You can search for an online template by using the PowerPoint search feature, or an Internet search engine.

The PowerPoint search feature allows you to search by a keyword and shows you online presentation templates associated with that keyword. The search feature shows you a preview of the template and the name of who provided it, and then downloads the template for you! Remember to download only files from websites that you trust.

Search for Templates Online

1 Click the **File** tab to show Backstage view.

2 Click **New**.

Templates available on your computer appear.

A You can search by clicking one of the suggested searches.

3 Type a keyword in the search text box and click (⊙).

This example uses Sports.

4 Click **Search** (⊙).

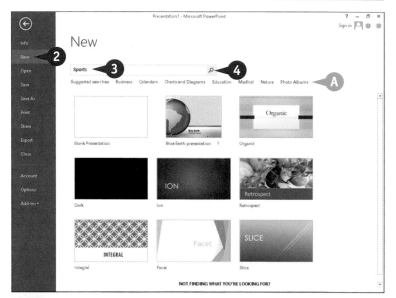

PowerPoint shows online templates that match the search text.

B Click the **Pushpin** button (＋) to pin a template to your list of templates (＋ changes to ＋).

5 Click the template of your choice.

A dialog box appears, showing a preview of the template.

C You can click **Back** (◉) or **Forward** (◉) to view other slides from this template.

D You can click **Back** (◉) or **Forward** (◉) to view other templates from the list.

E You can click the **Close** button (✖) to leave Backstage view.

6 Click **Create**.

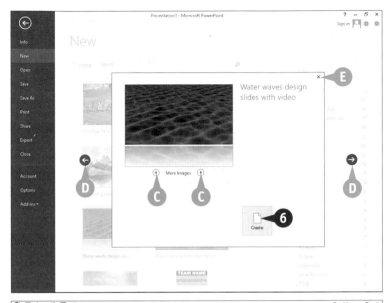

PowerPoint creates a presentation from the template.

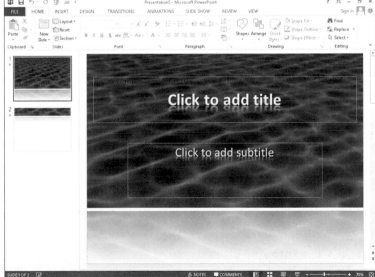

TIPS

Do templates come in different sizes?
Yes. Templates come in two slide sizes. The 16:9 aspect ratio is for widescreen, and the 4:3 aspect ratio is for conventional monitors. Your choice of template may require you to change the aspect ratio. See Chapter 6 to learn about changing aspect ratios.

I need more space to work. Can I hide the ribbon?
Yes. To hide the ribbon, simply double-click a tab and the ribbon disappears except for the tabs. Then click a tab and the ribbon appears temporarily so you can execute a command. Double-click a tab again to show the ribbon continuously.

Save a Presentation

After you create a presentation, you should save it for future use. You should also save the presentation often while working on it to avoid losing any changes. Saving a PowerPoint file works much like saving any other Microsoft Office program file: You need to specify the location in which to save the file and give the file a name. If you want to save a presentation that has previously been saved, you can click the Save icon in the upper-left corner of the PowerPoint window to quickly save it.

Save a Presentation

1 Click the **File** tab to show Backstage view.

2 Click **Save As**.

3 Click **Computer**.

4 Click **Browse**.

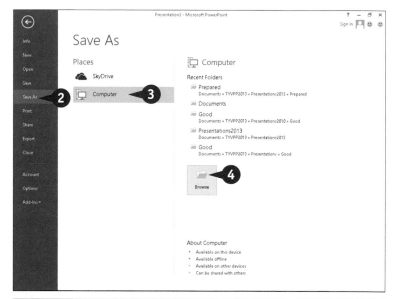

The Save As dialog box appears.

5 Click the folder where you want to save your file.

This example saves to My Documents.

6 Click in the **File name** text box to select the text and then type a filename.

A You can click and drag the scroll bar to find more folder locations.

B You can click **New folder** to create a new folder.

In this example, the filename is WaterWaves.

⑦ Click the **Save as Type** down arrow (⌄) to change the file type from the default.

Note: If you choose a format other than the default PowerPoint format, you may see a prompt about an issue such as version compatibility. Respond to the prompt to continue saving.

⑧ Click **Save**.

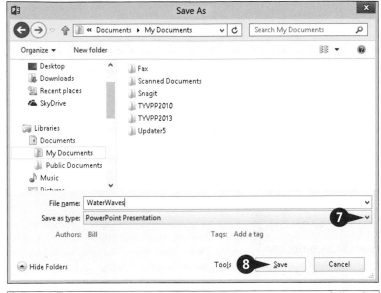

PowerPoint saves the presentation and the Save As dialog box closes.

⑥ The new filename appears in the title bar.

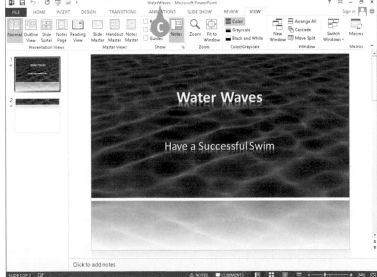

TIPS

I save presentations in a specific folder all the time. Is there a quick way to locate that folder in the Save As dialog box?

Yes. You can make your favorite folder the default local file location in the PowerPoint Options dialog box. When you perform a save, your favorite folder is the default location in the Save As dialog box. See Chapter 3 to learn how to change PowerPoint options.

Must I always use the Save As dialog box?

No. You can click the **Save** icon (💾) on the Quick Access Toolbar or press Ctrl+S. To save a copy of your presentation under a new name, click the **File** tab, click **Save As**, and then specify a new filename and save location.

Find a Presentation

Sometimes you want to open a presentation file but you forget what you named it or you forget which folder contains it. Finding that file is very important because you need it not only to design the presentation, but also to present the slide show. If it is not on the Recent Presentations list in Backstage view and browsing for it is unsuccessful, you can use the PowerPoint search feature to locate the file. You can also use the search feature on the Windows 8 Start screen to locate it.

Find a Presentation

Use the Open Dialog Box

1 Click the **File** tab to show Backstage view.

2 Click **Open**.

3 Click **Computer**.

4 Click **Browse**.

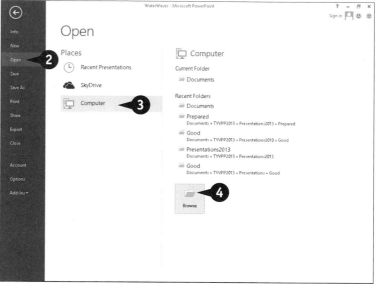

5 Click the parent folder that you think may hold the file, even if you think it is in a subfolder.

6 Type a keyword in the search text box.

Note: PowerPoint searches filenames and file contents.

This example searches for Water.

As you type, the Open dialog box shows files containing the keyword.

7 If PowerPoint finds your file, click it.

8 Click **Open**

The file opens.

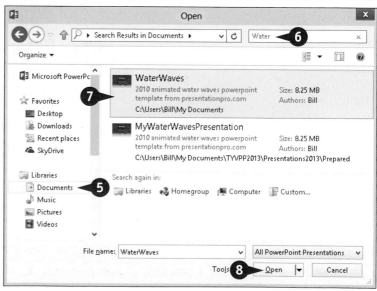

Use the Windows 8 Start Screen

1 Press ⊞ + F.

The Search screen appears.

2 Type a keyword in the text box.

3 Click the **Search** icon ( ).

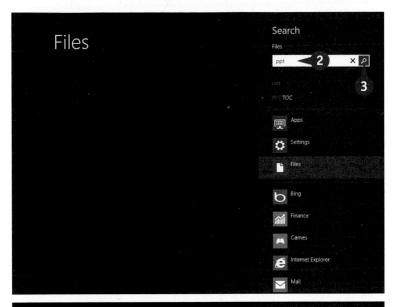

Files that contain the keyword appear in the search results.

4 If PowerPoint finds your file, click it.

A You can position your mouse pointer ( ) over the file to see details about the file.

The file opens.

TIP

I remember the date I last saved my presentation, but nothing else. How can I find it?

Repeat Steps **1** to **4** to start the search in the Open dialog box and click the search textbox. The textbox becomes a drop-down list, and on the bottom are two choices under Add a search filter. The two choices are Date modified and Size. If you click Date modified, a calendar appears — click a date on the calendar and you will see only files modified on that date. If you click Size, a list appears with ranges of file sizes — click one of the ranges to see only files of that particular file size.

Open an Existing Presentation

After you save and close a presentation, you must find it and open it the next time you want to use it — you need to open it to design it as well as to present the slide show. You can locate your presentation by using the Open dialog box to browse your computer for it. If you used the presentation recently, the quickest way to open it is to find it in the Recent Presentations list in Backstage view.

Open an Existing Presentation

1 Click the **File** tab to show Backstage view.

2 Click **Open**.

3 Click **Recent Presentations**.

The Recent Presentations list appears.

A You can click the **Pushpin** (📌) to pin a presentation to the list (📌 changes to 📌).

4 If you find your presentation on the list, click it and PowerPoint opens it.

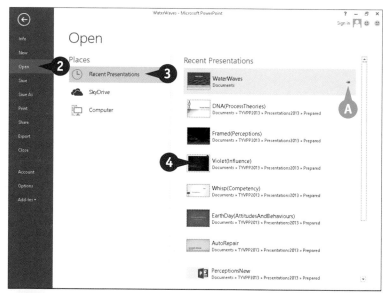

5 If your presentation is not on the Recent Presentations list, Click **Computer**.

B If you find your folder location in the Recent Folders, you can click it there.

6 Click **Browse**.

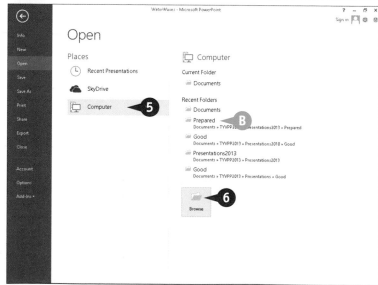

The Open dialog box appears.

7 Click the folder that contains the presentation file you want to open.

This example selects Documents.

8 Click the filename.

This example selects WaterWaves.

9 Click **Open**.

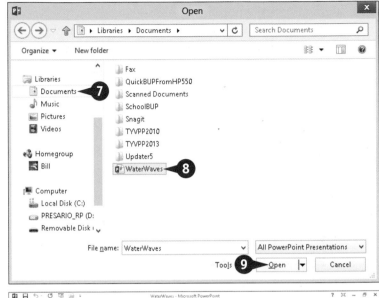

PowerPoint opens the presentation.

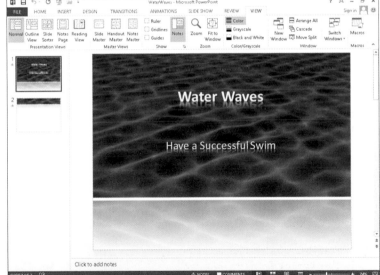

Is there a way to keep my presentation on the Recent Presentations list?

Yes. To pin a presentation to the Recent Presentations list, position the mouse pointer (⟨⟩) over a presentation on the Recent Presentations list and then click the **Pushpin** to the right of the name (⤴ changes to ⬆). To unpin a presentation, click **Unpin** (⬆).

Is there a command for exiting PowerPoint?

No. The PowerPoint application automatically exits when you close your last presentation. If you want to close PowerPoint directly, click the **Close** button (✖) in the upper-right corner of the PowerPoint window.

Close a Presentation

When you finish working with a presentation, you can close it. Closing the presentation gives you a less cluttered workspace on your computer and frees valuable computer memory to process other work that you need to do. If you share the file with others on a network, closing it allows them to access the file without worrying about sharing violations.

When you close a file with unsaved changes, PowerPoint prompts you to save the presentation to avoid accidentally losing your work. For more on saving a presentation, see the section, "Save a Presentation," in this chapter.

Close a Presentation

1 Click the **Close** button (✖).

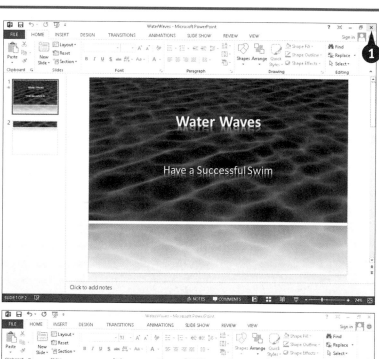

A message may appear, asking if you want to save changes.

2 Click **Save**.

Ⓐ If you do not want to save the changes to your presentation, click **Don't Save**.

Ⓑ To abort closing the presentation, click **Cancel**.

The file closes, but PowerPoint remains open.

Note: You can also close the presentation by pressing **Alt**+**F4**.

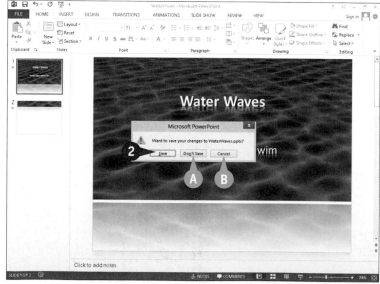

Delete a Presentation

Occasionally you will come across an old file while browsing for a presentation to open. This file may have out-of-date information or may be an unneeded backup copy. You can conveniently delete the file from the Open dialog box.

Deleting old files frees up space on your hard drive. However, you should make sure that the file is backed up somewhere in case you need it in the future.

Delete a Presentation

1 Click the **File** tab to show Backstage view.

2 Click **Open**.

3 Click **Computer**.

4 Click **Browse**.

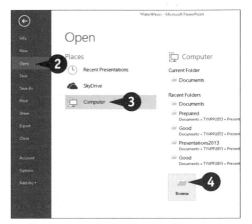

The Open dialog box appears.

5 Right-click the file you want to delete.

This example deletes WaterWaves.

The submenu appears.

6 Click **Delete**.

The Delete File dialog box appears.

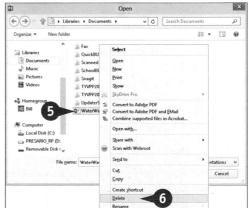

7 Click **Yes**.

PowerPoint deletes the file and puts it in the Recycle Bin.

Note: You also can browse files from Windows Explorer and delete any file.

CHAPTER 2

Navigating PowerPoint

Discover PowerPoint basics such as working in different views and navigating through PowerPoint. Knowing how to navigate through an application can save time, avoid frustration, and help you build a quality presentation. In this chapter, you learn the elements in the PowerPoint screen, and how to get help when you need it.

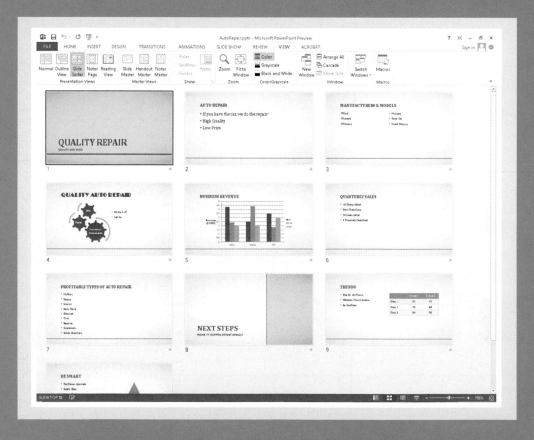

Explore Normal View

PowerPoint offers several views that you can use to work on different aspects of your presentation. Having different views is important because certain views are better for performing certain tasks. For example, arranging slides is easiest in Slide Sorter view.

You will usually work in Normal view, where you can create, position, and format objects on each slide. In Outline view, you can enter presentation text in outline form and the text automatically appears on the slide.

Ⓐ Navigation Buttons

You can change views using the command buttons on the View tab of the ribbon, or using the command buttons on the status bar. These buttons include *Normal view* (▤), *Slide Sorter view* (▦), *Slide Show view* (▤), and *Reading view* (▥).

Ⓑ Slides Thumbnail Pane

The Slides Thumbnail pane contains thumbnails of each slide. The thumbnails are numbered by the order in which they appear in the slide show. You can click and drag the thumbnails to change the order of slides and you can delete slides from this pane.

Ⓒ Slide Pane

The Slide pane is the largest pane in Normal view and shows a slide and all its contents. Here you can create and manipulate slide objects such as graphics and animations, and type text directly on to the slide.

Ⓓ Notes Pane

The Notes pane appears below the Slide pane. You can enter speaker notes associated with each individual slide into this pane. You can then refer to these notes while presenting a slide show without your audience seeing them.

Navigate PowerPoint Views

In addition to Normal view, you can use Slide Sorter view to organize slides, Notes Page view to create detailed speaker notes, and Slide Show view or Reading view to display your presentation. Each view has certain tasks that are easier to perform in that particular view.

Outline View

Outline view has a pane that enables you to enter text into your slides in a familiar outline format. In this view, the Outline pane replaces the Slides Thumbnail pane. Top-level headings in the outline are slide titles, and entries at the second level appear as bullet points. The outline is a great reference if you need to write a paper to accompany your presentation.

Slide Sorter View

Slide Sorter view is the best view to change the order of slides, delete slides, or duplicate slides. In Slide Sorter view, you can click and drag a slide to move it. If you double-click a slide, PowerPoint changes to Normal view and displays that slide in the Slide pane.

Reading View

You can click Slide Show view (🖵) to present your show. Slides appear one at a time at full screen size. Reading view (📖) is very similar to Slide Show view, but gives you more navigation flexibility because the status bar remains at the bottom of the screen. To exit either view, press Esc.

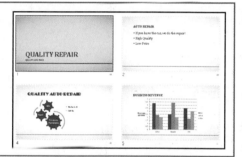

Notes Page View

In Notes Page view, you can display each slide and the associated speaker notes as one full page. You can also type notes on the page while viewing your slide — this is the most convenient view for typing presentation notes. From the View tab, click Notes Page to work with this view.

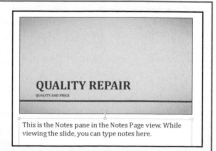

Work with Ribbon Groups, Commands, and Galleries

Y ou can find all the commands that you need to design and present your slide show on the ribbon. The *ribbon* is the user interface at the top of the PowerPoint window. Commands are necessary to design your presentation, and knowing their location allows you to find them quickly so you can work efficiently.

Related commands are grouped on the ribbon tabs. Commands are further arranged into groups on the tab, with the group names shown at the bottom of the group. Some command buttons include down arrows that display menus or galleries of commands when you click them.

Work with Ribbon Groups, Commands, and Galleries

1 Click any tab on the ribbon.

This example selects the View tab.

The commands for the particular tab you clicked appear on the ribbon.

2 Click the button or check box for any command.

This example selects Macro.

The Macro dialog box appears.

3 Click **Cancel** to cancel the command.

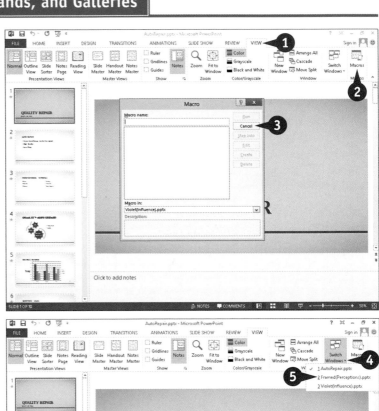

4 Click the down arrow (▼) next to any button to display a gallery.

Note: Clicking a down arrow (▼) displays a menu or menu.

5 Click the desired choice from the menu or gallery that appears.

6 Click a **dialog box launcher** (⌟).

Note: A dialog box launcher (⌟) displays a dialog box when you click it.

In this example, the Grid and Guides dialog box appears.

7 Click **OK** to accept any selections you have made in the dialog box.

The presentation reflects any changes you made.

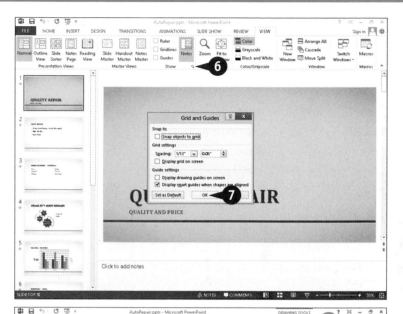

Ⓐ For some ribbon commands, such as those on a contextual tab, you must first select an object on the slide before choosing a command.

Ⓑ Note that the Drawing Tools Format tab does not appear until you click an object like a text box.

TIPS

How do I learn what a particular ribbon button does?
Position the mouse pointer (⌖) over the button, and a ScreenTip describing the button appears. You see ScreenTip that lists the button name, any available shortcut key, and a brief description of the button. By default, ScreenTip features are enabled, but you can disable them in the PowerPoint Options dialog box (described in Chapter 3).

What happens if I click the main part of a ribbon button that has a down arrow on it?
If the sole purpose of the button is to open a gallery or menu, PowerPoint does that. If the main part of the button executes a command, PowerPoint applies that command using either the settings you last used or the most commonly used settings for that command.

Arrange Presentation Windows

Sometimes you need to view multiple presentations on-screen at once — for example, when you want to compare their contents or copy a slide from one presentation to another. You can arrange PowerPoint in such a way that you can see multiple open presentations at the same time. This handy feature is found on the View tab.

You should limit the number of open presentations to three or four. Otherwise, you cannot see enough of each presentation to make this feature useful.

Arrange Presentation Windows

1 Open two or more presentations.

2 Click the **View** tab.

3 Click **Cascade** ( ).

The presentation windows move so they overlap.

Ⓐ You can click **Switch Windows** and then click a presentation in the menu to make that presentation active.

4 Click **Arrange All** ( ).

The presentation windows appear side by side.

Ⓑ You can drag a window's title bar to move the window.

5 Click the **Maximize** button ( ) on one of the windows.

The window appears full screen again.

Find and Use KeyTips

You can use the KeyTips feature to employ keyboard shortcuts to select and execute ribbon commands. You may be more comfortable using your keyboard instead of your mouse or touchpad. For example, you may use a notebook computer with a finicky touchpad. Alternatively, you may have your mouse pointer set up to go fast, which makes it hard to point at something with pinpoint accuracy. KeyTips allows you to run commands quickly without using the mouse or touchpad, making you more proficient in your presentation work.

Find and Use KeyTips

1 Press **Alt**.

A The KeyTips (shortcut keys) for the ribbon tabs and Quick Access Toolbar appear in boxes beside the ribbon tabs.

2 Press the shortcut key for the tab you want to use.

This example presses **S** to display the Slide Show tab.

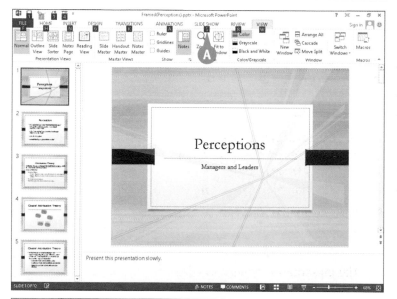

The Slide Show tab appears with KeyTips displayed next to the commands.

Note: To abort using KeyTips, press **Esc**.

3 Press the shortcut key for the command you want to execute.

The command executes, or a menu, gallery, or dialog box appears so you can finish choosing commands.

B This example presses **V** (☑ changes to ☐).

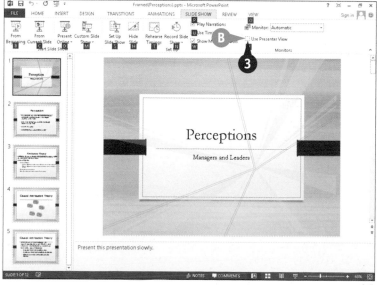

Using the Quick Access Toolbar

The *Quick Access Toolbar* appears above the File tab at the top of the PowerPoint application window. For your convenience, it contains command buttons for the most commonly used PowerPoint commands.

You can click the command buttons on the Quick Access Toolbar to execute these commands quickly. You can also easily add (or remove) some of these commonly used commands to (or from) the Quick Access Toolbar. You can even add your personal favorite commands to it.

Using the Quick Access Toolbar

1 Click the desired button on the Quick Access Toolbar.

PowerPoint executes the command.

Note: Finish executing the command if any menu or dialog box appears.

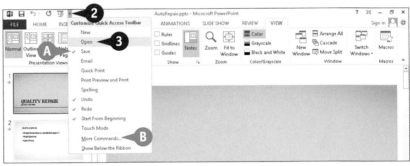

2 Click the down arrow (⤓) on the right side of the Quick Access Toolbar to access the menu.

A Note the check mark (✓) appearing next to commands on the Quick Access Toolbar.

B Click **More Commands** to see all available commands (see Chapter 3 for more information).

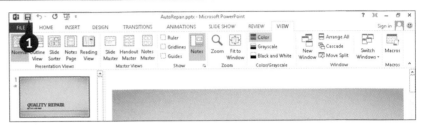

3 Click one of the commands from the menu list.

C The selected command appears as an icon on the Quick Access Toolbar and a check mark (✓) appears next to it in the menu.

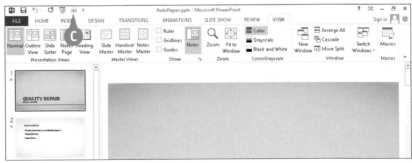

Resize the Notes Pane

It is often handy to have notes associated with slides. You may want to refer to notes while designing a slide or during a slide show presentation. You can enter notes into the Notes pane, which appears under the Slide pane in Normal view. Notes entered into the Notes pane are automatically displayed in Presenter view during a slide show presentation, but your audience cannot see the notes. (See Chapter 15 for more information on Presenter view.) You can resize the Notes pane to make it easier to enter and read the notes.

Resize the Notes Pane

① Click the **View** tab.

② Click **Notes**.

Ⓐ The Notes pane appears.

③ Position the mouse pointer ( ) over the pane divider until the mouse splitter pointer (↕) appears.

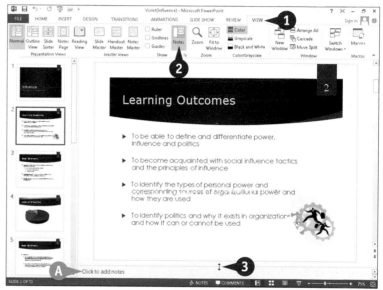

④ Click and drag upward.

The Notes pane resizes and the slide automatically resizes in the Slide pane to compensate.

⑤ Click **Notes** to hide the Notes pane.

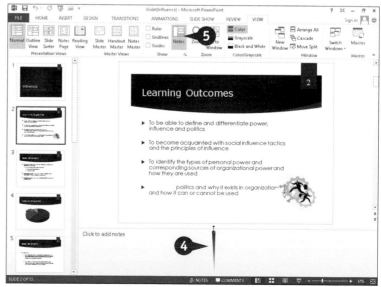

Zoom to Full Screen

There are times when you need maximum space to work on your presentation. For instance, while moving slides in Slide Sorter view, a little more space may allow you to see more slides or allow you to make the slides bigger so you can see them more clearly. You can zoom to full screen in design mode to take advantage of every little bit of space. When you zoom to full screen, the space occupied by the ribbon, status bar, and other elements is used to view the slides. You can zoom to full screen in any view.

Zoom to Full Screen

Hide the Ribbon

1. Click the **View** tab.

2. Click **Slide Sorter**.

   Slide Sorter view appears.

3. Click the **Ribbon Display Options** button (□) in the upper-right corner of the PowerPoint window.

4. Click **Auto-hide Ribbon**.

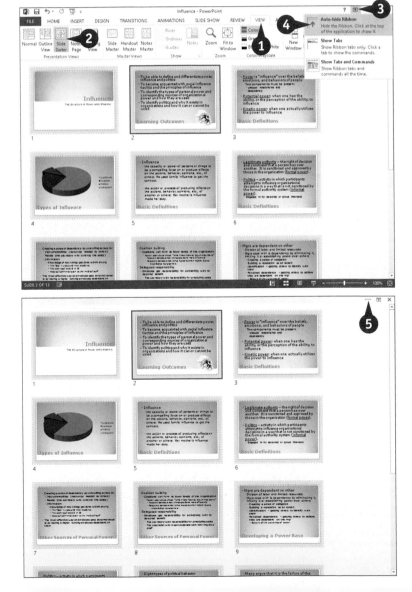

Slide Sorter view zooms to the entire screen.

5. Click the **Ellipsis** button (•••) in the upper-right corner of the screen.

The ribbon appears. You can now access the ribbon commands. The ribbon disappears after executing a command or clicking a slide. Repeat Step **5** each time you want to execute a command.

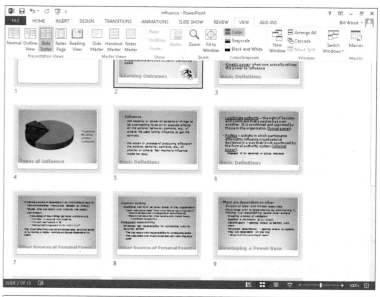

View the Ribbon Continuously

1 Click the **Ribbon Display Options** button (◻).

2 Click **Show Tabs and Commands**.

PowerPoint returns to the window view.

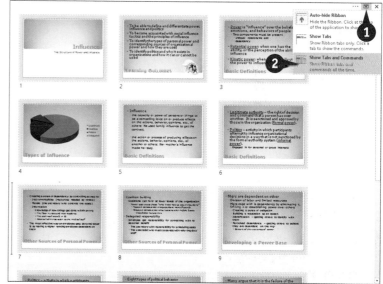

TIPS

I need more space to work, but I want to use the Quick Access Toolbar. Can I hide the ribbon?

Yes. To hide the ribbon, simply double-click a tab and the ribbon disappears except for the tabs. Click a tab and the ribbon appears temporarily so you can execute a command. Double-click a tab again to show the tab continuously.

Is there an advantage to using the Full Screen feature over using Reading view?

Yes. You cannot design the presentation in Reading view, so if you want to work on your presentation, use the Full Screen feature. If you want to quickly view the slide show and then quickly come back to design mode, use Reading view.

Navigate Slides

Slide show presentations generally contain many slides. As a result, PowerPoint provides different ways to navigate the slides so that you can choose one that is most efficient and effective for what you are doing. The way you work on your project determines the way you choose to navigate. You can use the various scroll bar buttons to navigate slides in Normal view, click a slide in the Slides Thumbnail pane to select a slide, or view slide thumbnails in Slide Sorter view.

Navigate Slides

Navigate Using the Scroll Bar

1 Click the **View** tab.

2 Click **Normal**.

3 Click and drag the scroll bar to scroll through slides.

4 Click the **Next Slide** button (⩒) to display the next slide.

5 Click the **Previous Slide** button (⩓) to display the previous slide.

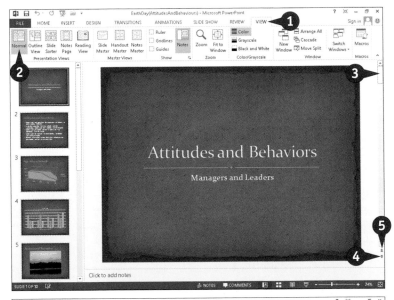

Navigate Using the Slide Thumbnail Pane

1 Click and drag the scroll bar to move through the slides.

2 Click a slide thumbnail.

   The selected slide appears in the Slide pane.

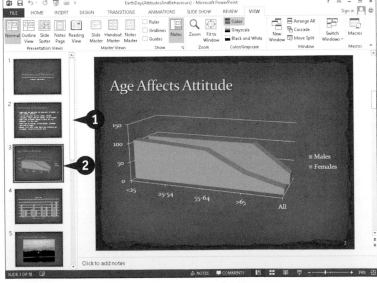

Navigate Using the Outline View

1 Click **Outline View**.

2 Click and drag the scroll bar to move through the slides.

3 Click a slide icon (⬜).

The selected slide appears in the Slide pane.

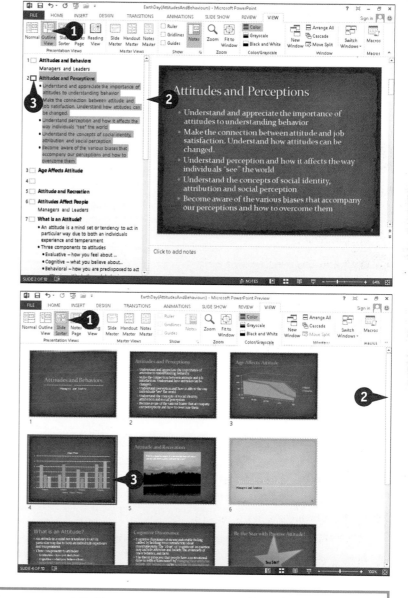

Navigate in Slide Sorter View

1 Click **Slide Sorter**.

Slide Sorter view appears.

2 Click and drag the scroll bar to move through the slides.

3 Click a slide.

PowerPoint selects the slide.

Note: Double-click a slide to view it in Normal view.

TIPS

Why are there no scroll bars in the Slide Thumbnails or Outline View panes?

If PowerPoint can display all slides in the presentation without scrolling down or up, it does not display a scroll bar. The fact that there is not a scroll bar means you are viewing all of the slides in the presentation.

Is there a way to see more slides in Slide Sorter view so I can easily find the one I want to view?

Yes. You can click and drag the Zoom slider in the lower-right corner of the PowerPoint window to make the slides smaller, which shows more slides. You can also click the **Zoom In** (➕) or **Zoom Out** (➖) buttons at each end of the slider.

Using Help

Microsoft Office PowerPoint Help offers two ways to get help. If you are connected to the Internet, it provides help from Microsoft Office Online. If an Internet connection is not available, PowerPoint uses Help files installed on your computer. PowerPoint also allows you to select between searching online and searching on your computer manually. You can find answers to your questions by selecting from a list of popular searches or by searching using keywords. The keyword searches are very similar, whether online or on your computer.

Using Help

1 Click the **Help** button (**?**).

The PowerPoint Help window appears.

2 Type a keyword in the search text box.

A Optionally, you can click in the Popular Searches list.

3 Click the **Search** button (🔍).

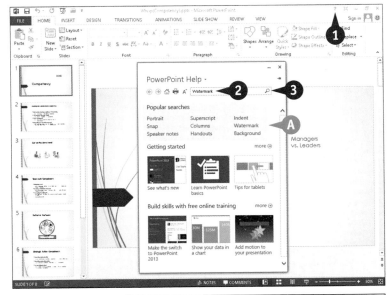

PowerPoint shows a list of online articles.

4 Click the **Home** button (⌂).

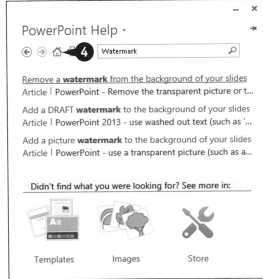

The Help home page appears.

Ⓑ You can click a graphic to show a help article for that topic.

5 Click the **PowerPoint Help** down arrow (▼).

The drop box opens.

6 Click **PowerPoint Help from your computer**.

The Basic Help home page appears.

Ⓒ Click **Back** (⊝) and **Forward** (⊛) to navigate back and forth.

Ⓓ Click **Print** (🖶) to print information.

Ⓔ Click **Use Large Text** (A˙) to increase font size.

7 Type a keyword in the search text box.

8 Click the **Search** button (🔎).

PowerPoint displays ribbon commands associated with the keyword you typed.

9 Click an item to display detailed information about that item.

10 Click **Next** to see more results.

11 Click the **Close** button (✖) to exit Help.

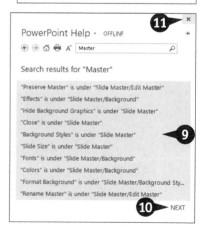

TIP

Is there a fast and easy way to open the Microsoft Office.com Help page from PowerPoint?

Yes. Click **more (Ⓐ)** after executing a search and PowerPoint launches your Internet browser and opens the Microsoft Office.com Help web page. From here, you can click various topics for help. You can even get a training video for PowerPoint 2013 for free!

CHAPTER 3

Changing PowerPoint Options

PowerPoint is a powerful tool that becomes even more powerful when you customize it the way you want it to perform. You can adjust various settings to personalize PowerPoint, so you can use it more efficiently and effectively.

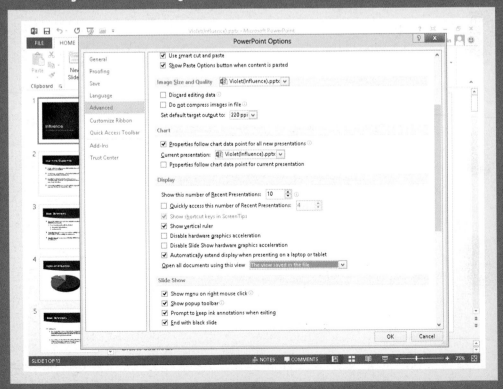

Introducing PowerPoint Options

PowerPoint provides a wide variety of option settings that enable you to customize how it performs. The options are grouped on tabs in the PowerPoint Options dialog box, and then further grouped into categories. You can change these settings to control the behavior of certain features in PowerPoint, and optimize less noticeable settings such as the default save location. Settings that are more visible include customizing the Quick Access Toolbar and the ribbon so that your favorite and most commonly used commands are at your fingertips. Changing PowerPoint options allows you to design presentations as effectively and efficiently as possible.

General Options

In the General options, you can enable or disable the Mini Toolbar and Live Preview. The *Mini Toolbar* is a floating contextual toolbar that gives you quick access to formatting commands when you select text. *Live Preview* shows how a feature affects your slide when you position the mouse pointer (⍌) over a choice in a gallery. You can enable or disable *ScreenTips*, which is the feature that gives you pop-up descriptions of command buttons when you position the mouse pointer (⍌) over a command button on the ribbon. You can also change the username, which appears in the properties of presentations.

Proofing Options

The Proofing tab affects the way that Microsoft Office checks for spelling and grammar errors in PowerPoint. Changes to these settings also affect the settings in the other Microsoft Office programs. You can add words to the custom dictionary and make exceptions to spelling rules. You can customize the powerful AutoCorrect and AutoFormat tools. While you type, *AutoCorrect* detects possible spelling errors and *AutoFormat* adjusts formatting to the surrounding formatting. You can control settings such as whether PowerPoint automatically capitalizes the first words of sentences and whether it checks the spelling of words that are in all uppercase.

Save Options

You can adjust the way PowerPoint saves presentations with the Save options. This tab controls the default file location for saving documents, and allows you to choose the default file format. *AutoRecovery* automatically saves your PowerPoint presentation at regular intervals so that if PowerPoint unexpectedly closes, it can recover your work. You can disable AutoRecovery or adjust how often AutoRecovery automatically saves presentations. You can even save the fonts you use in your presentation so you can guarantee that the presentation looks good even on a computer that does not recognize the fonts you use.

Language Options

The Language tab allows you to choose the language used for the ribbon, tabs, ScreenTips, and Help. You can include additional editing languages, which affect dictionaries, grammar checking, and sorting. This is useful if you use languages other than English in your presentations, such as when your organization has divisions or departments overseas. If you use languages other than English, setting up and using these options can make your experience with PowerPoint 2013 a delightful one.

Advanced Options

Advanced options allow you to customize settings for printing, some editing, and slide show features. Some settings, such as print options, only apply to individual PowerPoint presentations. Advanced options control what you see on the screen during slide show presentations. For example, you can control whether you see the pop-up toolbar during presentations. The *slide show pop-up toolbar* allows you to perform various tasks during a slide show presentation. Cut, copy, and paste options and display options are also found here.

Ribbon and Quick Access Toolbar Options

Although you can add a limited number of commands to the Quick Access Toolbar from the toolbar itself, you can add any command to it from the Quick Access Toolbar tab in the Options dialog box. Along with being able to add commands to the ribbon, you can also add tabs, add groups, and rename existing tabs and groups. An excellent use of this feature is to create a ribbon tab with your most commonly used commands so they are at your fingertips on a single tab, thereby making design work efficient and effective.

Add-ins

Add-ins are small chunks of programming that enhance the functionality of PowerPoint. Add-ins can be developed specifically for PowerPoint, or can be Component Object Model (COM) add-ins that enable you to use the functionality of another program in PowerPoint, such as a PDF writer or screen-capture program. You can get add-ins that give you special tools to design presentations or that add special functionality to your slide shows. Add-ins are available through third parties, or you can create them if you have programming experience.

Trust Center

In the *Trust Center*, you can read the Microsoft privacy statements and learn about security. Malicious programs can be attached to documents in various ways. You can customize settings to control the behavior of safeguards used against these threats. If you open only presentations that you trust, you can minimize security so there is no need to respond to security messages. If you open presentations of unknown origin, you can heighten the security so that malicious programs cannot affect your computer through a PowerPoint presentation.

Modify General Options

PowerPoint provides a wide variety of options that enable you to customize how it works. Options for features such as Live Preview, ScreenTips, and the Mini Toolbar are found in General options. These settings determine whether you see the Start screen when you open PowerPoint and which file extensions PowerPoint will open. You can also change the username, which PowerPoint records in the properties of each presentation to identify who creates it. You can change these options in the General tab of the PowerPoint Options dialog box.

Modify General Options

1 Click the **File** tab to show Backstage view.

2 Click **Options**.

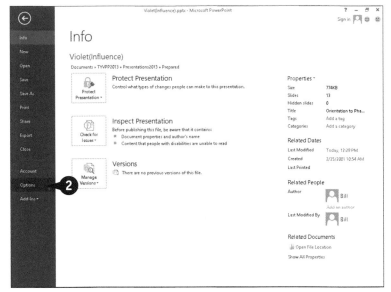

The PowerPoint Options dialog box appears.

3 Click **General**.

4 Click to enable (☑) or disable (☐) options under the User Interface options heading.

Ⓐ You can position your mouse pointer (🔍) over the Information icon (ⓘ) to see a brief description of an option.

Ⓑ You can click the **Office Background** down arrow (▾) and select a color scheme for the PowerPoint window.

Ⓒ You can click the **ScreenTip style** down arrow (▾) and select a ScreenTip style to display when you position the mouse pointer (🔍) over a command.

5 Click **Default Programs**.

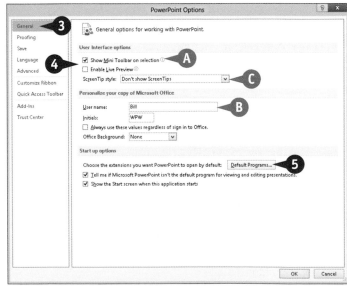

The Set Program Associations dialog box appears.

6 Click to enable (☑) or disable (☐) files whose extensions you want PowerPoint to open by default.

7 Click **Save**.

PowerPoint saves your changes and the dialog box closes.

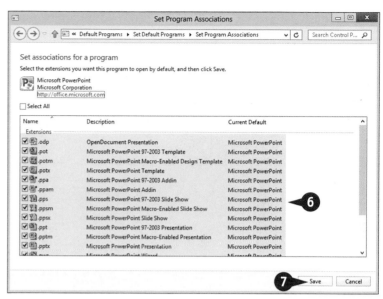

8 Type your username and Initials in the text boxes.

9 Click **Show the Start screen when this application starts** (☑ changes to ☐) to disable the Start screen page when PowerPoint starts.

10 Click **OK**.

PowerPoint applies your new settings and closes the PowerPoint Options dialog box.

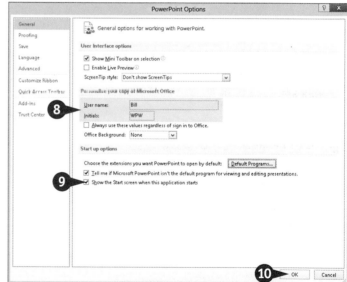

TIP

What is the Mini Toolbar?

The Mini Toolbar is a floating, contextual formatting toolbar that appears when you right-click an object to use the submenu. The Mini Toolbar contains the most commonly used formatting commands for the object that you select. For example, it shows the formatting commands from the Font group of the Home tab when you select text. If you enable the Mini Toolbar in the General options, the Mini Toolbar automatically appears when you click and drag across text in a placeholder.

Change Spelling Options

Misspellings in presentations are never good. The powerful spell-checker in Microsoft Office automatically and continually checks spelling in PowerPoint as you type. The spell-checker identifies possible misspellings by underlining them with a red, wavy line. To review a word, you can simply right-click it. You can use this tool to check spelling as you type text, or you can disable the tool. When you need to check spelling, you can always use the spell-checker manually. You can customize how the spell-checker handles possible misspellings in the PowerPoint Options.

Change Spelling Options

1 Click the **File** tab to show Backstage view.

2 Click **Options**.

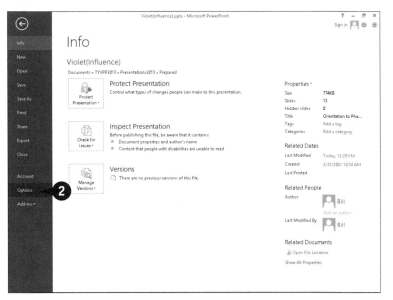

The PowerPoint Options dialog box appears.

3 Click **Proofing**.

4 Click to enable (☑) or disable (☐) options that determine how spell-checker flags certain errors.

Note: Changes that you make here also affect the spell-checker in the other Microsoft Office programs.

5 Click **Custom Dictionaries.**

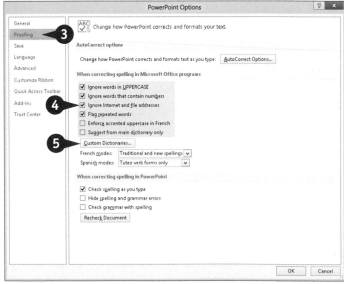

PowerPoint displays the Custom Dictionaries dialog box. PowerPoint automatically creates a custom dictionary (CUSTOM.DIC) when you add words during a spelling check. You can manually add words to your custom dictionary.

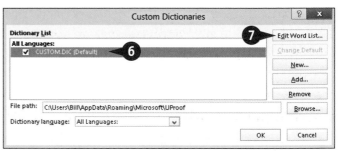

6 Click **CUSTOM.DIC** from the list so it is checked (☑).

7 Click **Edit Word List**.

The CUSTOM.DIC dialog box appears.

8 Type the desired word in the **Word(s):** text box.

9 Click **Add**.

PowerPoint adds the word to the Dictionary list.

10 Click **OK**.

The CUSTOM.DIC dialog box closes.

11 Click to enable (☑) or disable (☐) spell-checker options in PowerPoint.

A If you disable the **Check spelling as you type** option, you can run the spell-checker manually by clicking the **Spelling** command on the Review tab of the ribbon.

12 Click **OK**.

PowerPoint applies your new settings and closes the PowerPoint Options dialog box.

TIP

Can I delete words from the custom dictionary?

Yes. You can delete words from the custom dictionary by following these steps:

1 Follow Steps **1** to **7** in this section.

2 Click the word you want to delete.

3 Click **Delete**.

4 Click **OK** in each of the three open dialog boxes.

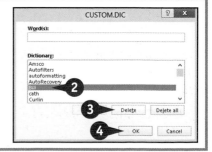

Change AutoCorrect Settings

The AutoCorrect feature automatically corrects common typing and spelling errors as you type. You can add words to a list of common misspellings, empowering AutoCorrect to automatically correct words that you routinely misspell. For example, you can tell it to change "actoin" to the word "action" automatically. You can also delete corrections that already exist on the list. For example, you can delete the automatic correction of changing (c) to ©. You can also make exceptions of words that you do not want to be marked as misspelled.

Change AutoCorrect Settings

1 Click the **File** tab to show Backstage view.

2 Click **Options**.

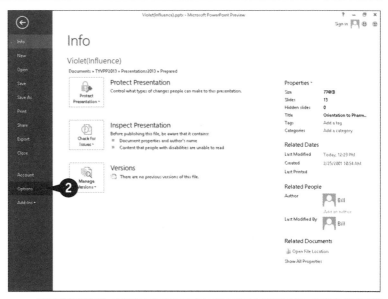

The PowerPoint Options dialog box appears.

3 Click **Proofing**.

4 Click **AutoCorrect Options**.

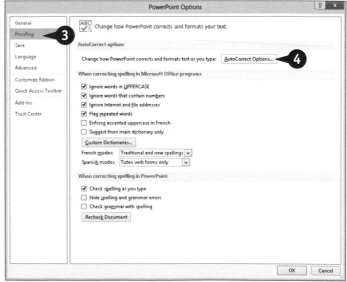

The AutoCorrect dialog box appears.

5 Click the **AutoCorrect** tab.

6 Click to enable (☑) or disable
(☐) any of the standard AutoCorrect options.

A To disable the misspelling correction feature,
click the **Replace text as you type**
option (☑ changes to ☐).

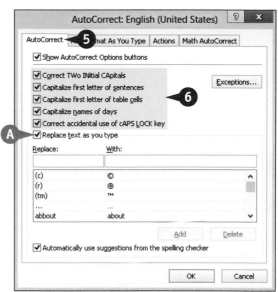

7 To add a word to the list, type the misspelled
version of the word in the **Replace:** text box.

8 Type the correct spelling of the word in the
With: text box.

9 Click **Add**.

B You can delete a word from the list by clicking it
and then clicking **Delete**.

10 Click **OK** in each of the two open dialog boxes.

PowerPoint applies your new settings.

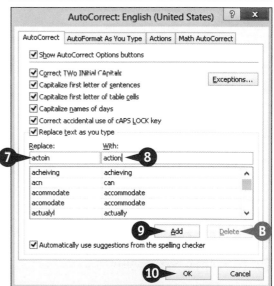

TIP

**AutoCorrect thinks the word "TO." is the end of a sentence and
capitalizes the next letter. How can I prevent this?**
You can add the word to a list of exceptions by following these steps:

1 Follow Steps **1** to **5** in this
section.

2 Click the **Exceptions** button.

3 Click the **First Letter** tab.

4 Type your exception in the
Don't capitalize after: text box.

5 Click **Add**.

6 Click **OK**.

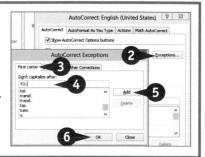

Change AutoFormat Settings

AutoCorrect has a feature called AutoFormat, which speeds up certain formatting that is cumbersome to perform. Examples include changing 1/2 to ½, replacing ordinals (1st) with superscript (1st), and changing Internet paths to hyperlinks (www.test.com). This is a very convenient feature because making these types of formatting changes can be tedious. It also automates bulleted and numbered lists, and automatically fits text to placeholders. You can customize these settings to suit your particular needs to streamline your work.

Change AutoFormat Settings

1 Click the **File** tab to show Backstage view.

2 Click **Options**.

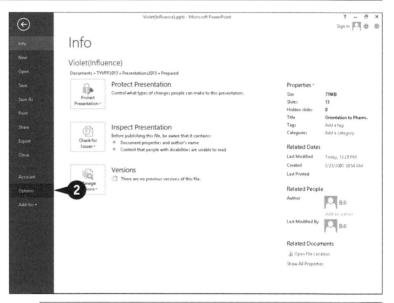

The PowerPoint Options dialog box appears.

3 Click **Proofing**.

4 Click **AutoCorrect Options**.

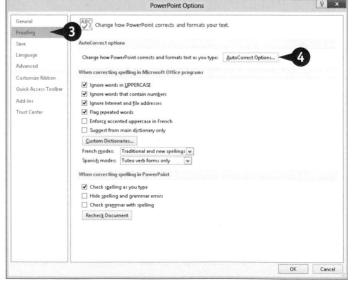

The AutoCorrect dialog box appears.

5 Click the **AutoFormat As You Type** tab.

6 Click to enable (☑) or disable (☐) any of the options under Replace as you type.

7 Click to enable (☑) or disable (☐) any of the options under Apply as you type.

These settings control whether text automatically sizes in the placeholders.

8 Click **OK** in each of the two open dialog boxes.

PowerPoint applies your new settings and closes both the AutoCorrect and PowerPoint Options dialog boxes.

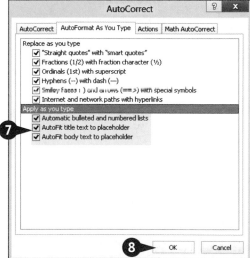

TIP

Why does PowerPoint change words that I type in all caps to lowercase?

AutoCorrect has a setting that corrects the accidental use of the Caps Lock key. To disable this option:

1 Follow Steps **1** to **4** in this section.

2 Click the **Correct accidental use of cAPS LOCK key** option (☑ changes to ☐).

3 Click **OK** to close each of the open dialog boxes.

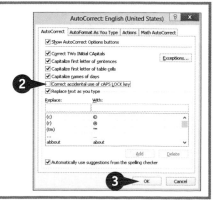

Customize Save Options

By default, PowerPoint saves a presentation in your user Documents folder with the PowerPoint 2013 format. For example, if your username is Bill and you save a presentation for the first time, the Save As dialog box uses the folder c:\Users\Bill\Documents\ as the default. If you share your presentations with colleagues who use an older PowerPoint version, you may want to change the settings so the default file format is the PowerPoint 2003 format because PowerPoint 2003 cannot open a file format later than that. You can also embed fonts in the saved presentation to preserve its look on any computer.

Customize Save Options

1 Click the **File** tab to show Backstage view.

2 Click **Options**.

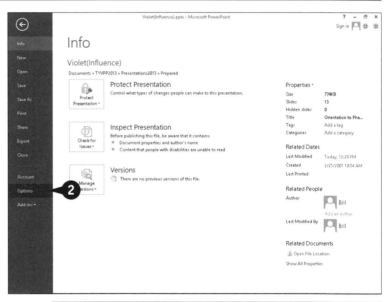

The PowerPoint Options dialog box appears.

3 Click **Save**.

4 Click the **Save files in this format** down arrow (▼).

5 Click a file format.

Note: The file type for PowerPoint 2013 is PowerPoint Presentation.

The next time you save a new file, the file type you specify here will appear as the file type in the Save As dialog box. You can choose a different file type during the save.

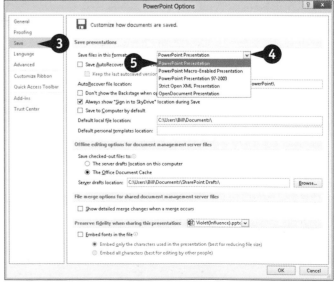

6 Click to enable (☑) or disable (☐) options under the Save presentations heading.

A If desired, click the spinner box (⬍) to change the number of minutes between AutoRecover saves.

B Click to deselect (☐) the **Save AutoRecover information every** option to disable the automatic saving feature.

C AutoRecover files are discarded when you close PowerPoint. Click to enable (☑) this option to retain the last file if you close without saving the file.

D To change the default save location, type a new default location.

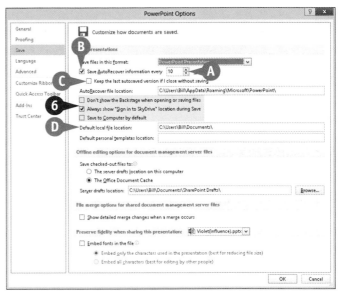

7 Click the **Embed fonts in the file** option (☐ changes to ☑).

E The fonts for this particular presentation are saved with it, so it will not appear differently when viewed on a system without those fonts.

F You can further specify whether to embed all characters or only those in use.

8 Click **OK**.

PowerPoint applies your new settings and closes the PowerPoint Options dialog box.

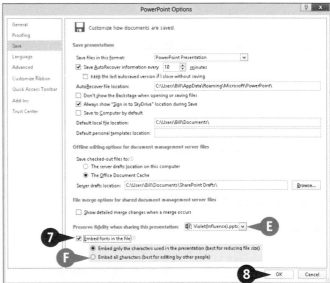

TIPS

What are the pros and cons of having the AutoRecover feature save frequently?

AutoRecover automatically saves your work at regular intervals in case PowerPoint closes unexpectedly. However, the pause you experience during the save might be lengthy if your presentation is large. You can disable AutoRecover if you do not want to be inconvenienced with this pause.

Why would I want to embed fonts in a presentation?

Some fonts are not available on every computer. If you view your presentation on a computer that is missing the fonts you used to design it, PowerPoint replaces the fonts with standard fonts from that computer. Embedded fonts travel with the presentation to ensure they are always in the presentation.

Modify View and Slide Show Options

You can change which features are available in the various PowerPoint views. The availability of these features may be determined by the option settings or by the type of presentation. In the Display and Slide Show options, you can select which view PowerPoint uses by default, such as Normal view or Slide Sorter view. You can also control whether the toolbar appears during the slide show presentation. These choices ensure that your preferred tools are on-screen when you need them.

Modify View and Slide Show Options

1 Click the **File** tab to show Backstage view.

2 Click **Options**.

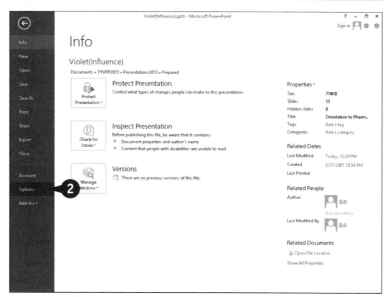

The PowerPoint Options dialog box appears.

3 Click **Advanced**.

4 Click and drag the scroll bar to locate the Display and Slide Show headings.

5 Click to enable (☑) or disable (☐) options under the Display heading.

6 Click the spinner box (⬍) to change the number of files displayed in the Recent list on the File tab.

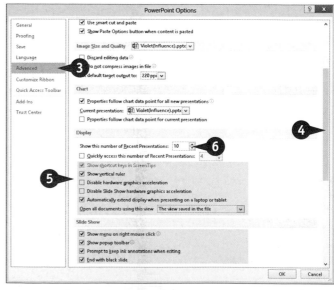

Ⓐ You can position your mouse pointer (🔖) over the information icon (ⓘ) to see a brief description of an option.

7 Click the **Open all documents using this view** down arrow (🔽).

8 Click a viewing choice.

PowerPoint uses the specified view when opening presentations.

9 Click to enable (☑) or disable (☐) options affecting behavior during a slide show.

Ⓑ Determines whether you can use the shortcut menu.

Ⓒ Controls the toolbar that faintly appears at the bottom-left corner of slides.

Ⓓ Determines whether you can save annotations you made on the slides upon exiting the slide show.

Ⓔ Determines whether the slide show ends with a blank, black slide.

10 Click **OK**.

PowerPoint applies your new settings and closes the PowerPoint Options dialog box.

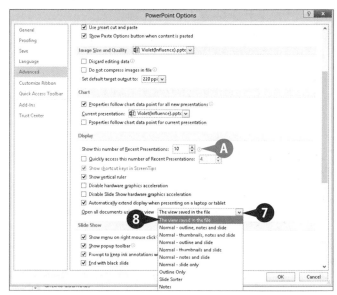

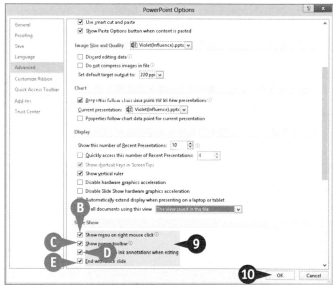

TIPS

What is the benefit of opening the presentation in Outline view?

If you start viewing the outline alone, you can concentrate on building the text for the presentation. This can be particularly helpful when you need a clean slate on which to organize your thoughts. The graphics of a slide can distract you from your outline because you may start thinking about the slide design.

Can I save annotations if I disable the Prompt to keep ink annotations when exiting option?

No. You can only save annotations by using the dialog box that prompts you to save them at the end of the slide show presentation. The prompt does not appear if you disable this option.

Change Editing Settings

You can change how certain editing tools work. For example, you can modify how the cutting and pasting, text selection, and Undo features perform. These features are useful, but can be annoying and cumbersome if not personalized through the settings in the options. You can also control the use of features such as the Paste Options button. This button appears when you paste a cut or copied object or text. It supplies convenient options for pasting, and you can click it to see commands for working with a pasted selection.

Change Editing Settings

1 Click the **File** tab to show Backstage view.

2 Click **Options**.

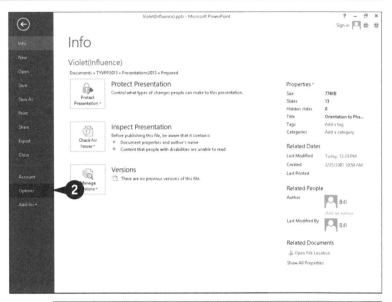

The PowerPoint Options dialog box appears.

3 Click **Advanced**.

4 Click to enable (☑) or disable (☐) options under the Editing options heading.

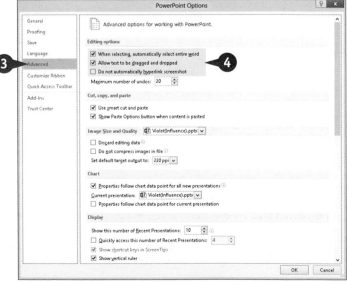

5 Click the spinner box (⬍) to change the number of undo edits you can perform with the Undo button (↶) on the Quick Access Toolbar.

This feature consumes considerable system memory, so if PowerPoint performs slowly, you should lower this number.

Ⓐ Some options apply to only one presentation. You can select which presentation.

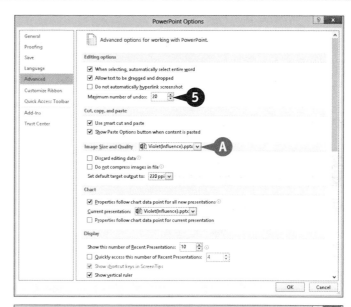

6 Click to enable (☑) or disable (☐) options under the Cut, copy, and paste heading.

Ⓑ Smart cut and paste is a feature where PowerPoint adds missing spacing around pasted text or objects.

Ⓒ Click to disable the **Paste Options** button (🖺(Ctrl)▾) that appears when you perform a copy-and-paste operation (☑ changes to ☐).

7 Click **OK**.

PowerPoint applies your new settings and closes the PowerPoint Options dialog box.

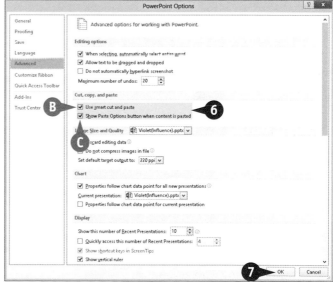

TIPS

What is the difference between the Paste Options button and Smart cut and paste?

The Paste Options button (🖺(Ctrl)▾) appears below a pasted object and offers formatting options. Smart cut and paste helps to eliminate errors when you paste. If spacing is not selected around copied text, Smart cut and paste makes sure that spaces are between words.

What number should I use for the maximum number of undos?

The default undo value is 20 and is probably about right. If you need to undo more than 20 actions, it might be faster to reconstruct a slide from scratch. You can also close the file without saving, and then open it again to get back where you started.

Work with Print Options

The PowerPoint Options dialog box offers several print options, making it easy to control presentation printing. For example, you can modify the way your printer handles fonts and the resolution of inserted graphics. You can also specify that a particular presentation always be printed with a particular printer and settings, saving you the trouble of choosing those settings every time you print that particular file. These settings can save time when printing presentations.

Work with Print Options

1 Click the **File** tab to show Backstage view.

2 Click **Options**.

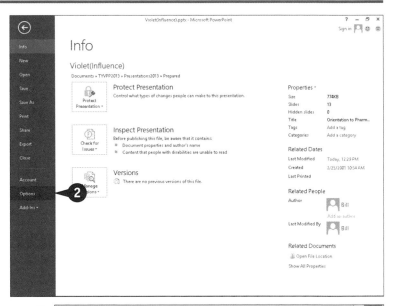

The PowerPoint Options dialog box appears.

3 Click **Advanced**.

4 Click and drag the scroll bar to the bottom of the PowerPoint Options dialog box.

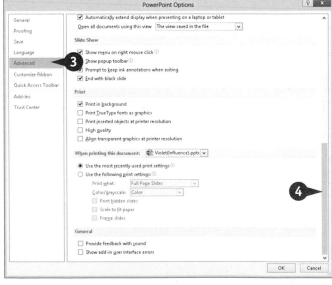

5 Click to enable (☑) or disable (☐) options under the Print heading.

A Print in background enables you to work in PowerPoint while printing.

B Print TrueType fonts as graphics prevents distortion of fonts.

C Enable this setting to use the printer's resolution settings to ensure quality printing of graphics.

D High quality increases the resolution of graphics, but can slow printing.

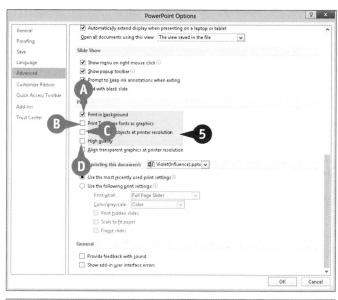

6 The next options apply to a single presentation; click the down arrow (☑) to select which presentation these options will affect.

7 Click the **Use the following print settings** option (○ changes to ◉).

The related settings become available.

8 Click to select print settings.

9 Click **OK**.

PowerPoint applies your new settings and closes the PowerPoint Options dialog box.

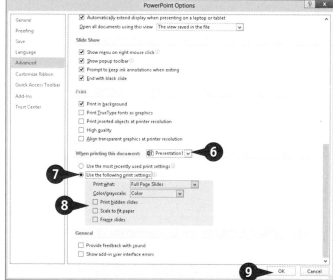

TIPS

How can I change print settings for a presentation that is not on the When printing this document drop-down list?

Only open presentations appear on this list; the current presentation is the default. Click **Cancel** to close the PowerPoint Options dialog box. Open the presentation file, and then reopen the PowerPoint Options dialog box. That presentation now appears in the list.

My printer prints slowly. How can I fix this?

You can try a couple of things. Enabling the **Print in background** option can slow down your printer, so try disabling this feature. Also, disable **Print inserted objects at printer resolution**. This option can slow printing because it may change the resolution of graphics, which can take considerable time.

Customize the Quick Access Toolbar

The Quick Access Toolbar appears above the ribbon in the upper-left corner of the PowerPoint window. You can move it below the ribbon if you like. This toolbar offers buttons for the most frequently used commands, providing even easier access than the ribbon.

You can add buttons to the Quick Access Toolbar to quickly access the commands you use the most, and you can remove buttons that you do not use. This allows you to reduce the number of clicks needed to run commonly used commands, thus streamlining your design work.

Customize the Quick Access Toolbar

1 Click the **Quick Access Toolbar** down arrow (▼).

2 Click **More Commands**.

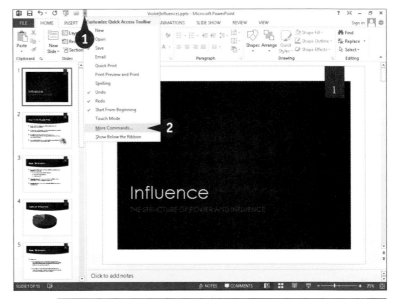

The PowerPoint Options dialog box appears, with Quick Access Toolbar displayed.

3 Click the down arrow (▼) and select the category or tab that holds the command button you want to add to the Quick Access Toolbar.

4 Find your desired command on the list and click it.

Ⓐ To add a command to the toolbar of a particular presentation, click the down arrow (▼) and select that presentation from the Customize Quick Access Toolbar list.

5 Click **Add**.

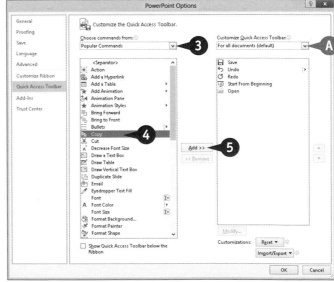

56

B The command appears on the list of commands under Customize Quick Access Toolbar.

C Click **Up** (▲) or **Down** (▼) to change a command's position.

D Click **Remove** to remove a command from the toolbar.

6 Click **OK**.

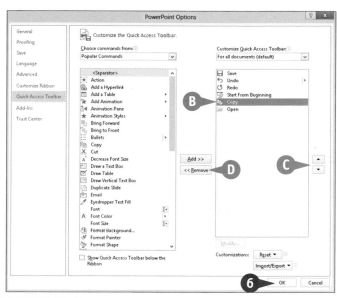

E The PowerPoint Options dialog box closes, and the Quick Access Toolbar reflects the changes you made.

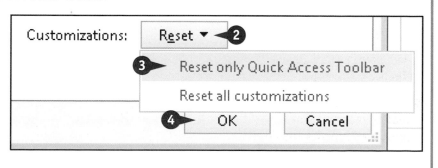

Customize the Ribbon

You can add commands to the PowerPoint ribbon, as well as add tabs and groups. Adding commands to the ribbon adds proficiency to the way you handle tasks and commands. An excellent use of this feature is creating a ribbon tab with your most commonly used commands so they are at your fingertips on a single tab, thereby making design work efficient and effective. You can add commands to existing tabs and rename existing tabs and groups.

Customize the Ribbon

Tour the Ribbon Tab Outline

1 Click the **File** tab to show Backstage view.

2 Click **Options**.

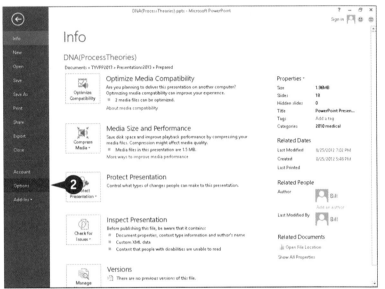

The PowerPoint Options dialog box appears.

3 Click **Customize Ribbon**.

4 Click the **plus sign** (⊞) to expand a level (⊞ changes to ⊟, which is used to collapse a level).

Ⓐ The first level of names on the list shows ribbon tabs.

Ⓑ The second level shows ribbon groups.

Ⓒ The third level shows ribbon commands, or ribbon menus and galleries.

Ⓓ The fourth level shows commands of ribbon menus and galleries that are on the third level.

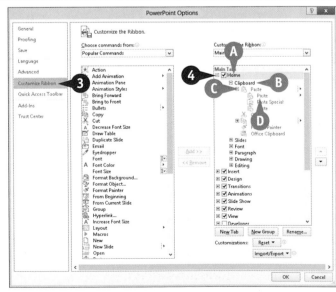

Add a Custom Tab to the Ribbon

1 Click the check box (☑) to disable a tab and remove it from the ribbon (☑ changes to ☐).

2 Click the **plus sign** (⊟) to collapse the Home tab (⊟ changes to ⊞).

3 Click a tab name from the list — your custom tab is inserted below it.

4 Click **New Tab**.

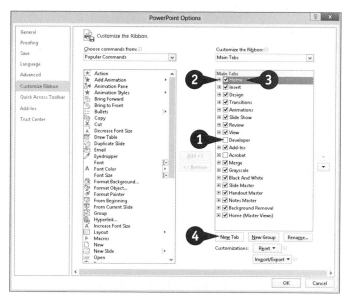

E A new tab appears with one new group.

5 Click **New Tab (Custom)**.

F You can use the **Up** (▲) and **Down** (▼) buttons to change the position of the tab.

G You can remove a custom tab by clicking **Remove**.

6 Click **Rename**.

The Rename dialog box appears.

7 Type a name in the text box.

8 Click **OK**.

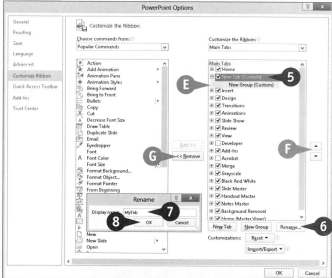

TIP

How do I make the ribbon look like it did when I first installed PowerPoint?

To reset the ribbon, follow these steps:

1 Follow Steps **1** to **3** in this section.

2 Click the **Reset** button.

3 Click **Reset all customizations**.

4 Click **OK**.

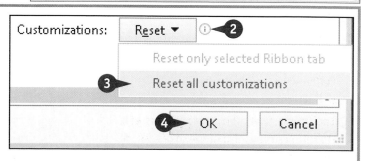

continued ▶ **59**

How people use ribbon commands depends upon how they work with PowerPoint. In fact, PowerPoint users often have a group of commands that they frequently use, and so many advanced users create a single tab with all of their favorite commands on it. You can group commonly used commands on a custom tab to make it easier than ever to design your presentation. Creating a presentation takes time, so you can make your design process faster and more effective by creating tabs with your favorite commands on it.

Customize the Ribbon (continued)

Ⓐ The tab name changes to MyTab.

Add a Group

1 Click the **plus sign** (⊞) to expand the Insert tab (⊞ changes to ⊟).

2 Click a group name from the list; your custom group is inserted below it.

3 Click **New Group**.

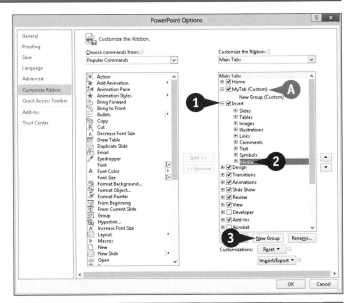

Ⓑ A new group level appears.

Add a Command

1 Click **New Group (Custom)**.

2 Click a command from the list.

3 Click **Add**.

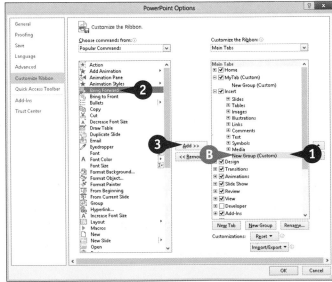

④ Repeat Steps **2** and **3** for any commands you want in any group, including existing groups.

⊙ PowerPoint adds your commands to New Group (Custom).

⑤ Click **OK**.

The PowerPoint Options dialog box closes, and the ribbon reflects the changes you made.

⊙ PowerPoint adds MyTab to the ribbon.

⊙ PowerPoint adds the group, New Group, to MyTab.

⊙ PowerPoint adds the selected commands to New Group.

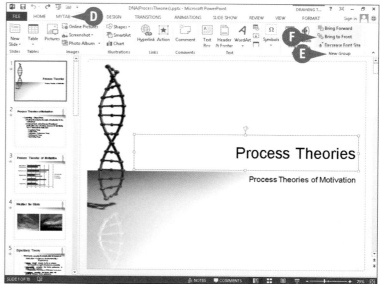

TIPS

Why do some of the commands that I added to my custom group not work?

Some commands require you to select an object or text before you can use them. Select an object or text, and then try using the commands — they should now be available to use.

On the left side of the Options dialog box, I cannot find the command I want in the selected category. Is there another place to look?

Yes. Click the down arrow (▾) on **Choose commands from**, and then click **All Commands**. If the command is currently available, it appears in the list of all commands. Keep in mind that PowerPoint 2013 may have removed some commands.

CHAPTER 4

Writing and Formatting Text

A professional presentation commands respect and conveys ideas easily. Nice formatting makes text easier to read and helps make your slides more attractive and polished. Changing the formatting can completely change the look, feel, and mood of a presentation.

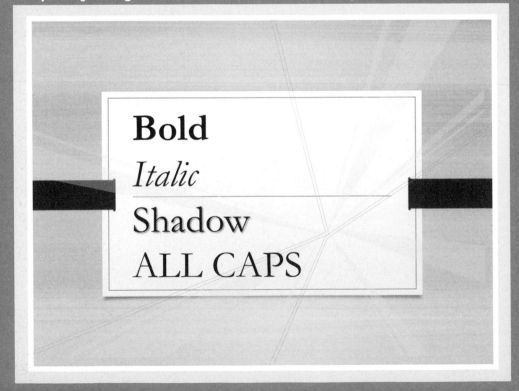

Understanding Slide Structure

You use PowerPoint to build a presentation slide by slide. Those slides, whether shown as a slide show or printed, make up your presentation. Different types of slides (slide layouts) serve different functions in your presentation. The slide layout controls which objects a slide contains and the placement of those objects on the slide. You can learn more about layouts in Chapter 5. The structure of the presentation affects flow and visual appeal.

Title Slide

The Title slide typically appears first and includes the presentation title or topic, and a subtitle. The subtitle might be the presenter's name or the name of the presenting company, or it might be the date and location of the presentation. There is usually just one title slide in a presentation, though they are sometimes used at the beginning of slide sections.

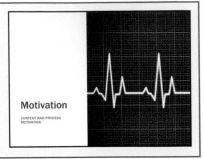

Title and Content Slide

A Title and Content slide is perhaps the most frequently used slide layout. It includes a title plus a placeholder where you can add one of several types of content: a bulleted list, table, chart, clip art, picture, SmartArt graphic (diagram), or media clip (sound or video).

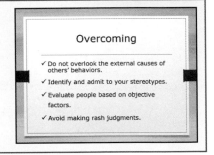

Other Slide Content

PowerPoint provides other slide layouts for your convenience: Two Content, Comparison, Content with Caption, Picture with Caption, and Blank. Each layout includes placeholders to position your information. Choose the layout that best presents your concepts and the associated data or graphics.

Slide Sections

You may need to divide a presentation into logical sections. Section breaks allow your audience to ask questions or for the group to take a break. You can easily change the slide theme of each section, possibly to denote a change in topic. You can introduce a new section with a slide using the Section Header or Title Only layout.

Explore Text Formatting Options

You can use various text formatting tools in PowerPoint to change the appearance of selected text. The Font and Paragraph groups on the Home tab of the ribbon provide most of the tools you need, or you can make formatting changes in the Font or Paragraph dialog boxes. You can also change the formatting of entire placeholders using the Quick Styles command on the Home tab.

Change the Font

When you type text on a slide, it is formatted with a font that is determined by the presentation theme you apply. The font (lettering type) gives a certain look and feel to your presentation, such as formal or informal. Changing the formatting of text can emphasize a certain word or line. You can change the font for selected text or for all text in a title or bulleted list.

Resize Text

Properly sizing presentation text makes the text more readable and attractive. You can modify the text size to reflect the environment where you make the presentation. Smaller text may be readable for a presentation viewed on a kiosk, but larger text may be needed to ensure clarity in a lecture hall. You can also use size to emphasize words.

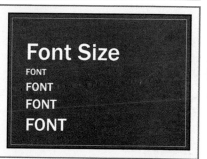

Change Text Color and Other Attributes

You can use text color for both design and practical purposes. The text color should be appealing to the eye. More importantly, it should provide a good contrast against the slide background so that the text is easy to read. You can also apply attributes such as bold, italic, and underline to slide text. Use colors and attributes to add emphasis to important words or phrases in your presentation.

Selecting Text or Placeholders

You can change the formatting of the text in a placeholder — how you select the placeholder determines which text changes. To select text in a placeholder, simply click the text, click and drag across it, or double-click a word. The placeholder border becomes a dashed line. To select the entire placeholder, click the border. The border becomes solid and your changes affect all of the text in the placeholder.

Add a Slide

When you open a new presentation, PowerPoint creates a blank title slide. To build your presentation, you can add as many slides as you like — just select one from the several slide templates that are available in the slide gallery by default.

Determine the number of slides in your presentation based upon how many topics you want to cover and the time you have available to cover them. Each slide should cover or detail a new topic.

Add a Slide

1 With a presentation open, click the **Home** tab.

2 Click the **New Slide** down arrow (▼).

3 Click the desired slide layout from the gallery.

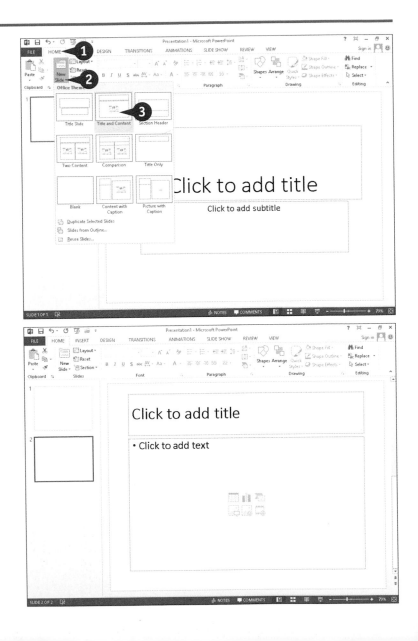

A new blank slide appears with the specified layout.

Note: Depending on circumstances, clicking the top half of the **New Slide** button inserts a slide with either the Title and Content layout or the same layout as the current slide.

Delete a Slide in Normal View

As you build your presentation, you may decide you do not need a particular slide. In this case, you can simply delete that slide. It is common to use an existing presentation as the basis for other presentations. In that situation, you may need to delete several slides that are irrelevant or out of date. You can either hide or delete slides. If you are confident that you do not need a slide, delete it to keep your presentation uncluttered.

Delete a Slide in Normal View

1 Click the **View** tab.

2 Click **Normal**.

Note: For more on Normal view, see Chapter 2.

3 Right-click the slide you want to delete.

The submenu appears.

4 Click **Delete Slide**.

PowerPoint deletes the slide.

Note: You can also click the slide, and then press Delete.

A Click the **Undo** button (↺) on the Quick Access Toolbar if you decide you need the slide and want it back in the presentation.

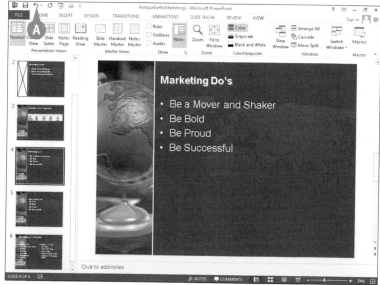

Type and Edit Text on a Slide

You can type text into a placeholder on a slide so you can convey information to the presentation audience through the written word. There are three types of placeholders that can hold text: title, content (bulleted list), and subtitle. You simply click the placeholder and then start typing. You can also go back and edit text you have already typed. Bullet points are discussion points, not detailed sentences. Remember to keep them short.

Type and Edit Text on a Slide

Enter Text

1 With a presentation in Normal view, add a **Title and Content** Slide.

Note: See the section "Add a Slide" in this chapter to learn how to add a slide.

2 Click the title placeholder.

The insertion point appears and the "Click to add title" text disappears.

3 Type your text.

4 Click outside the placeholder.

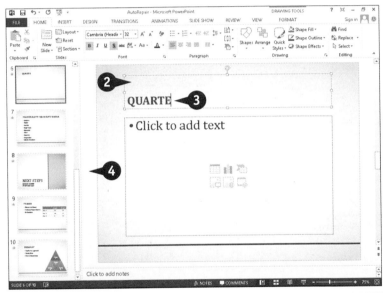

Ⓐ PowerPoint adds the text.

5 Click the content placeholder.

6 Type your text.

7 Press **Enter**.

Ⓑ The insertion point moves to the next line.

8 Repeat Steps **6** and **7** for all bullet points for that slide.

9 Click outside the placeholder.

PowerPoint adds the text.

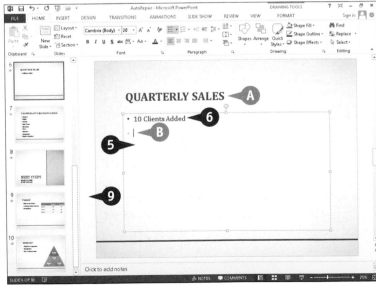

Edit Text

1 Click anywhere within a title, subtitle, or text placeholder.

2 Click the existing text where you want to change it.

The insertion point appears where you clicked. You can press Backspace to delete text to the left, or press Delete to delete text to the right of the insertion point.

3 Press Backspace.

This example deletes the number '2.'

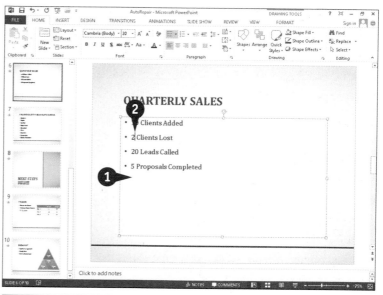

4 Type any text you want to add.

This example types the text 'Two.'

5 Click and drag over one or more words.

6 Press Delete.

PowerPoint deletes the selected text.

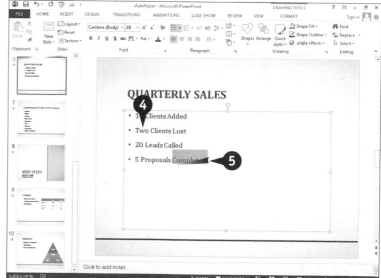

TIPS

Why does my placeholder say, "Click to add text"? Will this appear if I print or run my presentation?

That is simply an instruction to let you know that this placeholder currently has no text entered in it. The words and the placeholder neither print nor appear when you present the slide show. When you click the placeholder to type, it disappears.

When I type text in Outline view, where does it appear?

Text that you type in the Outline tab appears on the currently displayed slide. The top-level heading in a slide corresponds to the title placeholder on the slide. Second-level entries become the bullet items in the text placeholder. Third-level entries are bullet items, and so on.

Format Text Color and Style

Color adds flair to any presentation. You can use text color to make your text more readable and more attractive. Choose text colors that are a good contrast with the background so your audience can easily read the text during the slide show. You can select colors from a standard palette or work with custom colors. Use text colors along with text styles such as bold or shadow to add emphasis to the words in your presentation.

Format Text Color and Style

1. Click a placeholder to select it.

2. Click and drag over one or more words.

3. Click the **Home** tab.

4. Click the **Font Color** down arrow (▾).

   A color palette appears.

5. Select a color from the palette.

A. For a custom color, click **More Colors**.

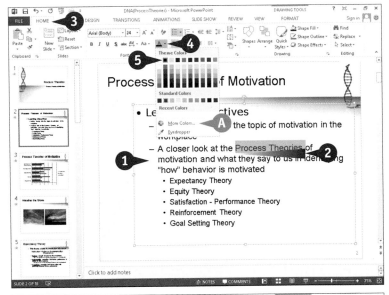

B. The text you selected changes to the color you chose.

6. Click and drag over one or more other words.

Note: You can also double-click to select a single word.

7. Click the **dialog box launcher** button (🖿) in the Font group.

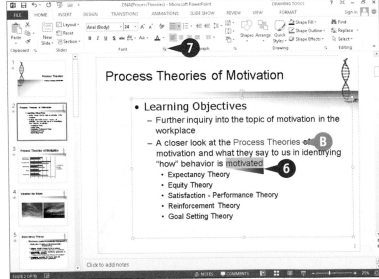

The Font dialog box appears.

8 Click the **Font style** down arrow (⌄).

9 Click a style from the list.

10 Click an effect to apply to your text (☐ changes to ☑).

11 Click **OK**.

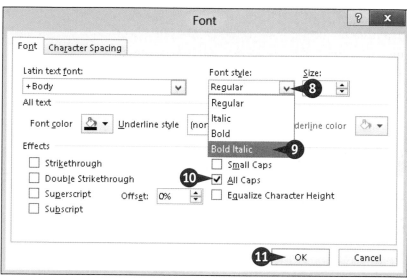

C PowerPoint changes the text to the style that you selected.

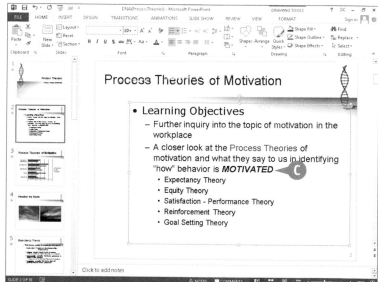

What is the difference between applying formats with the Home tab buttons and the Font dialog box?

The Font dialog box enables you to apply several formats at one time from a single location. All possible options are there, including some specialized attributes, such as superscript and subscript, which you do not see in the Font group on the Home tab.

What are superscript and subscript?

These formats either raise (superscript) or lower (subscript) the selected text a set distance from the regular text. Superscript and subscript are often used for footnote or scientific notation, such as 4^2 representing 4 to the second power, or f_x to represent a function of x. Unless you customized the ribbon, these attributes are only found in the Font dialog box.

Format Text Font and Size

The font you choose for text portrays a certain look and feel. Some fonts are playful, and others more formal. Fonts are divided into four main types: serif fonts, with cross strokes on the letter ends; sans serif fonts, which do not have cross strokes on the letter ends; script fonts, which look like handwriting; and decorative fonts such as Algerian, which are heavily stylized. Font size is important because your audience should be able to read all of the text in your presentation without straining their eyes.

Format Text Font and Size

1 Click a placeholder to select it.

2 Click and drag over one or more words.

3 Click the **Home** tab.

4 Click the **dialog box launcher** button (⬚) in the Font group.

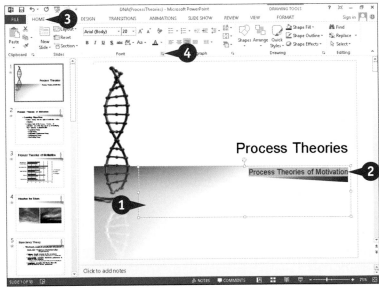

The Font dialog box appears.

5 Click the **Latin text font** down arrow (⌄).

6 Click the desired font.

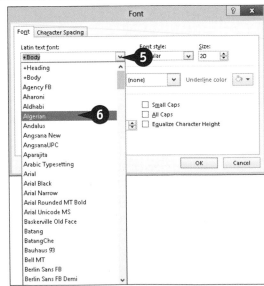

7 Double-click the number in the **Size** text box and type a new font size.

A You can also click the spinner (↕) beside the Size text box to increase or decrease the font size.

8 Click **OK**.

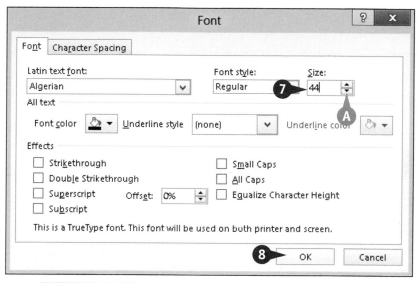

B PowerPoint applies the new formatting to the text.

Note: If the placeholder is not wide enough to accommodate the size of the font with the number of characters in one line, then the auto-formatting feature makes the text two lines.

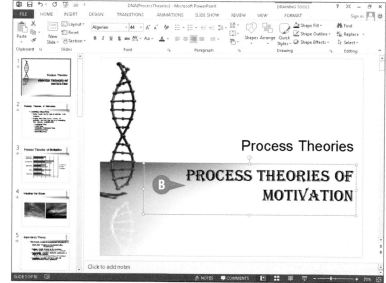

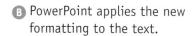

TIPS

There is a Character Spacing tab in the Font dialog box. What does it allow you to do?
The Character Spacing tab allows you to kern the font, or in other words, adjust the character spacing of the text. You can kern the font and specify above which font size you want to start kerning.

Are there limitations on how large or small text can be?
No. You can type whatever font size you like, with the lower limit being 1 and no practical upper limit. However, remember to keep the text readable for the viewer. A very small text size is difficult to see; a huge text size can make text look like a design element.

Cut, Copy, and Paste Text

When you edit your presentation, you can move text by using the Cut, Copy, and Paste features. Using these features assures accuracy and saves time because you avoid typing the text manually. *Cut* removes text from its original location. *Copy* duplicates the text, leaving the original in place. *Paste* places either cut or copied text into another location. You can also cut, copy, and paste objects like placeholders and pictures. If you change your mind or make a mistake, you can use the undo feature to reverse the commands you made.

Cut, Copy, and Paste Text

1 Click the **Home** tab.

2 Click the **dialog box launcher** button (⬚) in the Clipboard group.

The Clipboard task pane appears.

3 Click a text placeholder to select it.

4 Click and drag to select text.

5 Click the **Cut** button (✂).

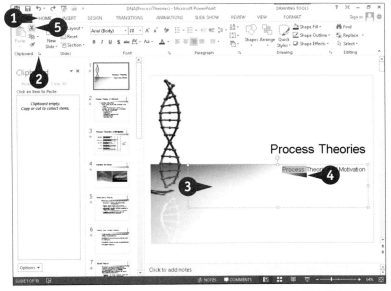

A PowerPoint removes the selected text and places it on the Windows Clipboard.

6 Click and drag to select different text.

7 Click the **Copy** button (📋 ▾).

Note: If you do not open the Clipboard, it holds only your most recent copied or cut text.

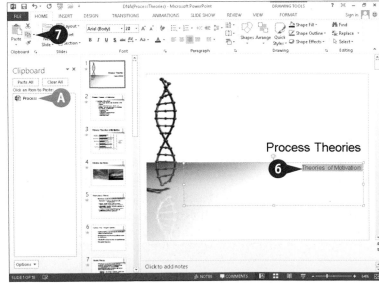

ⓑ PowerPoint copies the selected text to the Clipboard.

❽ Select the slide where you want to paste the text.

Note: For more information on navigating slides, see Chapter 2.

❾ Click within the placeholder to position the insertion point where you want to paste the text.

ⓒ The insertion point appears in the placeholder.

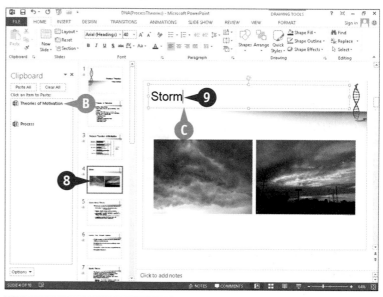

❿ To paste an item that you copied, click it in the Clipboard.

ⓓ PowerPoint pastes the cut or copied text into the placeholder.

ⓔ You can also click **Paste** to paste the most recently copied item, which is always the first item on the Clipboard.

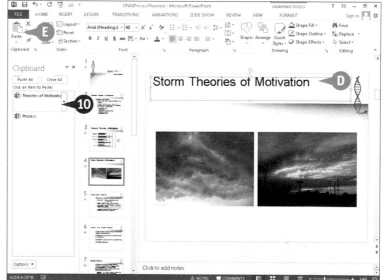

TIPS

Is there an easier and faster way to cut, copy, and paste?

Yes. You can perform these commands by using keystrokes. Press `Ctrl`+`X` to cut, `Ctrl`+`C` to copy, and `Ctrl`+`V` to paste. Use these keystrokes to perform these commands with text, objects, and even files. They work throughout Microsoft Windows.

The text that I copied in Word appears on the Clipboard. Can I delete it?

Yes. Move your mouse pointer (⇖) over the item that you want to delete and then click the down arrow (▼). Click **Delete** on the drop-down list that appears and the item disappears from the Clipboard.

Format Bulleted Lists

Bulleted lists are the heart of any presentation. They summarize key points the presenter wants to make. You can format bulleted lists with different styles of bullets. For example, you can use check marks as bullets in a list of points for a project. You can use pictures and symbols as bullet points and dictate the size of bullet points as well.

If you place the insertion point within the text of a placeholder, only the bullet for that line changes. To change all bullets, click the placeholder border to select the entire placeholder.

Format Bulleted Lists

1. Click the border of a placeholder containing a bulleted list.

2. Click the **Home** tab.

3. Click the **Bullets** down arrow (▾).

4. Click a bullet style from the gallery.

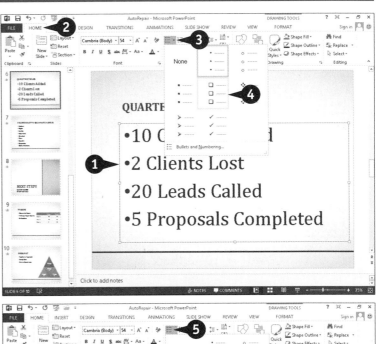

Ⓐ The bullets change to the new style.

5. Click the **Bullets** down arrow (▾).

6. Click **Bullets and Numbering** at the bottom of the gallery.

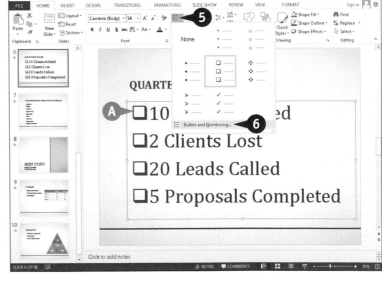

The Bullets and Numbering dialog box appears.

Ⓑ You can change the bullet color.

Ⓒ You can click **Customize** to use a symbol as a bullet.

7 Click **Picture**.

The Insert Pictures dialog box appears.

Ⓓ You can use a picture from your computer.

8 Type a keyword into the **Office.com Clip Art** text box.

9 Click the **Search** button (🔎).

10 Click a picture from the selection.

11 Click **Insert**.

Ⓔ The picture appears as a bullet.

TIPS

How can I make the bullets larger?
The Bullets and Numbering dialog box includes a size setting. This setting is expressed in percentage of the text size. If you increase the text size, the bullet size increases proportionally. Double-click in the **Size** text box, type the size you want, and then click **OK** to apply the sizing.

Can I apply a new bullet style to every bullet in the presentation without having to change each individually?
Yes. You can use the master slides to make formatting changes that apply to every slide in the presentation. Chapter 9 covers master slides in detail.

Using the Spelling Check Feature

You should check the contents of your presentation for spelling accuracy because good presentations do not have spelling errors. Not all of us are spelling bee winners, but your audience will definitely notice spelling errors. Fortunately, PowerPoint offers a spelling check feature to improve your spelling accuracy without using a dictionary. You can check the spelling of all the words throughout your presentation so it is as professional as possible.

Using the Spelling Check Feature

1 Click the **Review** tab.

2 Click **Spelling**.

Note: You can also press **F7** to start the spelling check.

A The Spelling task pane appears, displaying the first questionable word and suggested spellings.

3 Click a suggestion from the **Suggestions** list.

4 Click **Change** to replace the misspelling.

B You can click **Change All** to replace all instances of the misspelled word.

C You can click **Ignore** to leave the spelling as is.

D You can click **Ignore All** to leave all instances of this spelling as they are.

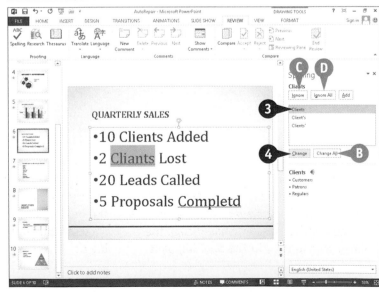

E The spelling check proceeds to the next questionable word.

5 Repeat Steps **3** and **4** until the spell check is complete.

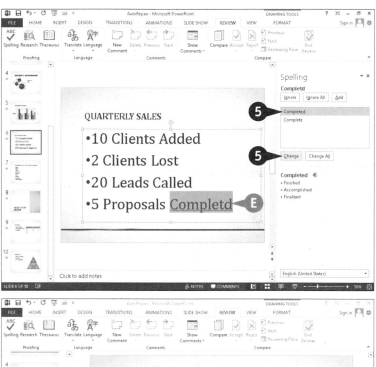

A dialog box appears notifying you when the spelling check is complete.

6 Click **OK**.

The Spelling task pane closes.

Note: If PowerPoint options are set to check spelling as you type, red wavy lines may appear under possibly misspelled words after you type them. You can right-click the word and then click an option in the shortcut menu that appears.

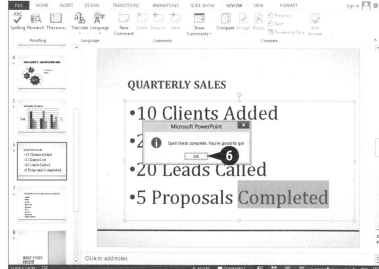

Is it possible to check spelling for a specific word?

Yes. Select the word before you run the spelling check. The spelling check starts with the word you select. After taking the appropriate action, simply click the **Close** button (✖) in the Spelling pane.

Is there a way to get PowerPoint to stop flagging a particular word as misspelled?

Yes. In the Spelling pane, click **Add**. This adds the word to your custom dictionary, so it recognizes the spelling as legitimate in the future. Keep in mind that your custom dictionary affects all Microsoft programs, so the word you add will be viewed as a legitimate spelling in all Microsoft programs.

Using the Research Feature

As you type text in a presentation, you may need to check definitions or facts. PowerPoint gives you the convenience of researching a topic without a dictionary, thesaurus, or any other references; you can research the topic without leaving PowerPoint! If your computer has an Internet connection, you can use the Research feature to search reference books and research sites for relevant information on your topic. PowerPoint finds relevant references so you can open them with a click of your mouse button!

Using the Research Feature

1 Click the **Review** tab.

2 Click and drag across the text you want to research.

3 Click **Research**.

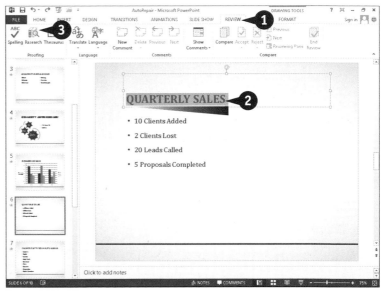

The Research task pane appears with the selected text in the Search for text box.

4 Click the **Search** button (→ changes to ◎).

You can click the **Stop** button (◎) to cancel the search.

Ⓐ The search results appear.

Ⓑ If you want to change the search topic, type it in the **Search for** text box and click the **Search** button (→).

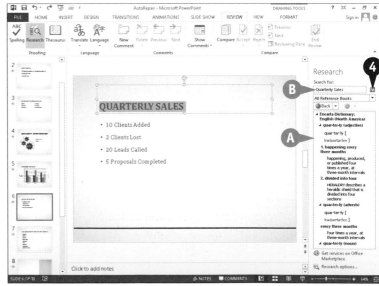

5 Click the **Search for** down arrow (▼) to change where the Research feature looks for information.

6 Click to select a research site from the drop-down list.

PowerPoint changes the search results to reflect your change.

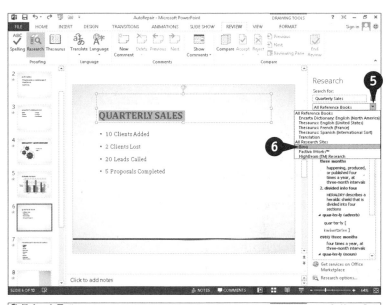

C Click the **Expand** icon (▷) to expand a listing (▷ changes to ◢).

D Click the **Collapse** icon (◢) to collapse a listing (◢ changes to ▷).

E Click **Next** to see the next listings.

7 Click a link.

Additional information appears or a Web site opens, depending on the type of link it is.

8 Click the **Close** button (✖) to close the Research task pane.

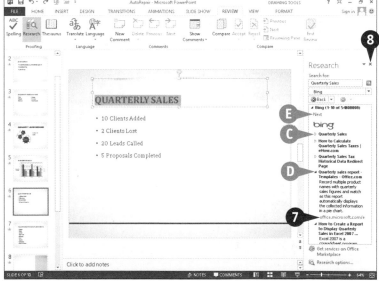

TIPS

Can I specify which research sites PowerPoint will check?

Yes. With the Research task pane displayed, click the **Research options** link at the bottom. A dialog box appears with a list of all resources. Click the check box beside any listed reference, and then click **OK**. The references you selected now appear in the drop-down list.

I followed a link but it did not contain the information I wanted. Is there a way to go back to the original item that was displayed?

Yes. Working within PowerPoint, you can click the **Back** button (⬤Back ▼) in the Research task pane. You can also choose another topic in the Research task pane.

CHAPTER 5

Working with Layouts

Slide layouts are templates that consist of different combinations and arrangements of placeholders. *Placeholders* are rectangular objects on slides that hold text, graphics, charts, tables, SmartArt, and multimedia. Slides may contain one or more placeholders. You use the various slide layouts and place content into placeholders to create your presentation. Slide layouts save you the time and trouble of designing slides from scratch.

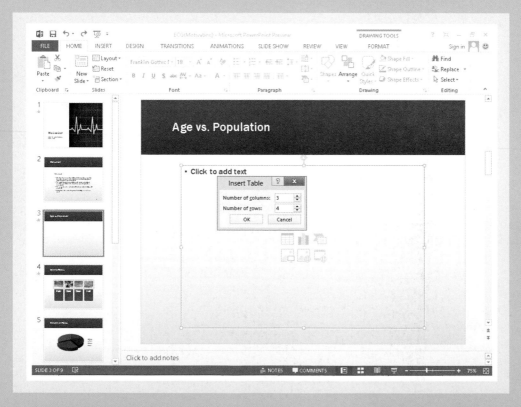

Understanding Layouts and Placeholders

Many presentation slides combine a slide title, graphic elements, and slide text in the form of a bulleted list or table. Your selection of slide layout determines where the title, graphics, and text appear. Slide titles, bullet lists, and other text usually exist in placeholders. Content placeholders can also contain graphic elements, tables, charts, pictures, and SmartArt. The layout of a slide is established by the placement of placeholders on the slide. PowerPoint offers several standard slide layouts. You can use one of these layouts to quickly and easily create a presentation.

Slide Layout Gallery

Clicking the bottom part of the New Slide button opens the Slide Layout gallery. You will find a New Slide button on both the Home and Insert tabs. You can use the gallery to insert a slide with a particular layout. With some exceptions, if you click the top part of the New Slide button, PowerPoint inserts a slide with the same layout as the selected slide.

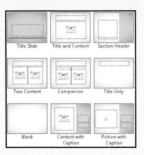

Placeholders

Each slide layout has an arrangement of placeholders. Text placeholders accept only text. Content placeholders accept either text or a graphic element. A content placeholder contains icons that help you insert graphics. You can move placeholders to design slides that suit your particular needs.

Types of Slide Layouts

The Slide Layout gallery enables you to choose a layout for a slide. Some layouts hold only text, such as the Title Slide, Section Header, and Title Only layouts. Other layouts include a title, plus content placeholders. Layouts that feature placeholders include Title and Content, Two Content, Comparison, and Content with Caption.

Slide Layouts Remain Flexible

You can adjust a layout to meet your particular needs. There are handles on the border of the placeholder — dragging any handle resizes the placeholder. To move a placeholder, click its border and then drag it to another location. If a placeholder does not contain any content, it is not visible when you print or show your presentation.

Insert a New Slide with the Selected Layout

To insert a new slide with a particular layout, you can click the bottom part of the New Slide button and choose the desired layout from the Slide Layout gallery. The various slide layouts allow you to give your presentation diversity and to accomplish different objectives such as comparing two lists or showing data in chart form. PowerPoint inserts slides after the currently selected slide. With some exceptions, if you click the main part of the New Slide button, PowerPoint inserts a slide with the same layout as the selected slide.

Insert a New Slide with the Selected Layout

1 Select a slide.

2 Click the **Home** tab.

3 Click the **New Slide** down arrow (▼).

The Layout gallery appears.

4 Click the desired layout.

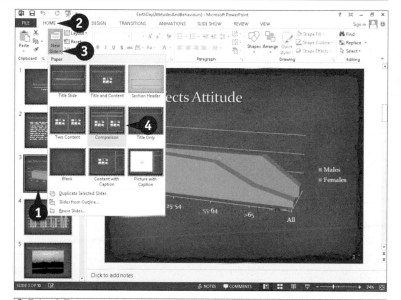

A The new slide with the specified layout appears in the presentation.

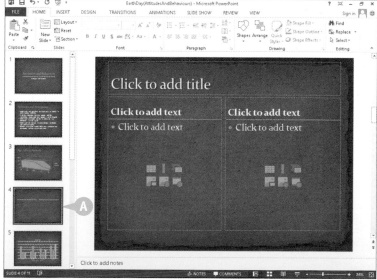

Change a Slide Layout

If you decide a slide's original layout no longer works, you can apply a different slide layout in Normal view or Slide Sorter view. This allows you to change the layout without designing the slide again. If the configuration of the new layout does not include an element from the original layout — such as a chart that you have set up — PowerPoint keeps that additional element on the slide, even with the new layout.

Change a Slide Layout

1 Select the slide whose layout you want to change.

Note: To learn how to select a slide, see Chapter 2.

2 Click the **Home** tab.

3 Click the **Layout** down arrow (⏷).

The Layout gallery appears.

4 Click a slide layout from the gallery.

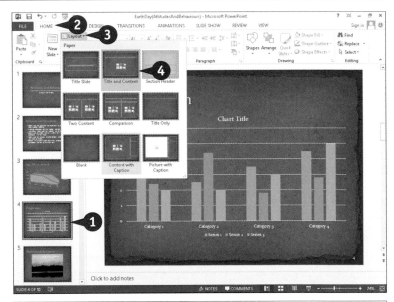

The slide changes to the selected layout.

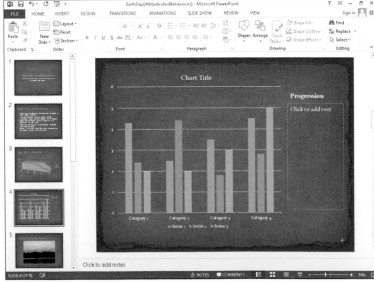

Using Layouts with a Content Placeholder

Content placeholders appear on most of the slide layouts that you will use. You can use content placeholders to build your presentation effectively and efficiently. Content placeholders are convenient containers that allow you to place text or graphics on a slide. They are easy to move and simple to change. Placeholders enable you to insert text, or one of six types of graphical objects onto the slide. You can use text to convey ideas, and graphics to make your presentation more aesthetically dynamic and visually appealing.

Ⓐ Bulleted List

Click the bullet to add text or type a list of items. Press **Enter** at the end of each item.

Ⓑ Tables

Click the **Insert Table** icon (▦) to create a table. You can specify the number of columns and rows in the table.

Ⓒ Charts

Click the **Insert Chart** icon (▮▮) to generate a chart using a chart type that you specify, and data that you type into a spreadsheet.

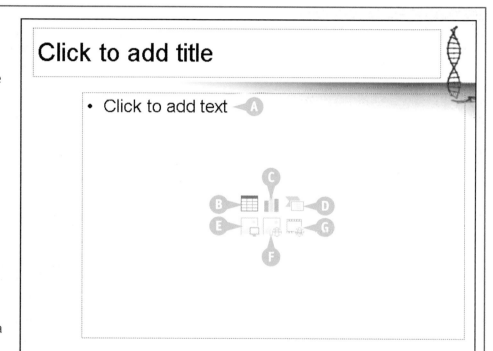

Ⓓ SmartArt

Click the **Insert a SmartArt Graphic** icon (▧) to insert a diagram using one of the many diagram styles provided by PowerPoint.

Ⓔ Pictures

Click the **Insert Picture** icon (▨) to insert a picture file such as a bitmap or JPEG that you have stored on your computer or other storage media.

Ⓕ Online Pictures

Click the **Insert Online Picture** icon (▨) to select an image from the built-in clip art collection, or import clip art from Microsoft Office Online.

Ⓖ Videos

Click the **Insert Video** icon (▨) to insert a video file that plays during the slide show. You can specify that it plays on command or automatically.

Insert a Table

You can use a table to arrange information in rows and columns for easy data comparison. For example, you might list age groups in the far-left column of a table, and then compare population demographics between males and females in two other columns. Tables are useful for showing important data to your audience. For example, you might use a table to show the data for a chart. You can use a content placeholder to insert a table, and then type data into the table cells.

Insert a Table

Insert a Table

1. Select a slide with a content placeholder.

2. Click the **Insert Table** icon ( ).

   The Insert Table dialog box appears.

3. Click and type the number of columns you want in your table.

4. Click and type the number of rows you want in your table.

Note: Alternatively, you can click the **spinner** ( ) to select the number of columns and rows.

5. Click **OK**.

   The table appears on the slide.

Note: By default, most of the table styles assume that you will enter column headings in the top row of the table.

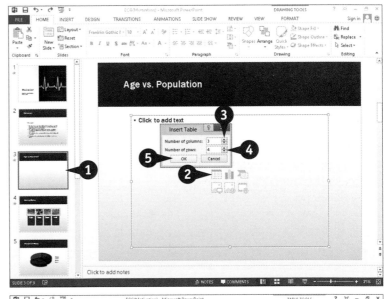

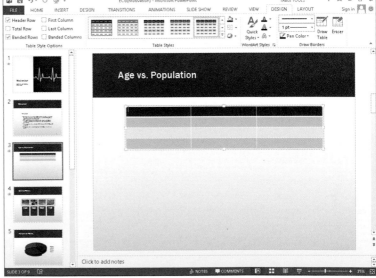

Type Text in a Table

① Click in the first cell and type a column heading.

This example types Age Group.

② Press **Tab**.

Ⓐ The insertion point moves to the next cell.

Note: You can also click in a cell to type data into it.

③ Continue adding column headings and cell entries by repeating Steps **1** and **2**.

④ Click outside the table when finished.

Ⓑ To change table data, click in the cell, edit your entry, and then click outside the table when finished.

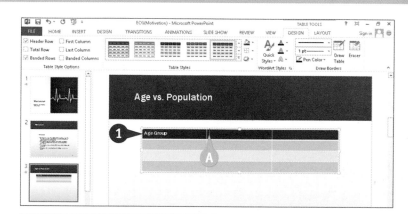

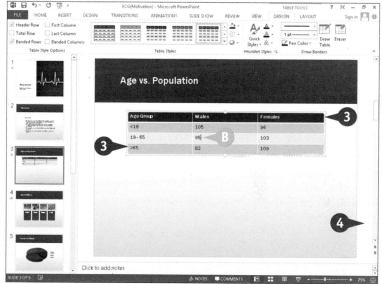

TIP

Can I add and delete rows or columns to tables?

Yes. You can insert and delete rows or columns by following these steps:

① Click a row or column.

② Click the **Table Tools Layout** tab.

③ To insert, click an Insert option.

④ To delete, click **Delete**.

⑤ Select an option from the menu.

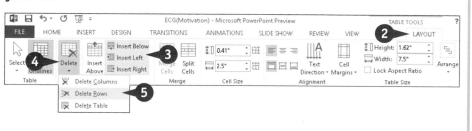

Format a Table

When you insert a table, PowerPoint automatically applies a style to the table based on the theme of the slide. You can add visual impact to your presentation by changing the format of your table. You can add and delete rows and columns, format the text and background, and change the style of the table. There are a variety of ways to select cells, rows, and columns in a table, so experiment with clicking and dragging them!

Format a Table

1 Select a slide with a table.

Note: To learn how to select a slide, see Chapter 2.

2 Click the table.

3 Click the **Table Tools Design** tab.

4 Click the **Table Styles** down arrow (⩣).

5 Click a style from the gallery.

Ⓐ You can click **Clear Table** to remove any previously applied styles.

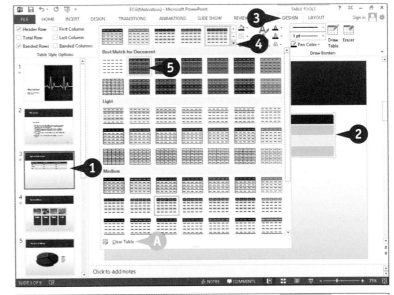

PowerPoint applies the style to the table.

6 Click a row to select it.

You can also click and drag across cells or text.

This example selects the header row.

7 Click the **Quick Styles** down arrow (⩢).

8 Select a style from the gallery.

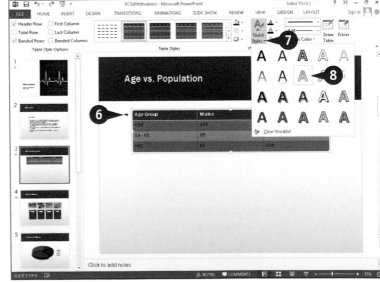

PowerPoint applies the style to the selection.

9 Click and drag across rows to select them.

This example selects all of the rows.

10 Click the **Borders** down arrow (▼).

11 Click a border from the menu.

12 Click the **Home** tab.

13 Click the **Bold** button (B).

14 Click the **Italic** button (I).

15 Click the **Center** button (≡).

PowerPoint applies the formatting changes to the selection.

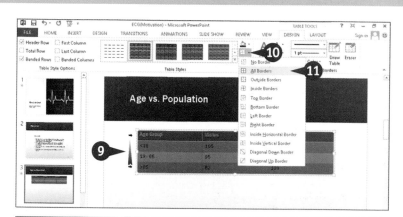

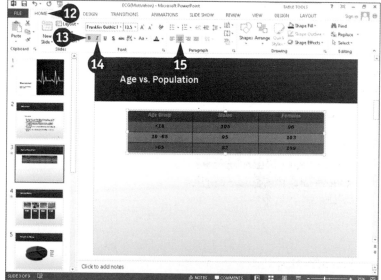

TIP

Can I make size adjustments to the table?

Yes. You can resize your table as follows:

1 Click in the table.

2 Position the mouse pointer ( ) over a handle.

3 Click and drag the handle to size the table.

4 Position the mouse pointer ( ) over a cell border separating rows or columns.

5 Click and drag the border.

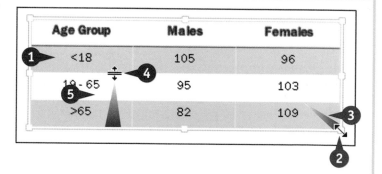

Insert a Chart

Charts present information visually and make a presentation aesthetically pleasing. They give an instant impression of trends, or they compare sets of data, such as sales growth over a several-year span. Charts tell a story with a brief viewing and can convey statistical information quickly. You can add these visual-analysis tools to your presentation to convey summarized information quickly to your audience. PowerPoint allows you to choose the chart type and then type chart data into a spreadsheet.

Insert a Chart

Create a Chart

1 Select a slide with a content placeholder.

Note: To learn how to select a slide, see Chapter 2.

2 Click the **Insert Chart** icon ( ).

The Insert Chart dialog box appears.

3 Click a chart type category.

4 Click a specific chart type.

5 Click **OK**.

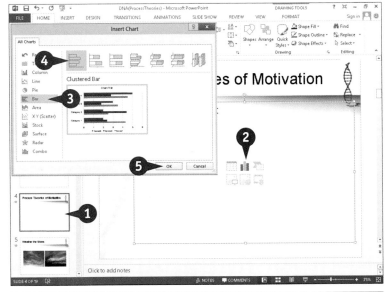

The chart appears, along with sample data in a separate spreadsheet window.

Note: Entering data is similar to entering data into an Excel worksheet.

6 Click in the grid to activate the spreadsheet.

7 Delete any unneeded information in rows or columns.

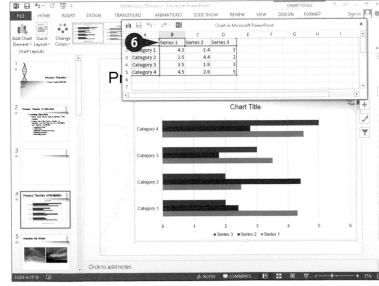

Enter Chart Data

1 Type column headings in Row 1.

2 Type row labels in Column A.

A The borders containing the chart data range automatically expand as you enter information.

3 Type your data values in the cells.

Note: You can click a cell and type to enter new data, and double-click a cell to edit existing data.

4 Click the **Close** button (×) to close the Excel worksheet.

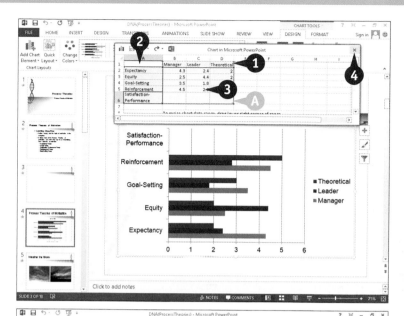

The spreadsheet window closes and the chart appears on the slide.

5 Click outside the chart when finished.

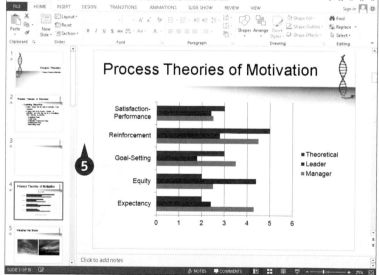

TIP

Can I change the type of a chart?
Yes. Follow these steps:

1 Click anywhere in the chart.

2 Click the **Chart Tools Design** tab.

3 Click **Change Chart Type**.

4 Click a chart type category.

5 Click a specific chart type.

6 Click **OK**.

PowerPoint changes the chart type to the one you selected.

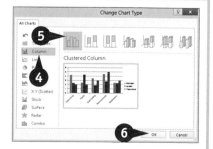

Format a Chart

When you insert a chart, PowerPoint automatically applies a style to the chart based on the theme of the slide. Charts present information visually, so choice of color is important. You can change the formatting of charts to convey a particular mood or to make specific data stand out. To format any object on a chart, you click it and then use the formatting tools on the Chart Tools Design and Home tabs to change it to your liking. Try to keep the chart relatively simple, though — the less complicated and cluttered it is, the easier it is for the audience to understand.

Format a Chart

1 Click anywhere on a chart.

2 Click the **Chart Tools Design** tab.

3 Click the **Chart Styles** down arrow (⤓).

4 Click a chart style from the gallery.

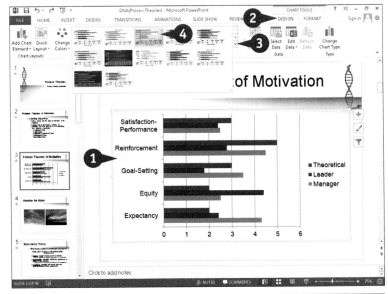

The chart reflects the change in chart style.

5 Click the **Plus** icon (+).

The Chart Elements box opens. You can add or remove chart elements using this box.

6 Click the **Data Labels** down arrow (▶).

7 Click an item from the selection (☐ changes to ☑).

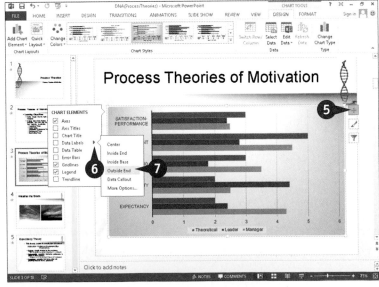

The data labels appear.

8 Click the plot area.

9 Click the **Chart Tools Format** tab.

10 Click **Shape Fill**.

Ⓐ You can alternatively make a selection from the Shape Styles gallery.

Ⓑ You can choose from specialized fill options such as a picture, or different gradients and textures.

11 Click a color from the gallery.

The plot area changes color.

12 Click a data series.

Note: To format a data series (series of bars), click a bar in that series. To format a single bar in the series, click it twice (not a double-click). The same applies to the data labels.

13 Click the **Shape Effects**.

14 Click **Glow**.

15 Click an item from the gallery.

Ⓒ You can change the border color by clicking **Shape Outline**.

PowerPoint applies the formatting to the bars.

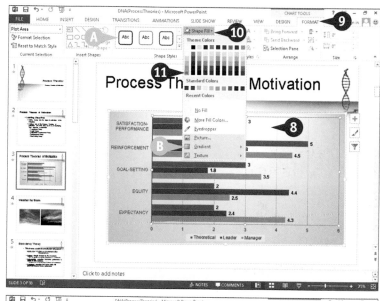

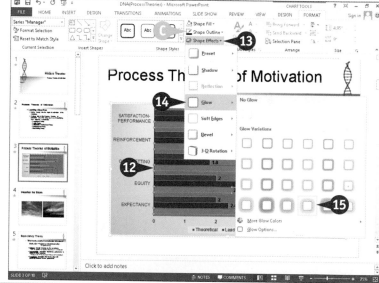

TIP

Can I format the numbers on the axis?

Yes. You can format text in a chart just like other text in PowerPoint by using the Home tab.

1 Click a chart axis.

2 Click the **Home** tab.

3 Click the **Font Size** down arrow (▾).

4 Click a font size from the drop-down list.

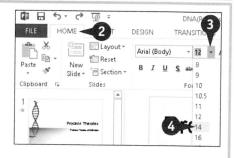

Edit Chart Data

It is not unusual for chart data to change over time. You can update your chart with the most recent information by opening the data spreadsheet and changing the data. You need not show all of the spreadsheet data in the chart. If you decide not to display all of the data, you can remove data elements such as data series or categories from the chart without deleting that information from the spreadsheet. You can later bring removed data back by reversing the process. Alternatively, you can delete the data from the spreadsheet.

Edit Chart Data

1 Click anywhere on a chart.

2 Click the **Filter** icon (▼).

The Chart Filters box opens. You can add (☑) or remove (☐) the data elements with this box.

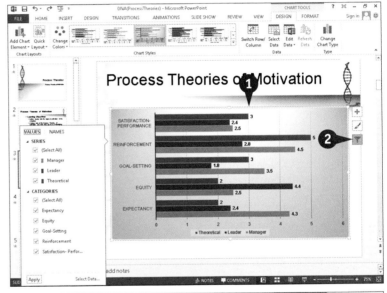

3 Click a series (☑ changes to ☐).

This example hides the Manager series.

4 Click a category (☑ changes to ☐).

This example hides the Satisfaction – Performance category.

5 Click **Apply**.

PowerPoint removes the data elements.

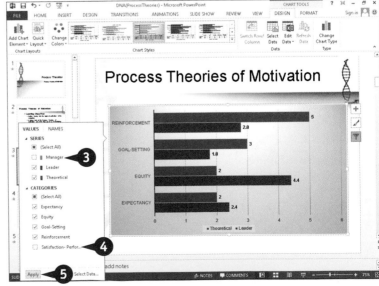

6 Click the **Chart Tools Design** tab.

7 Click **Edit Data**.

The data spreadsheet appears.

8 Double-click a cell to edit the data.

This example is editing Cell A6.

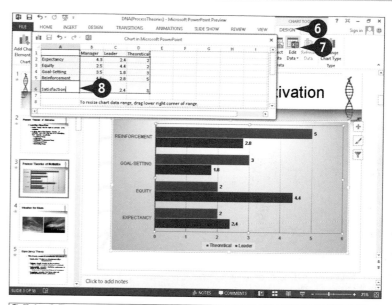

9 Type a column heading and data in Column E.

10 Type a row label and data in Row 7.

Note: The colored borders around the table adjust automatically.

Ⓐ The chart updates with a new series for the added column.

Ⓑ The chart updates with a new category for the added row.

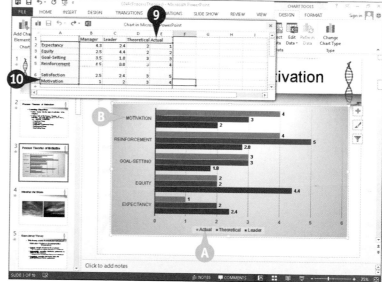

TIP

Are there other ways to show chart data?
Yes. Switching the categories and series gives the data a different, revealing perspective. Follow these steps:

1 Click the **Chart Tools Design** tab, then click Select Data.

2 Click **Switch Row/Column**.

3 Click **OK**.

Insert Pictures

You can illustrate and enhance your slide show presentation using pictures. You can insert various types of pictures into placeholders, including digital camera shots, scanned images, clip art, and bitmaps. These pictures can come from your own collection on your computer, Microsoft Office Online, or a Bing search of the Internet. Bing provides a link to the website that holds the picture and even tells you if the picture is free to use! All pictures found at Microsoft Office Online are royalty-free.

Insert Pictures

1 Select a slide with a content placeholder.

Note: To learn how to select a slide, see Chapter 2.

2 Click the **Insert Picture** icon ( ).

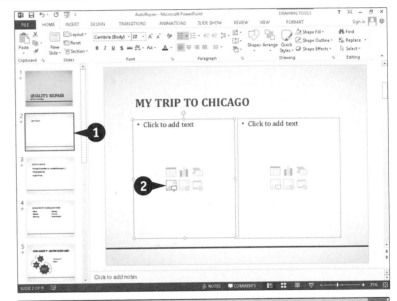

The Insert Picture dialog box appears.

3 Click the folder that contains the picture file you want to insert.

4 Click a picture file.

5 Click **Insert**.

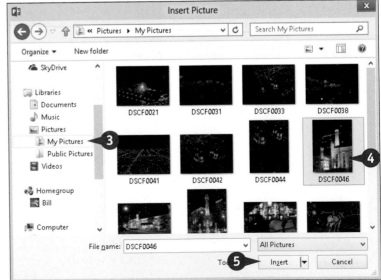

A PowerPoint inserts the selected picture into the placeholder.

6 Click the **Insert Online Picture** icon (▣).

The Insert Online Pictures dialog box appears.

7 Type a keyword in the Office.com ClipArt text box or Bing Image **Search** text box.

8 Click the **Search** icon (🔍).

9 Click a picture from the gallery.

10 Click **Insert**.

B PowerPoint inserts the selected picture into the placeholder.

Note: You can resize the pictures as desired. See Chapter 10 to learn how.

When I click a picture, a Picture Styles group appears on the Picture Tools Format tab. What can I do with this group of tools?

These tools include many ways to make pictures more interesting — several of which involve changing the border. For instance, you can give the picture a reflection such as one you would see in a lake. You can make the picture border glow or give it soft edges. You can frame the picture as though it is hanging from a wall. You can even rotate the picture to give it a three-dimensional look.

Insert Video

Showing instructional videos is a great way to present an information segment in your slide show. You can also show interesting or funny video captures to make your presentation exciting. You can insert videos directly into a placeholder without using an intermediate program to handle the video. Inserting videos directly into PowerPoint saves time and avoids the cost of a program that you otherwise may not use. PowerPoint recognizes videos in a variety of different formats, such as Windows Media Video (WMV) files and Motion Pictures Experts Group (MPEG) files.

Insert Video

1 Select a slide with a content placeholder.

Note: To learn how to select a slide, see Chapter 2.

2 Click the **Insert Video** icon (▣).

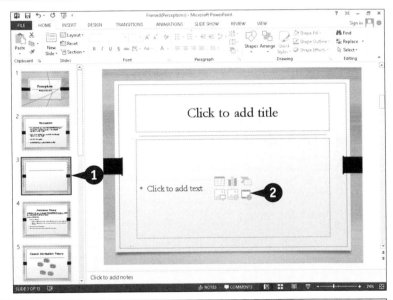

The Insert Video dialog box appears.

Ⓐ You can search for and insert a video file directly from the Internet.

Ⓑ You can insert a file from the Internet using the embed code.

3 Click **Browse**.

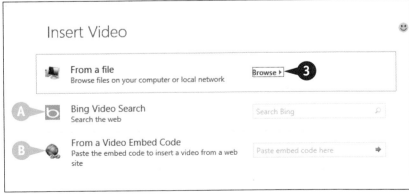

The Insert Video dialog box appears.

4 Click the folder that contains the video file you want to insert.

5 Click a video file.

6 Click **Insert**.

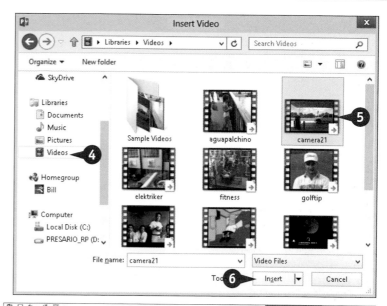

PowerPoint inserts the selected video into the placeholder.

7 Click the video.

8 Click the **Video Tools Playback** tab.

9 Click **Play** (▶ changes to ▌▌).

The video begins to play.

C You can click the **Forward** (▶) and **Back** (◀) buttons to browse the video.

D You can use the **Volume** button (◀») to adjust the sound.

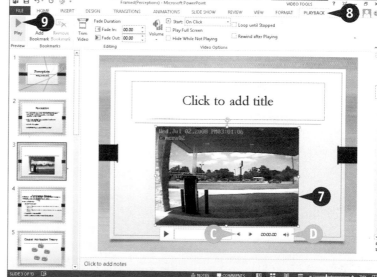

TIP

There is a Hide While Not Playing check mark on the Video Tools Playback tab. What does this option do?
Presenters often do not want a video to be visible when it is not playing. A slide appears uncluttered if the video is hidden, and it can provide a dramatic effect by fading in when it starts playing. If you click to the **Hide While Not Playing** option (□ changes to ☑), the video will not be visible during the slide show if it is not playing. There is a disadvantage, though: To use this feature, you must set the video to play automatically, so you lose some control over when the video plays.

Insert a SmartArt Graphic

SmartArt graphics are diagrams that illustrate a process, workflow, or structure. You can use SmartArt graphics or SmartArt diagrams to quickly present concepts in a visually interesting way. For example, a diagram can show the workflow of a procedure or the hierarchy in an organization. Some SmartArt layouts are text only, while others involve text and pictures. You might use a SmartArt picture layout to show the four seasons, and a SmartArt text graphic to describe the steps for starting a race. PowerPoint offers many SmartArt layouts to help you communicate with your audience graphically.

Insert a SmartArt Graphic

1 Select a slide with a content placeholder.

2 Click the **Insert a SmartArt Graphic** icon ( ).

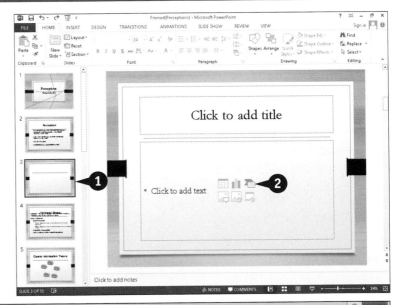

The Choose a SmartArt Graphic dialog box appears.

3 Click a diagram category.

Ⓐ You can drag the scroll bar to see all of the layouts.

4 Click a specific diagram layout.

5 Click **OK**.

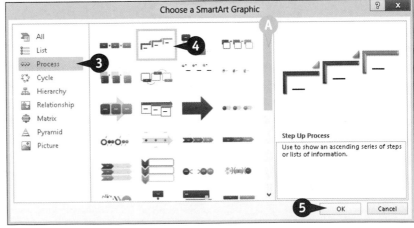

The dialog box closes and the SmartArt graphic diagram appears on the slide.

6 Click the left arrow (◄) to open the Text pane (◄ changes to ►).

7 Click **[Text]** next to a bullet.

[Text] disappears and the insertion point takes its place next to the bullet.

Note: You can also edit text directly in the graphical element.

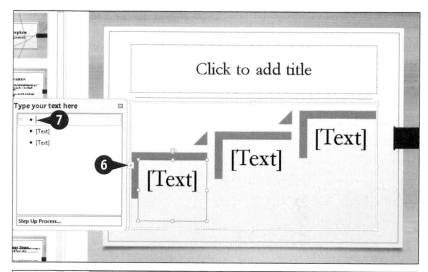

8 Type the text for the element.

9 Repeat Steps **7** and **8** to type text into other graphical elements.

10 Press **Enter** to add a graphical element.

11 Click outside the SmartArt graphic when you are finished.

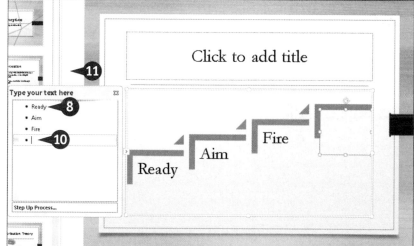

Can I add more elements in the SmartArt graphics diagram if I am not using the Text pane?

Yes. Click an element next to where you want the additional element. Click the **Smart Tools Design** tab. Click the **Add Shape** down arrow (▼). The list gives you options about where to place the new element. Click a selection from the list.

How do I add a picture to a SmartArt graphic?

It is just like inserting a picture, as described in this chapter. Make sure the graphic is a picture-specific SmartArt graphic. Click the **Insert Picture** icon in the center of the graphic and follow the same steps as for inserting a picture.

Edit SmartArt

After you create a SmartArt graphic, you can change its look and contents at any time. For example, you can change a SmartArt graphic to a different layout, edit the text, change its color, give it a 3-D effect, or even mix different shapes. You can also format text by changing the font color or style, or by making the font bold or italic. This versatility allows you to create the perfect diagram that sends a specific message to your audience.

Edit SmartArt

1 Click anywhere in the SmartArt graphic to select it.

2 Click the **SmartArt Tools Design** tab.

3 Click the **Expand** button (◄) to open the Text pane (◄ changes to ►).

4 Click any text in the Text pane or on any element to edit the text.

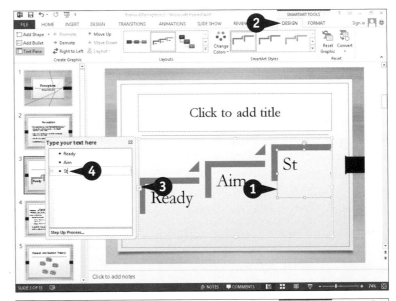

5 Click the **Collapse** button (►) to close the Text pane (► changes to ◄).

6 Click the **SmartArt Styles** down arrow (▼).

The SmartArt Styles gallery appears.

7 Click a style from the gallery.

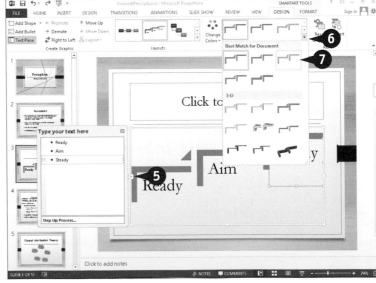

The SmartArt graphic changes style.

8 Click the **SmartArt Layout** down arrow (☰).

The SmartArt Layout gallery appears.

9 Click a layout from the gallery.

The SmartArt graphic changes layout.

10 Click a single element to select it.

11 Click the **SmartArt Tools Format** tab.

12 Click **Smaller** or **Larger** to change the element's size.

13 Click a Shape Styles command to change the color, border color, or special effect of the shape.

14 Click a WordArt Styles command to change the color, border color, or special effect of the font.

The element reflects the changes you made.

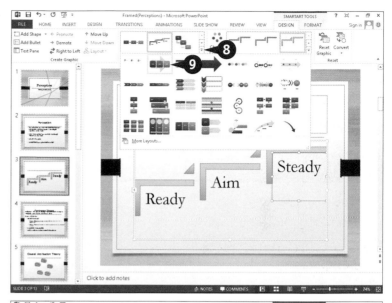

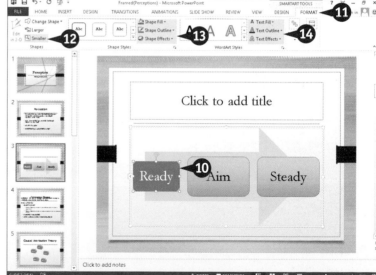

TIP

Are there color themes for the SmartArt graphics?
Yes. Follow these steps to choose from a variety of color themes.

1 Click a SmartArt graphic to select it.

2 Click the **SmartArt Tools Design** tab.

3 Click **Change Colors**.

4 In the Primary Theme Colors gallery, click a color theme.

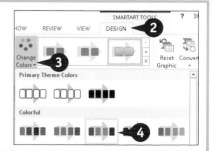

Insert a Slide from Another File

You can insert a slide from one presentation file into another. This can be a great timesaver when you have created a slide with a highly detailed chart, table, or diagram in another presentation. You may want to use a favorite slide in several presentations. For example, a slide showing sales growth may go into a presentation for the sales team, a different one for management, and yet another presentation for potential customers. Importing the slide from the other presentation saves you the trouble of reentering data and reformatting the object on the slide.

Insert a Slide from Another File

1 Select the slide after which you want to insert the new slide.

Note: You can also perform this task in Slide Sorter view. See Chapter 2 to learn how to switch views.

2 Click the **Home** tab.

3 Click the **New Slide** down arrow (˅).

The Layout gallery appears.

4 Click **Reuse Slides**.

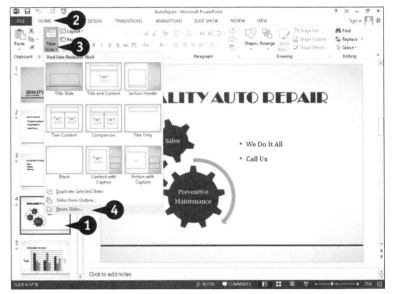

The Reuse Slides task pane appears.

5 Click **Open a PowerPoint File**.

The Browse dialog box opens.

6 Click the folder that contains the presentation file you want to view.

7 Click the presentation file that contains the slide you want to insert.

8 Click **Open**.

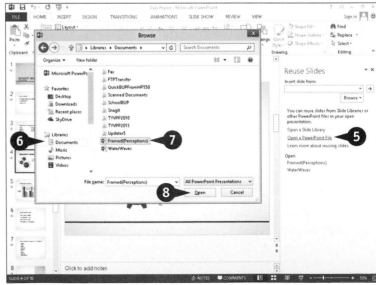

The slides of the selected presentation appear in the Reuse Slides task pane.

9 Drag the scroll bar to find the slide you want to insert.

10 Click the slide.

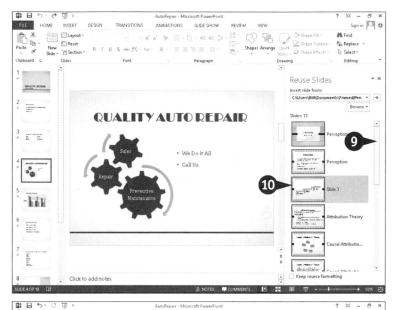

A PowerPoint inserts the slide you clicked after the slide you originally selected.

11 Click the **Close** button (✖) to close the Reuse Slides task pane.

Note: If you have two presentations open, you can drag slides from one to another.

TIP

Is there an easy way to import slides from multiple presentations?
Yes. Repeat Steps **1** to **8** and then follow these steps:

1 Click the **Browse** down arrow (▼) in the Reuse Slides task pane.

2 Click **Browse File**.

The Browse dialog box appears so that you can open a different presentation file in the Reuse Slides task pane.

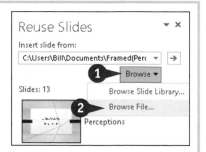

CHAPTER 6

Organizing Slides

After you have created a number of slides, you should check to ensure that the overall flow of your presentation makes sense. A great place to organize your slides is in Slide Sorter view. This view displays a thumbnail (little picture) of each slide. You can use the thumbnails to move, delete, or copy slides with ease.

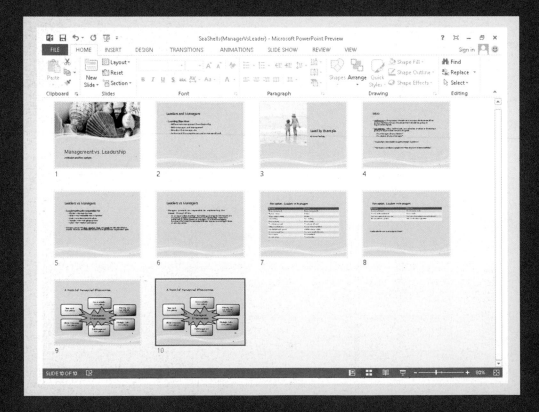

Move a Slide

Agood presentation conveys a sequence of ideas in a logical progression. When creating a presentation, you often must reorganize slides to get that sequence right. For example, a presentation on how to build a house would start with building the foundation; continue with rough carpentry, roofing, plumbing, electrical, and drywall; and conclude with finish carpentry and cleanup — all in that order. PowerPoint has the ability to easily move slides so you can quickly order them as necessary.

Move a Slide

1 Click the **View** tab.

2 Click **Slide Sorter**.

Slide Sorter view appears.

3 Click and drag a slide thumbnail to the desired location.

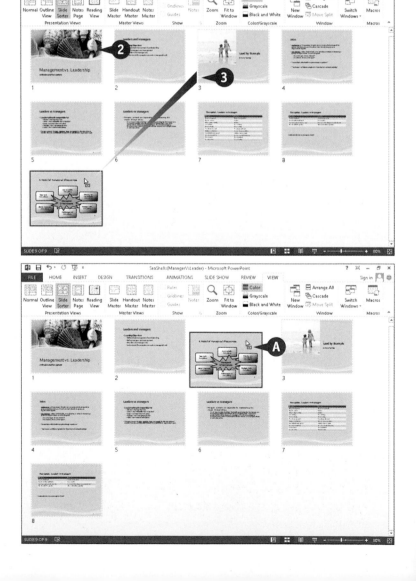

A When you release the mouse button, the slide appears in its new position.

Note: Press and hold Ctrl as you drag to create a duplicate slide in the new position.

Copy and Paste a Slide

If you create presentations about similar subjects, you may want to copy a slide from one presentation to another to save time. For example, you may need to copy a slide that contains a table of data. The ability to copy the slide from one presentation to another saves you time because you do not need to re-create the slide; you can simply copy and paste it. You can also click and drag a slide from one presentation to another to copy it.

Copy and Paste a Slide

① Select the slide(s) you want to copy in Slide Sorter view.

Note: You can also perform this task in Normal view.

Note: To select multiple slides, click the first slide, and then press Ctrl while clicking additional slides.

② Click the **Home** tab.

③ Click the **Copy** button (🖹 ▾).

④ Switch to a presentation that is open.

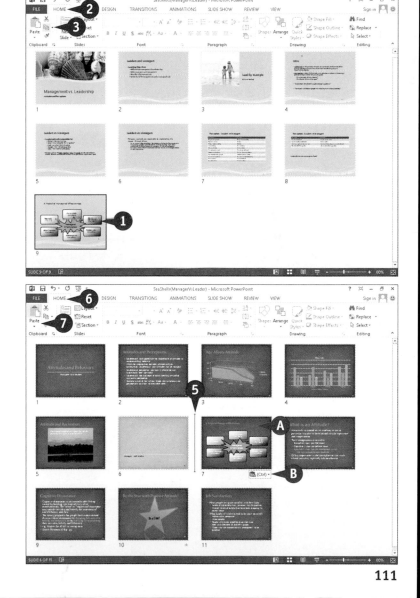

⑤ In Slide Sorter view, click in between the slides where you want the copied slide to appear.

The insertion point appears.

⑥ Click the **Home** tab.

⑦ Click **Paste**.

Ⓐ The copied slide(s) appear in the presentation.

Ⓑ You can change the slide back to its original formatting by clicking the **Paste Options** button (🖹 (Ctrl) ▾) and then clicking the **Keep Source Formatting** button.

Delete a Slide in Slide Sorter View

As you build your presentation, you may decide that you do not need particular material. For example, you may need to delete slides if a presentation is outdated or if you decide not to use a slide that you designed. In some cases, you might use a copy of a particular presentation as a template for a presentation that you are designing and you only need certain slides, so you need to delete some of them. When you decide to remove a slide, PowerPoint makes it quick and easy to do so.

Delete a Slide in Slide Sorter View

1 Select the slide(s) you want to delete in Slide Sorter view.

Note: To select multiple slides, click the first slide, and then press **Ctrl** while clicking additional slides.

2 Right-click any selected slide.

The shortcut menu appears.

3 Click **Delete Slide**.

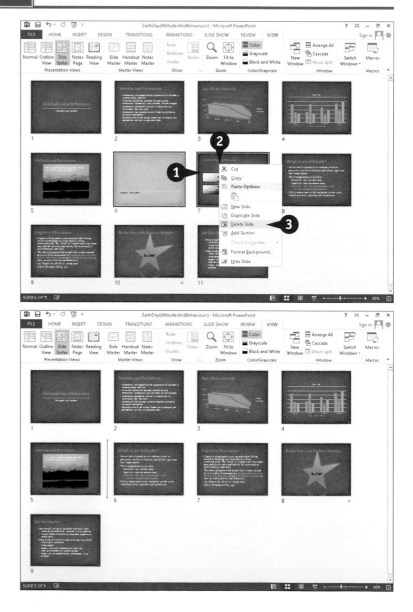

PowerPoint deletes the selected slide(s) from the presentation.

Note: PowerPoint does not prompt you to confirm the deletion. If you want to get the slide back, click the **Undo** icon (↺) on the Quick Access Toolbar.

Note: You can also delete a slide by selecting it and then pressing **Delete**.

Make a Duplicate Slide

If you need to make two slides that are very similar, you can design the first one, duplicate it using the Duplicate Slide feature, and then make minor changes to the new slide. For example, if a slide at the beginning of a presentation lists key topics, you can duplicate it, make minor changes, and use it as a summary. You may want to make a duplicate slide in one presentation, modify it while looking at both slides, and then move it. Duplicating a slide can save time and ensure accuracy of the information on the slide.

Make a Duplicate Slide

1 Select the slide(s) you want to duplicate in Slide Sorter view.

Note: To select multiple slides, click the first slide, and then press **Ctrl** while clicking additional slides.

2 Click the **Home** tab.

3 Click the **New Slide** down arrow (▼).

4 Click **Duplicate Selected Slides**.

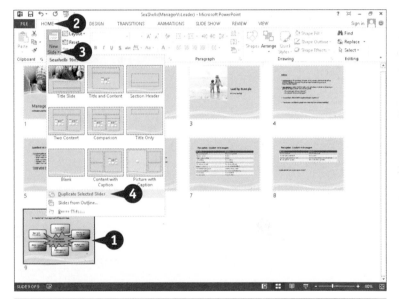

A PowerPoint duplicates the selected slide(s).

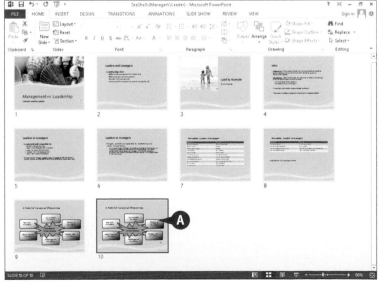

Hide a Slide

Hiding a slide prevents it from appearing during the slide show. By hiding slides, you can create an abbreviated slide show from a presentation without deleting any slides. For example, you may need to give an abbreviated slide show to executives, but a more detailed presentation of the same slide show to managers. You can hide slides, give the presentation, and then unhide them. Hiding slides saves you time by allowing you to prepare only one slide show for two audiences. Hiding slides is also a good way to temporarily remove them to see how your presentation flows without them.

Hide a Slide

1 Select the slide(s) you want to hide in Slide Sorter view.

Note: To select multiple slides, click the first slide, and then press **Ctrl** while clicking additional slides.

2 Click the **Slide Show** tab.

3 Click **Hide Slide**.

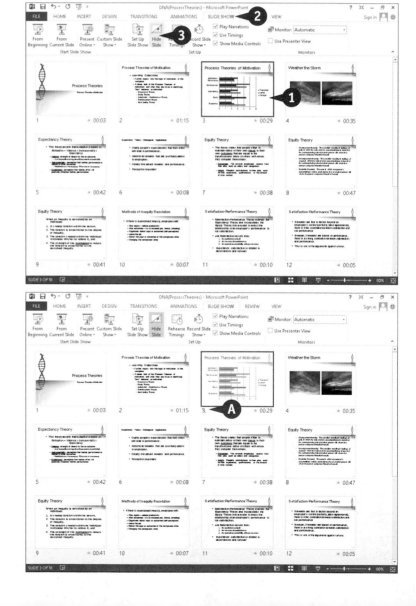

A A diagonal line appears through the slide number, indicating that the slide will not appear during the slide show.

Note: To redisplay hidden slide(s), repeat Steps **1** to **3**.

114

Zoom In the View

I n Slide Sorter view, you can view a slide in greater or less detail by changing the zoom level. If you want to view many slides at once, you can select a smaller zoom percentage so that the slides are smaller and more fit in the available space. That approach can help you find a slide more quickly. You can also apply a larger zoom percentage so that you can see fewer slides but in more detail. The appropriate zoom for any particular task can make the task more efficient, thus saving you a lot of time.

Zoom In the View

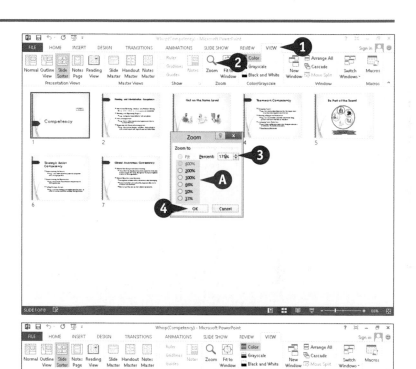

1 In Slide Sorter view, click the **View** tab.

2 Click **Zoom**.

The Zoom dialog box appears.

3 Double-click the **Percent** text box and enter a number.

A You can also click a zoom percentage option.

4 Click **OK**.

B You can also click and drag the **Zoom** slider to zoom, or click the **Zoom In** button (**+**) or the **Zoom Out** button (**−**) at each end of the slider.

PowerPoint displays the slides at the specified zoom level.

Go to an Individual Slide

hen you are working in Slide Sorter view, it is sometimes useful to go to Normal view, where you can view a slide in detail. Sometimes you will see a slide in Slide Sorter view and want to design it. While in Slide Sorter view, you can quickly and easily change to Normal view while keeping the slide selected to see it in detail. Although you can select a slide and then click the Normal view icon, these steps show a faster way to display an individual slide.

Go to an Individual Slide

1. Click the **View** tab.

2. Click **Slide Sorter**.

3. Double-click the slide that you want to see in detail.

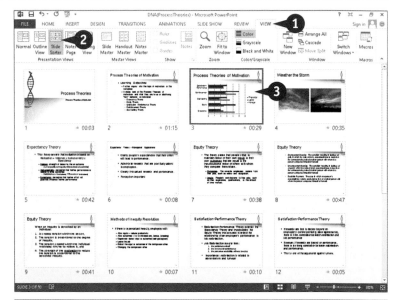

Ⓐ The slide appears in Normal view.

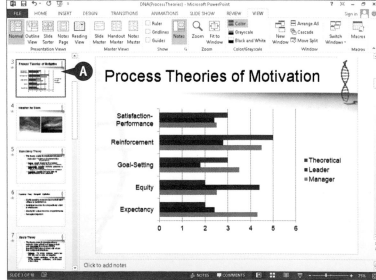

Change Slide Orientation

Typically, slide shows are presented horizontally in the landscape orientation; portrait orientation is vertical, like a business letter. The landscape orientation is made to fit a monitor, widescreen monitor, or projector screen. There are times when you may want your presentation in the portrait orientation — possibly while you print the slide show or to show two slide shows side by side on a screen. You can change the orientation of your presentation, though changing orientation distorts objects on the slides; if you want to show it in the portrait orientation and have it look good, you should change the orientation first, and then design it.

Change Slide Orientation

1. In Slide Sorter view, click the **Design** tab.

2. Click **Slide Size**.

3. Click **Custom Slide Size**.

   The Slide Size dialog box appears.

4. Click **Portrait**.

5. Click **OK**.

   The scaling dialog box appears.

6. Click **Ensure Fit**.

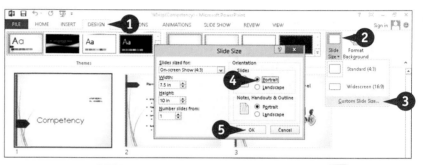

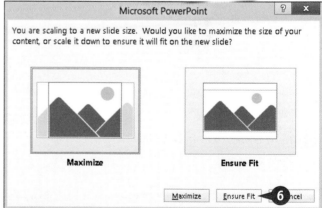

The slides change to the chosen orientation.

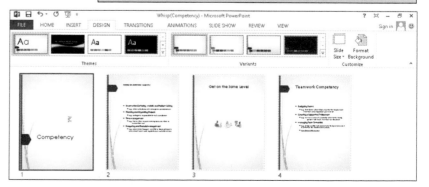

Change Aspect Ratio

You may find yourself presenting a slide show on a variety of screens, such as a widescreen or standard monitor, a notebook monitor, or an LCD or plasma projector. Most of these devices have screens that have one of two aspect ratios: 4:3 (standard) or 16:9 (widescreen). Presentations and templates come in either aspect ratio. You can change the aspect ratio of a presentation so that you can show a slide show on any device and use any template to design a presentation.

Change Aspect Ratio

① Click the **View** tab.

② Click **Normal**.

Note: This particular presentation is a 16:9 aspect ratio.

③ Click **Design**.

④ Click **Slide Size**.

⑤ In the Slide Size menu, click an aspect ratio from the list.

Ⓐ You can also customize an aspect ratio by clicking **Custom Slide Size**.

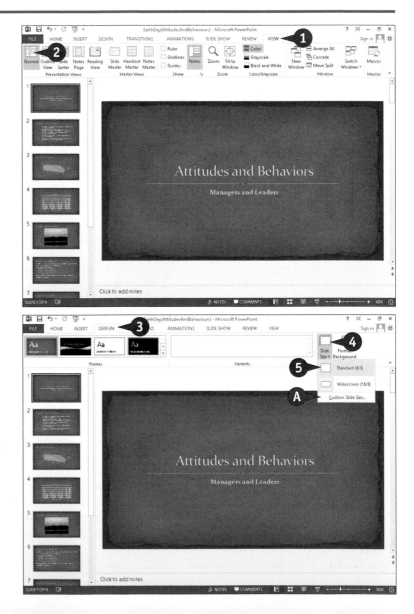

A sizing dialog box may appear.

6 Click **Maximize** or **Ensure Fit** in the dialog box.

Note: Ensure Fit resizes objects to ensure that they fit on the slide. Maximize does not resize objects, but objects may fall off the edge of the slide as a result.

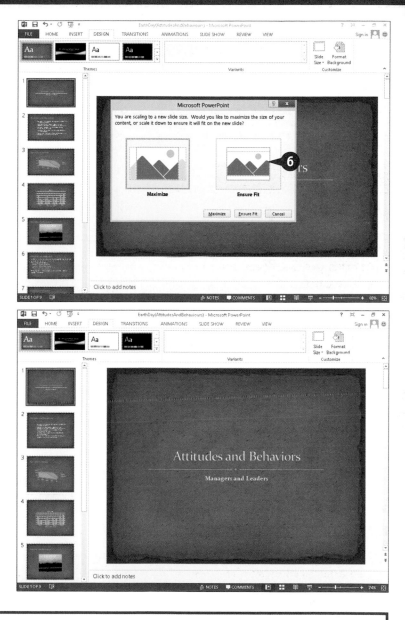

PowerPoint changes the aspect ratio of the presentation.

TIP

The background of my presentation seems a little different after I changed the aspect ratio. Did it change?

Yes, it may have changed — it depends on the circumstances. When you change aspect ratio, AutoFormat may adjust fonts and lines. Changing the aspect ratio in a presentation may skew the slide background and may resize and distort objects. Always inspect your presentation after changing the aspect ratio to see if anything changed. Better still, try to design your presentation in the proper aspect ratio. If you must change the aspect ratio of a template, do it before any design work so that potential distortion only affects the background.

View Slides in Grayscale

There are times when you may want to view your design work in black and white or grayscale. For example, in a presentation with a lot of color in the background, it can be easier to view slide content in grayscale. If you plan to print the slides in grayscale, you may want to switch to grayscale periodically during the design to see how it looks. You can view grayscale slides in Normal, Slide Sorter, or Notes Page view.

Grayscale presents slides in shades of gray. Black and white is extreme because it uses no shading.

View Slides in Grayscale

1 In Normal view, click the **View** tab.

2 Click **Grayscale**.

The presentation appears in grayscale and an additional tab called Grayscale appears.

3 Click the **Grayscale** tab.

4 Click an object in the presentation.

5 Click **Inverse Grayscale**.

A The object changes appearance.

6 Click **Back to Color View**.

The presentation returns to color view.

TIP

Can I print my presentation in grayscale or black and white on a color printer?

Yes. If you use a black-and-white printer, PowerPoint automatically adjusts the presentation to print in grayscale. If you use a color printer, do the following:

1 Click the **File** tab to go to Backstage view.

2 Click **Print**.

3 Click the **Color** down arrow (▾).

4 Click **Grayscale**.

5 Click **Print**.

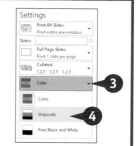

Group Slides into Sections

You may need to present multiple topics in your slide show, calling for a logical separation between topics. For example, you may want to have different themes for morning and afternoon. A presentation on Microsoft Office may need three distinct sections for three different applications, Word, Excel, and PowerPoint. Instead of creating separate presentations, you can easily separate one presentation into sections. The sections exist independently, enabling you to easily apply different themes and color schemes to each section while keeping the sections together in one presentation.

Group Slides into Sections

1 In Slide Sorter view, click the slide that you want to begin your new section.

2 Click the **Home** tab.

3 Click **Section**.

4 Click **Add Section**.

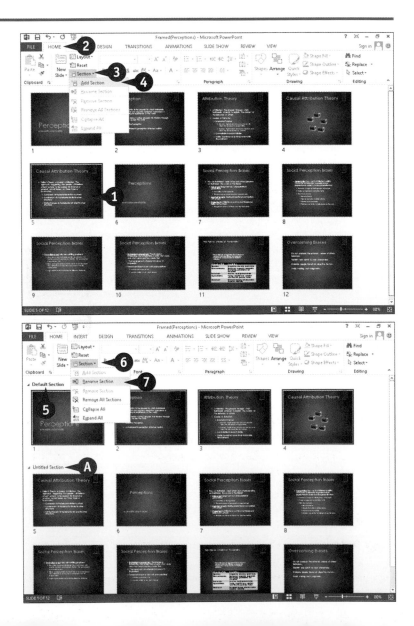

A PowerPoint inserts a section before the slide that you selected.

Note that the beginning part of the presentation becomes a section, too.

5 Click a section you want to rename.

6 Click **Section**.

7 Click **Rename Section**.

The Rename Section dialog box appears.

8 Type a new name.

9 Click **Rename**.

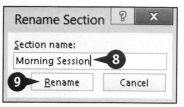

B PowerPoint renames the section.

10 Click a **Section**.

11 Click the **Design** tab.

12 Click a variation from the Variants group.

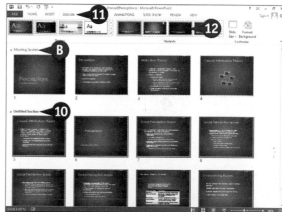

PowerPoint changes the theme for the section.

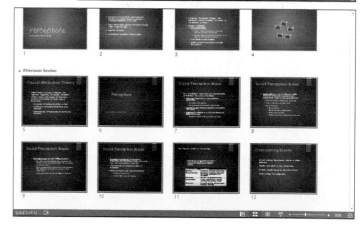

TIP

Can I get rid of a section of my presentation?

Yes. You can remove a section or simply collapse it, depending on your needs. To remove a section:

1 Click the section.

2 Press Delete.

A To collapse or expand a section, you can click the collapse icon (◢) next to the section name.

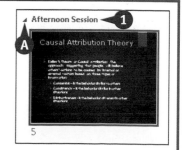

CHAPTER 7

Working with Outlines

Outline view provides the easiest and most convenient way to enter text into your presentation. It helps you organize your thoughts into a simple outline form and hierarchy so that you can focus on the flow of ideas in the presentation. It is a great place to view and make changes to text. If you need to write a paper or report to accompany your presentation, the outline is an excellent resource to write that, too.

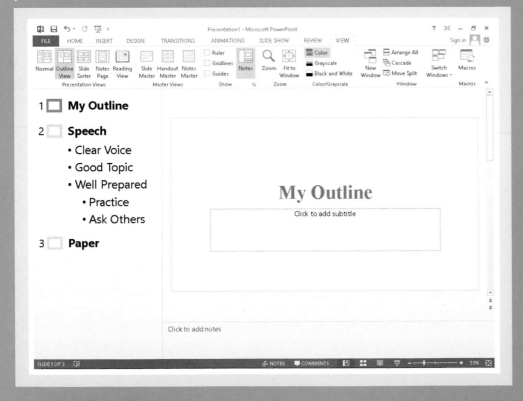

Display Outline View

Outline view is the same as Normal view except the Outline pane replaces the Slides Thumbnail pane. Typing text into a slide in Normal view can be cumbersome — you need to move and manage text and bullets. In Outline view, you simply type text into an outline and PowerPoint adds slides, inserts text into them, and manages bullets. When you finish working with the text, you can switch to Normal view to work on the slide design. You can easily move between Outline view and other views so that you can alternate between typing text and designing the slides.

Display Outline View

1 Click the **View** tab.

2 Click **Outline View**.

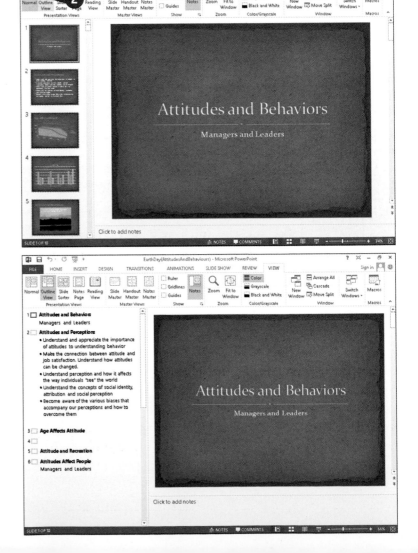

PowerPoint displays Outline view.

Understanding How Outline and Slide Content Relate

Y ou can enter presentation text in Outline view or directly on a slide in Normal view. Typing text into a slide in Normal view can be cumbersome and time consuming — you need to move and manage text and bullets, possibly from slide to slide. In Outline view, you type text in a familiar outline form. To take advantage of Outline view, you must first become familiar with it. You can work more effectively when you understand how the contents of the outline and slides relate to each other.

One Heading, One Slide

Every top-level heading (a heading at level one in the outline) is the title of a slide. When you type text in a title placeholder on a slide, it appears as a level-one heading in the outline. When you type a level-one heading in the outline, PowerPoint adds a slide and the level-one heading appears in the title placeholder on the slide.

AUTO REPAIR
- Fast repair!
- High Quality
- Low Price

Bullet to Bullet

The second level of headings in an outline becomes the bullets in the content placeholder on the corresponding slide. If you have more than one level of bullets in the outline, there will be multiple levels of bullets on the slide, and vice versa. As you type, PowerPoint manages the bullets, but you can change the way they look.

Graphics

Graphics never appear in the outline. You place graphics on slides and you see them in the Slide pane. You can insert graphics in a content placeholder, in a header or footer, or in any available location on the slide. An advantage of Outline view is that graphics do not appear in the outline, so you can concentrate on text.

Special Text

Special text elements include headers, footers, text boxes, tables, charts, and in some cases, WordArt. Many of the graphics have text elements. Text elements such as these are some of the graphics that appear on a slide — they do not appear as part of the outline.

Enter Presentation Content in an Outline

Outline view provides the easiest way to enter text into your presentation. You can build the text for a presentation very quickly with Outline view. You build your outline by typing text and using the Enter and Tab keys, just like any other outline. PowerPoint automatically adds slides for each first-level item in the outline. You can watch the slide develop as you type the text. The first slide in your outline automatically becomes the presentation's Title slide. Additional slides use a Title and Content slide layout automatically, although you can change the layout later.

Enter Presentation Content in an Outline

1 Start a new presentation.

Note: See Chapter 1 to learn how to start a new presentation.

2 Click **View**.

3 Click **Outline View**.

Outline view appears.

4 Click in the Outline pane next to the slide icon (▢).

5 Type a line of text; the text appears on the slide as you type.

6 Press Enter.

Ⓐ The insertion point advances to the next line and PowerPoint adds a second slide, a Title and Content slide.

7 Click the **Home** tab.

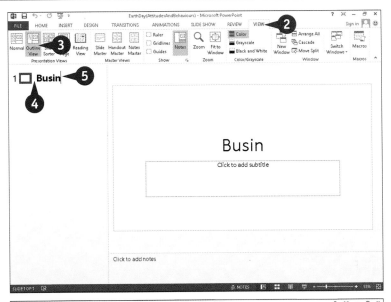

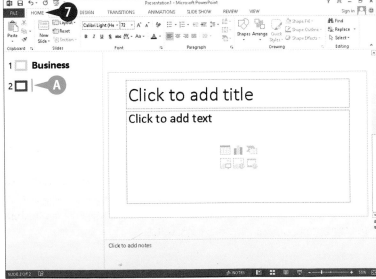

8 Type a second line of text; the text appears on the slide as you type.

9 Press **Enter**.

The insertion point moves to the next line.

10 Press **Tab**.

Ⓑ The insertion point moves one tab to the right, becoming the first bullet on the second slide.

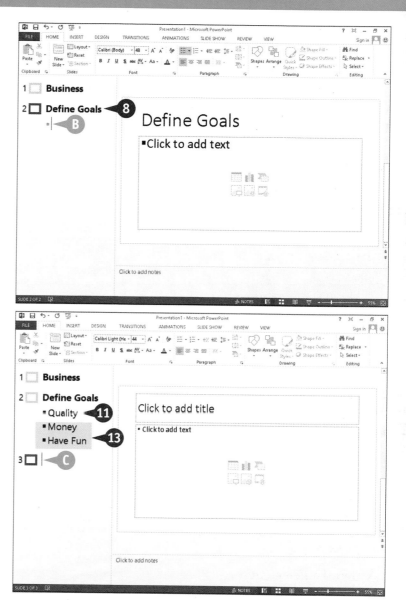

11 Type text for the bullet item.

12 Press **Enter**.

The insertion point moves to the next line.

13 Repeat Steps **11** and **12** to add bullet items as needed.

14 Press **Shift** + **Tab**.

Ⓒ The insertion point moves left, a slide icon appears, and PowerPoint adds a third slide, a Title and Content slide.

TIP

Is there a way to enlarge the Outline pane and make the font bigger to view my outline text?
Yes. Position the mouse pointer (⟨⟩) over the border between the Outline pane and the slide pane until it changes to the mouse splitter (↕). Click and drag the border to the right to enlarge the pane, and click and drag to the left to make it smaller. To increase the font size of the outline, click anywhere in the Outline pane and then click **Zoom** on the View tab. When the Zoom dialog box appears, select a bigger zoom percentage and then click the **OK** button.

Move Slides and Bullet Points in an Outline

As with the content of other types of documents, presentation content evolves. For example, you may review your presentation and decide on a more logical flow for the information. A great advantage of Outline view is the ability to move bullet points easily and text around — even from slide to slide. You can also easily promote and demote bullet points from one level to another. You can even rearrange slides, bullet points, and text in your presentation by dragging and dropping them in the Outline pane.

Move Slides and Bullet Points in an Outline

1 Click the **View** tab.

2 Click **Outline View**.

3 In the Outline pane, click the **Slide** icon (⬜) for the slide you want to move.

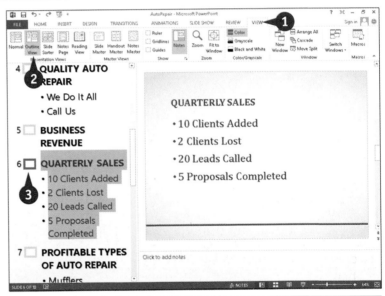

4 Click and drag the **Slide** icon (⬜) to the desired position using the horizontal line as a guide.

Note: You can use the **Undo** button (↩) on the Quick Access Toolbar if you make a mistake.

Note: You can also cut, copy, and paste text in the Outline pane.

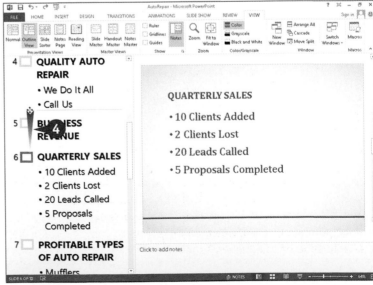

Ⓐ When you release the mouse button, the slide content moves to where you dragged it.

5 Click the bullet of a bullet point.

6 Click and drag the bullet item to a new location in the bulleted list.

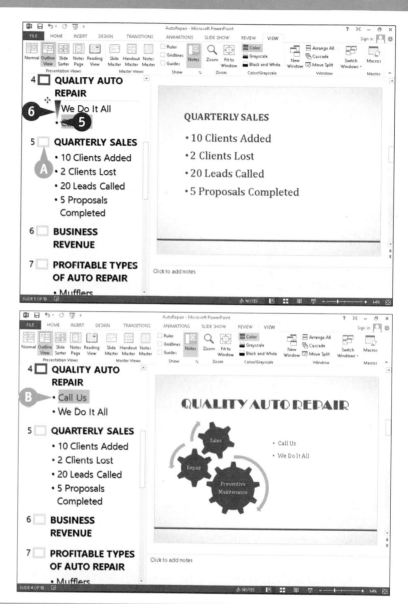

Ⓑ When you release the mouse button, the bullet item moves to where you dragged it.

Note: You can use this method to move a bullet item from one slide to another.

Note: You can click and drag text to select it and then drag it to another location.

TIPS

I dragged my slide to another location and now I have more bullet points on the slide. What happened?

You probably dragged the slide to a spot inside another slide. Dragging a slide into a group of bullet points on a second slide breaks the second slide apart and places the bottom bullet points of the second slide on the moved slide.

Are there any other actions I can execute by dragging bullets?

Yes. You can promote and demote bullet points in the outline. Click and drag a bullet left or right until the vertical line representing its outline position reaches the desired outline level. Release the mouse and the bullet point moves.

Promote and Demote Items

As you build and reorganize presentation content, you may need to move bullet points, or possibly slides, in the outline so that they become lower-level bullet points, a method called *demoting*. Conversely, you can move lower-level bullet points to become higher-level bullet points or even slides, which is called *promoting*. Changing the levels of bullet points and slides is cumbersome if you are working on the actual slide. You can save a lot of time and effort using the Outline pane, where you can easily promote and demote items with keystrokes and command button clicks on the ribbon.

Promote and Demote Items

1 In Outline View, click the **Home** tab.

Note: See Chapter 2 to learn how to switch views.

2 Click anywhere in a bullet point.

3 Click the **Demote** button (⇥≡).

Note: Alternatively, you can press **Tab**.

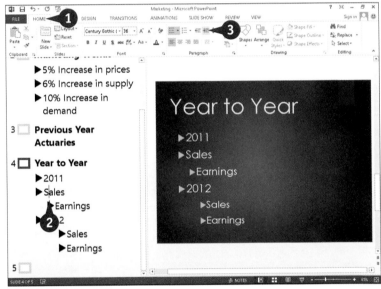

A The bullet point moves to the right, down one level in the outline hierarchy.

4 Click and drag across bullet points to select them.

Note: You can click and drag across bullet points at different hierarchy levels to perform this task.

5 Click the **Promote** button (⇤≡).

Note: Alternatively, you can press **Shift** + **Tab**.

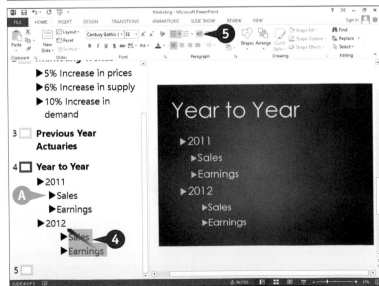

B The bullet points move left, up one level in the outline hierarchy.

6 Click a second-level bullet point, one tab to the right of the slide level.

7 Click the **Promote** button (⇤).

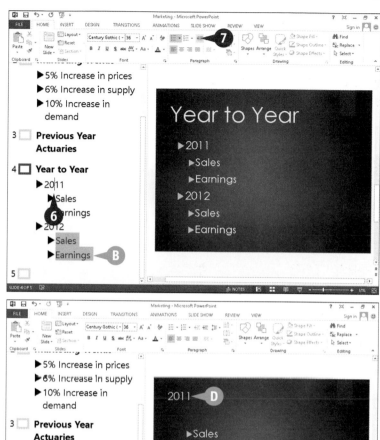

C PowerPoint promotes the bullet point to a slide and adds a slide.

D The bullet point becomes the title of the new slide.

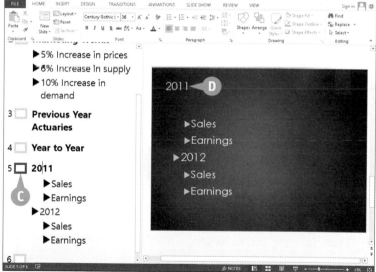

Can I promote and demote headings directly on a slide?

Yes. However, you cannot promote or demote a slide title. This is a true advantage of using Outline view. In Normal view, you need to add a slide and then cut and paste bullet points to promote a bullet point to a slide. To change the level of a bullet point on a slide, click the bullet and then click either **Promote** (⇤) or **Demote** (⇥) in the Paragraph group on the Home tab. The change in promotion or demotion occurs both on the slide and in the outline. If you click the bullet point text on the slide, it does not work — you must click the bullet.

Collapse and Expand an Outline

With a lengthy presentation, you can sometimes work more effectively if you collapse an outline so you see only slide titles and expand only certain slides to look at the details on them. Collapsing parts of the outline helps you to easily scroll through the presentation and identify outline items quickly. For example, you may want to collapse the slides that you are finished designing and expand the slides that still need work. You can collapse and expand any part or all of the outline. You can collapse or expand multiple slides. Simply select multiple slides before performing these steps.

Collapse and Expand an Outline

1 Click the **View** tab.

2 Click **Outline View**.

3 Right-click any text within a slide.

The submenu appears.

4 Click **Collapse**.

Ⓐ Click **Collapse All** to collapse all slides in the presentation.

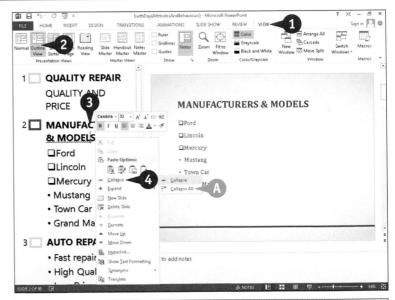

PowerPoint collapses all details and displays a wavy line under the slide title.

5 Right-click a collapsed slide title.

6 Click **Expand**.

Ⓑ Click **Expand All** to expand all slides in the presentation.

The slide details reappear.

Note: You can also double-click the **Slide** icon (▢) to collapse or expand slide details.

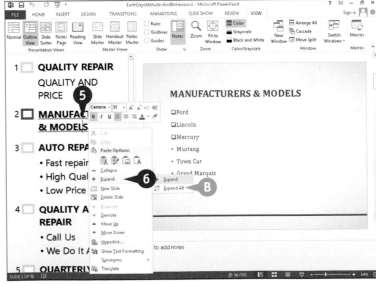

Edit Outline Content

Rarely does a first draft become a final presentation. You can edit the text in your presentation to make it as professional as possible. You typically want to change your presentation text to polish it, or fix typos and other errors. Many times a second read or proofread produces ideas to improve the wording. For example, maybe you need to update a favorite presentation because it has become outdated. Editing an outline is much like editing text anywhere else in PowerPoint, or in any other application for that matter.

Edit Outline Content

1 Click the **View** tab.

2 Click **Outline View**.

3 Click the point where you want to add or delete text.

4 Type to add text, or press Delete or Backspace to delete the text.

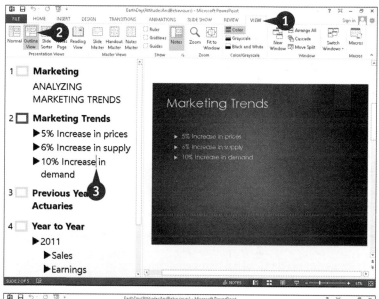

A The outline reflects the changes you made.

5 Click the bullet for any bullet point to select the entire bullet point.

Note: You can also click a **Slide** icon (▢) to select an entire slide.

6 Press Delete.

PowerPoint deletes the entire bullet point or slide.

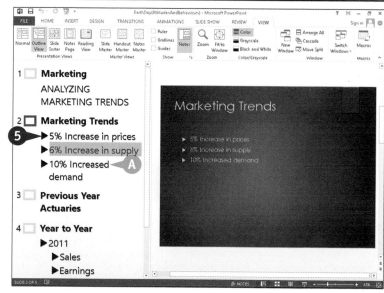

Insert Slides from an Outline

If you already have an outline that you want to use as a basis for your presentation, you do not need to retype it in PowerPoint. For example, you may already have an outline that you used to give a speech or to write a paper. To save time, you can import an outline into a new PowerPoint presentation, and then edit and format that content like any other presentation.

PowerPoint imports outlines that are created in Outline view in Microsoft Word. It also imports text file outlines written in text editors such as Notepad.

Insert Slides from an Outline

1 Click the **File** tab to show Backstage view.

2 Click **Open**.

3 Click **Computer**.

4 Click **Browse**.

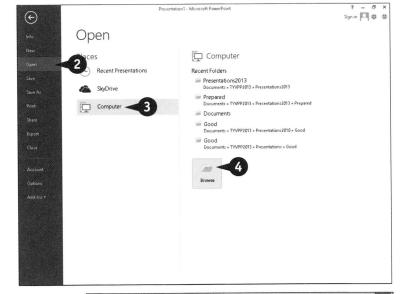

The Open dialog box appears.

5 Click the down arrow (⌄).

6 Click **All Outlines**.

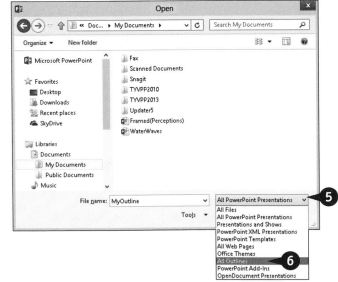

PowerPoint shows all file types that can hold an outline, such as Word files (.docx), text files (.txt), and rich text files (.rtf).

7 Click the folder that holds the outline file you want to import.

8 Click the outline file.

9 Click **Open**.

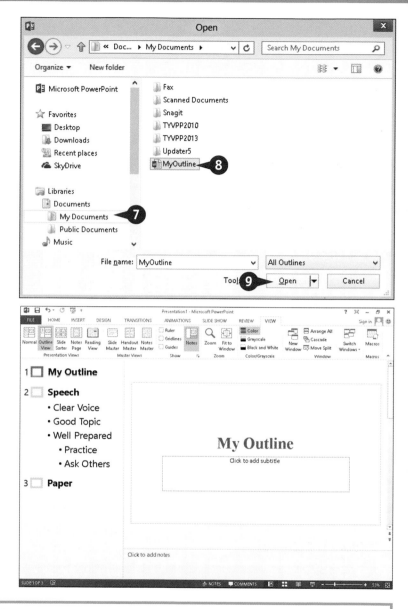

The new presentation appears in Outline view.

All of the content in my Microsoft Word outline became slides. What went wrong?

The outline is not in the proper format. The outline needs to be created with the Outline view in Word, which is very similar to typing an outline in PowerPoint. If you need an outline in both Word and PowerPoint, you can create it in either application and export it to the other application.

How does PowerPoint know where to start each slide?

Each top-level heading in the imported outline becomes the title for a new slide — just like a PowerPoint outline. So, be sure to review the outline before importing it. Make sure each slide title is at the top level in the outline.

CHAPTER 8

Using Themes

You can use the themes that are built into PowerPoint as well as online themes to apply a professional-looking design to your presentation. Although it is possible to design slides by applying slide backgrounds and graphics manually, or by formatting elements on slides or master slides one by one, people most commonly use slide themes to develop their presentations.

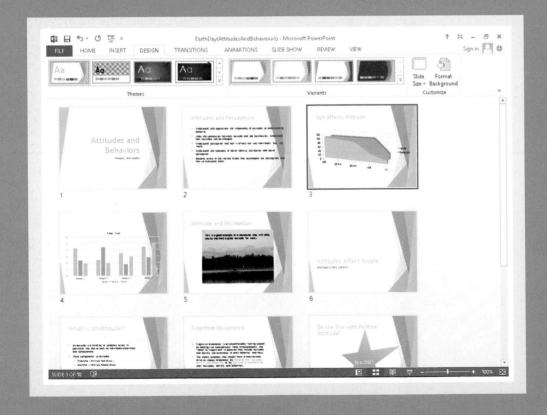

Understanding Themes

A theme is the look, color, and graphics that the slides in your presentation have in common. You can use a theme from the PowerPoint program, get one from Microsoft Office Online, or use a theme from an existing presentation. You can also create a blank presentation, and then apply a background and graphics to create your own theme — and then save the theme.

Theme Elements

By default, each new presentation you create uses a blank design theme. When you choose a specific theme, PowerPoint applies a set of colors, fonts, and placeholder positions to the slides. All of these elements vary greatly from theme to theme. The theme can also include a background color, background graphics, and effects for background graphics.

Apply Themes

It is easy to apply a theme to a single slide, a section, or the entire presentation. Generally it is better to use one theme for an entire presentation so that the slides have a consistent look and feel. However, you can also choose to apply a different theme to a particular slide for emphasis.

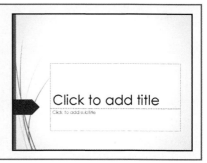

Modify Themes

Although PowerPoint provides professionally designed slide themes, you can tailor existing themes to meet your specific needs. You can change the background, background color, or the color scheme of the entire theme. Once you design a theme you really like, you can save it to the theme gallery to use again.

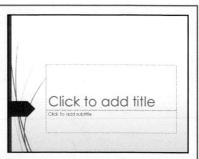

Themes and Masters

Slide masters determine where placeholders and objects appear on each slide layout. Each theme has a master slide for the Title slide, a master slide for the Title and Content Slide, and so on. After you apply a theme, you can modify the masters. Any changes you make to the master slides automatically appear in your presentation slides. You can also change the fonts on the master slides.

The Anatomy of a Theme

Themes control several aspects of your slide design. The theme determines the locations of placeholders, the color scheme, the slide background, and any graphics that may be part of the theme. These characteristics vary considerably from theme to theme. For example, the title may be on the top of slides in one theme and on the bottom of slides in another theme. These variations give each theme its own flavor and personality.

A Placeholder Position

Placeholder positions vary from theme to theme. Each theme has a set of slide masters that control where placeholders appear on each slide layout.

B Graphic Elements

Some themes include graphic elements that are typically part of the background. To avoid accidentally changing them, you can modify them on the slide masters, but not on individual slides.

C Color Scheme

Themes control the colors applied to slide text, the background, and objects such as tables, charts, and SmartArt Graphics. You can change colors on individual slides.

D Background

Themes specify the background applied to slides. The background might be a solid color, a gradient, or a pattern, and may include graphics.

E Effects

Effects give a dimensional appearance to graphics by adding shadows, transparency, 3-D, and more. A theme may apply a particular style of effect to graphics.

Apply a Theme to Selected Slides

You can apply a different theme to a single slide in either Normal or Slide Sorter view. You may want to apply a different theme to a single slide to emphasize the slide or make it stand out. If you apply a different theme to a single slide, you will normally want it to complement the design of the theme used on the other slides in the presentation. As you advance slides, the transition from one theme to another affects your viewers.

Apply a Theme to Selected Slides

1 Click **View**.

2 Click **Slide Sorter**.

3 Select a slide or slides.

Note: To select multiple slides, click the first slide, and then press **Ctrl** while clicking additional slides.

4 Click the **Design** tab.

5 Click the **Themes** down arrow (▼).

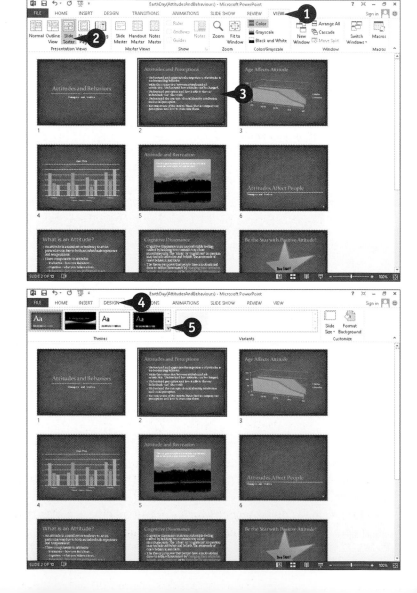

The gallery of themes appears.

6 Right-click a theme.

The shortcut menu appears.

7 Click **Apply to Selected Slides**.

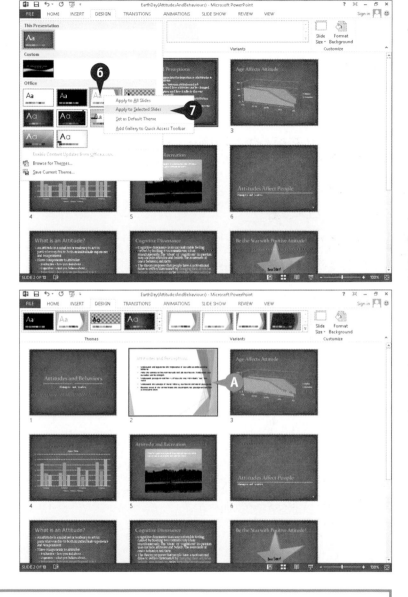

A PowerPoint applies the theme to the slide(s) you selected.

TIPS

If I change a few slides to a different theme, can I use the master slide features for those slides?

Yes. When you apply a theme to a presentation, PowerPoint creates a set of master slides for that theme. You get a set of master slides for every theme in your presentation — any of which you can modify. In Chapter 9, you learn about using master slides.

Why does my shortcut menu sometimes have an option called Apply to matching slides?

Apply to matching slides appears on the Themes shortcut menu if you are using more than one theme. You can apply your chosen theme to all slides that have the same theme as the currently selected slide.

Apply a Theme to All Slides

You can apply one theme to all the slides in a presentation. It is important to give your slides a consistent appearance so your presentation looks professional. While the slide layouts may vary, the theme supplies common colors, graphics, and more. This allows you to focus on content rather than design and formatting. You may design a presentation and then decide that the theme you originally chose does not set the proper mood for the presentation. No problem, just apply a different theme for the proper feeling. You can change the theme in either Normal or Slide Sorter view.

Apply a Theme to All Slides

1 In Slide Sorter view, click at least one slide.

2 Click the **Design** tab.

3 Click the **Themes** down arrow ($\overline{\overline{}}$).

The gallery of themes appears.

4 Click a theme.

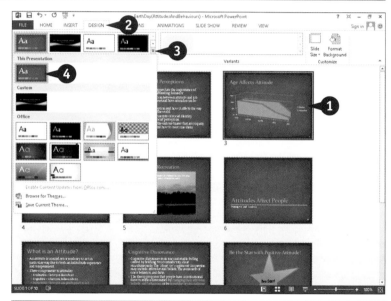

PowerPoint applies the theme to all slides in the presentation.

Note: You can also right-click a thumbnail in the gallery and then click **Apply to All Slides**.

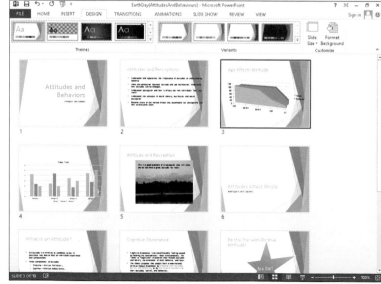

Apply a Theme to a Section

It is common to change topics during a presentation. For example, a person teaching a class about Microsoft Office changes topics when moving from teaching PowerPoint to teaching Excel. If you change topics, you might want to alter the mood to one that is more appropriate for the new topic. You can apply themes to sections of a presentation. Doing so gives each section a look and feel that is consistent with the others, yet makes it obvious that that particular section of your presentation is dedicated to a specific topic. You can change the theme in either Normal or Slide Sorter view.

Apply a Theme to a Section

1 In Slide Sorter view, click a section heading.

2 Click the **Design** tab.

3 Click the **Themes** down arrow ($\overline{\overline{}}$).

The gallery of themes appears.

4 Click a theme.

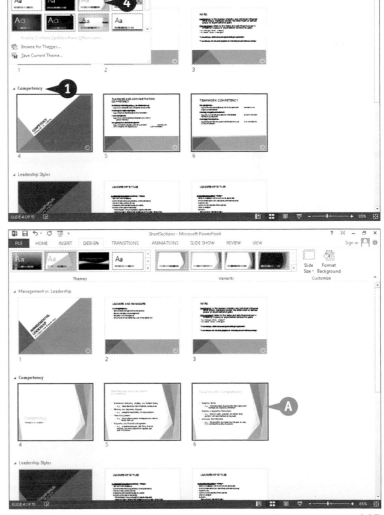

A PowerPoint applies the theme to all slides in the section.

Change Theme Colors

Each theme includes a color scheme. You can add variety or emphasize certain slides by changing the color scheme of only those particular slides. You can also change the color scheme of an entire presentation or a section of a presentation. When you alter the color scheme, the other aspects of the theme, such as placeholder position and background objects, stay the same — only the colors change. You can change the color scheme in Normal view or Slide Sorter view.

Change Theme Colors

① In Slide Sorter view, click a slide or slides.

Note: To select multiple slides, click the first slide, and then press Ctrl while clicking additional slides.

② Click the **Design** tab.

③ Right-click a color scheme from the Variants gallery.

④ Click **Apply to Selected Slides**.

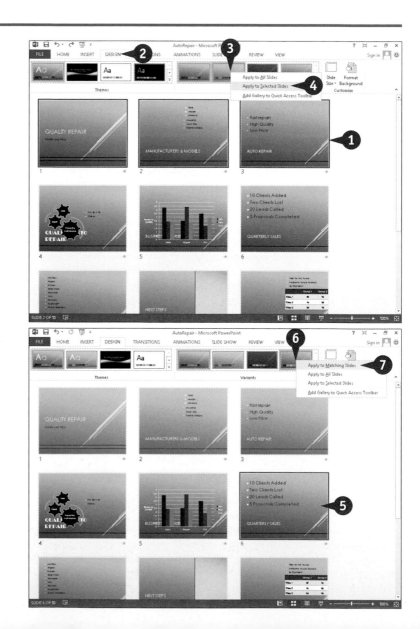

PowerPoint applies the color scheme to the slides you selected.

⑤ Select a slide designed with the theme you want to change.

⑥ Right-click a color scheme from the Variants gallery.

⑦ Click **Apply to Matching Slides**.

PowerPoint applies the color scheme to all slides whose theme matches the selected slide.

8 Right-click a color scheme from the Variants gallery.

9 Click **Apply to All Slides**.

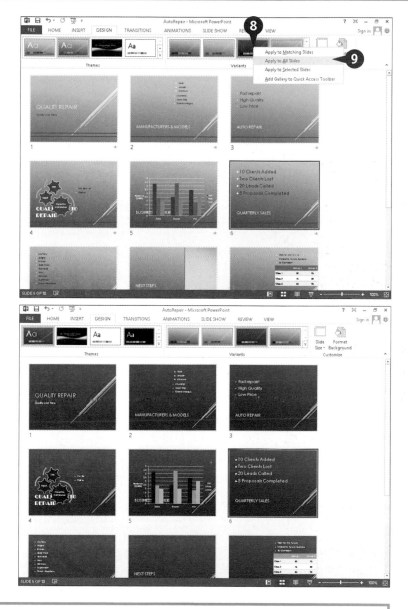

PowerPoint applies the selected color scheme to all slides in the presentation.

Is changing the background color of the theme different than changing the color scheme of the theme?
Yes. When you change the color scheme, it changes the colors of the background plus all of the geometric shapes on the slide, including charts and tables; when you format the background and change its color, it changes only the background and not the geometric shapes. Objects such as pictures and clip art are not affected by either type of change. You can change the background and foreground of objects such as clip art and pictures by formatting them. Some backgrounds are complicated, and changing the color of a complicated background produces a similar effect to changing the color scheme.

Modify the Background

A theme applies a background on which all slide elements sit. You can make the background a color or plain white, or you can even use a texture or digital picture as a background. For example, you can use a digital photo of a new product as a slide background for a presentation introducing the product. You can change the background for one slide, for a theme, or throughout the presentation and you can do this in Normal or Slide Sorter view. Be careful with your choice of background — a complicated background can make a presentation hard to read or distracting.

Modify the Background

1 Select the slide(s) you want to modify in Slide Sorter view.

Note: To select multiple slides, click the first slide, and then press `Ctrl` while clicking additional slides.

2 Click the **Design** tab.

3 Click **Format Background**.

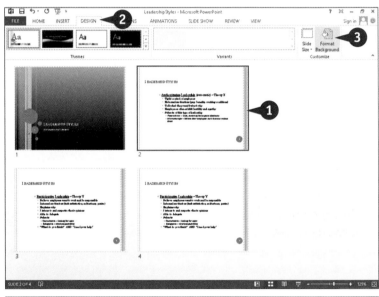

The Format Background pane appears.

4 Click the **Fill** icon (⬧).

5 Click **Solid fill** (○ changes to ⦿).

6 Click the **Color** button (⬚▾).

7 Click a color.

Ⓐ You can click **Apply to All** to apply the color to all slides.

PowerPoint applies the background color to the selected slides.

8 Click **Gradient fill** (○ changes to ◉).

PowerPoint applies a preset gradient to the background.

B You can adjust gradient options to change the direction and gradient type.

C You fine-tune the gradient by adjusting its characteristics, such as brightness and transparency.

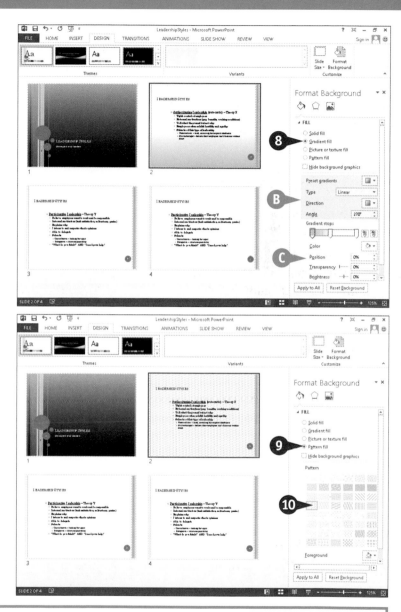

9 Click **Pattern fill** (○ changes to ◉).

10 Click a pattern from the gallery.

PowerPoint applies the background pattern to the selected slides.

TIPS

In PowerPoint 2010 I could change the font scheme. Can I still do that?

No, you can no longer change the font scheme as part of the theme. In past PowerPoint versions, you could change the font scheme in the theme or the master slides — both accomplished the same result. In PowerPoint 2013, you can only change the font scheme in the master slides.

Why does PowerPoint give me a pattern as soon as I click the Pattern fill option?

PowerPoint applies a preset pattern when you click the **Pattern fill** option. You can either select a different pattern version, or you can click the **Solid fill** option to get rid of the pattern.

Apply a Texture or Picture Background

If you really want to make a slide more dramatic, you can push design limits by using either a texture or a digital picture as a background. For example, you can use a digital photo of a landscape and sunrise for a slide introducing a new idea. Typically, you would not do this for an entire set of slides because a complicated background makes a slide difficult to read and can be hard on the audience's eyes. You can add a picture to the background of a slide in either Slide Sorter or Normal view.

Apply a Texture or Picture Background

1 Select the slide(s) to which you want to add a background in Slide Sorter view.

Note: To select multiple slides, click the first slide, and then press `Ctrl` while clicking additional slides.

2 Click the **Design** tab.

3 Click **Format Background**.

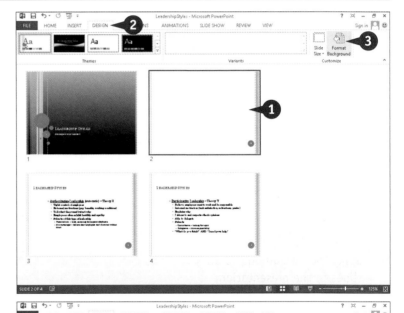

The Format Background pane appears.

4 Click the **Fill** icon (🖋).

5 Click **Picture or texture fill** (○ changes to ◉).

The slide fills with a preset texture.

Ⓐ Click the **Texture** button (🖼▾) to apply a texture to the background.

6 Click **File**.

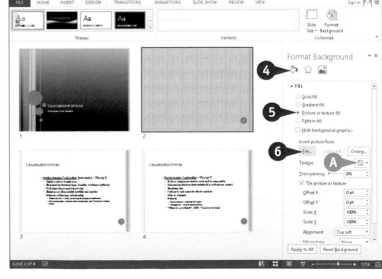

The Insert Picture dialog box appears.

7 Click the folder that contains the picture file you want to insert.

8 Click the picture file.

9 Click **Insert**.

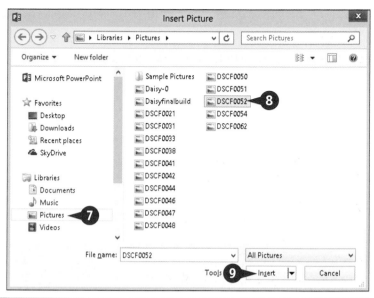

The Insert Picture dialog box closes and the picture becomes the background.

10 Click the **Picture** icon (🖾) to apply color corrections to the picture.

B You can click **Apply to All** to apply the background to all slides in the presentation.

TIP

How can I remove a texture or picture from the background?
With the Format Background pane open, follow these steps:

1 Click the **Fill** icon (🖎).

2 Click **Solid fill** (○ changes to ⦿).

3 Click the **Color** button (🖎▾).

4 Click **Automatic**.

PowerPoint removes the background.

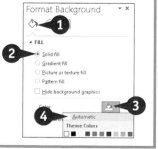

Save Your Own Theme

If you spent a lot of time creating your own theme, you may want to use it again. For example, say you designed a theme from scratch or modified an existing theme, where you applied a color scheme and background that really works, and possibly some graphics. If you do not want to do all this work again, you can save the results as a theme. This enables you to quickly apply that combination of color, background, and graphics to other presentations.

Save Your Own Theme

1 Click the **Design** tab.

2 Click the **Themes** down arrow (⤓).

The gallery of themes appears.

Ⓐ If you save your theme in the PowerPoint theme default folder, it will appear under Custom.

3 Click **Save Current Theme**.

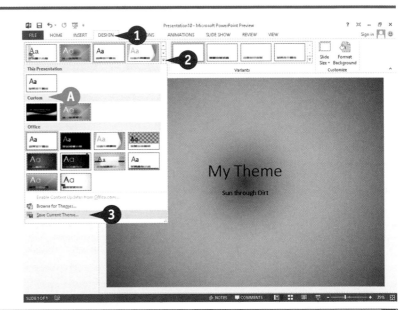

The Save Current Theme dialog box appears.

4 Type a filename.

Ⓑ This is the default folder location for themes.

Note: Do not change the folder location. Your themes appear in the gallery of themes because they are in this folder location.

5 Click **Save**.

PowerPoint saves the theme and adds it to the Custom section of the gallery.

152

Make a Theme the Default for New Presentations

By default, a new presentation has a blank background and uses the Calibri font in varying sizes and weights for the various placeholders. If you have a theme that you use often, you can make that theme the default for new presentations so it is automatically applied to future blank presentations. This gives you a fast start in designing a new presentation. If the default theme is not right for any particular presentation, you can always change it to one you prefer.

Make a Theme the Default for New Presentations

1 Click the **Design** tab.

2 Click the **Themes** down arrow (⩦).

The gallery of themes appears.

3 Right-click the theme you want to set as the default.

4 Click **Set as Default Theme**.

The theme immediately becomes the default theme. Any blank presentation you create uses that theme.

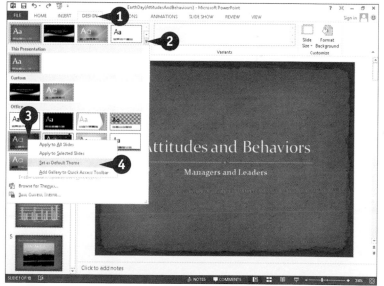

5 Click the **File** tab to show Backstage view.

6 Click **New**.

Ⓐ The selected theme appears as the default theme.

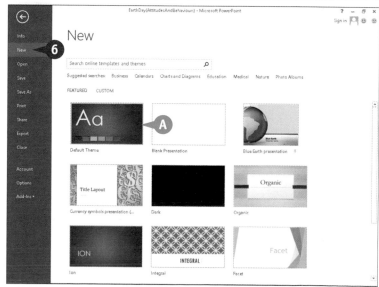

Save a Template

A template is a boilerplate presentation that you use repeatedly but change certain items each time you use it. It includes a presentation design plus reusable content such as slides that you would often use in a particular type of presentation. For example, you may have a template presentation for selling to a purchasing group's clients — content about the purchasing group does not change from client to client, so you would have slides about them in the template along with slides that you would tailor to each client. You can save a lot of time by using templates for repeatable presentations.

Save a Template

1. Click the **File** tab to show Backstage view.

2. Click **Save As**.

3. Click **Computer**.

4. Click **Browse**.

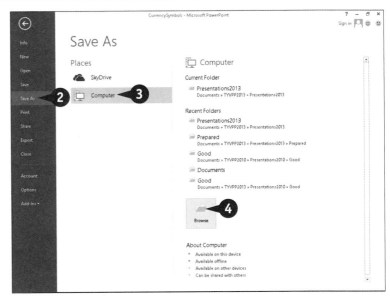

The Save As dialog box appears.

5. Click the **Save as type** down arrow (∨).

6. Click **PowerPoint Template**.

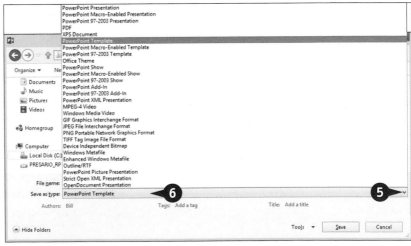

Ⓐ This is the default folder location for themes and templates.

Note: It is best not to change this folder location. Your templates appear in the templates gallery because they are in this folder location, which is the same as the theme folder location.

⑦ Type a filename.

⑧ Click **Save**.

PowerPoint saves the presentation as a template.

⑨ Click the **File** tab to show Backstage view.

⑩ Click **New**.

⑪ Click **Custom**.

Ⓑ Your template appears in the Custom template gallery.

Note: You may need to close and open PowerPoint for the template to appear in the Custom template list.

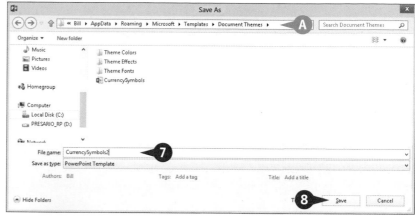

TIP

What is the difference between using a template and using a regular presentation as a template?
A PowerPoint presentation has a .pptx file extension and a template has a .potx file extension. If a template (.potx) is in the Template folder, it appears in the template list — you simply click it and PowerPoint creates a new presentation from a copy of the template. If you double-click a presentation (.pptx) in Windows Explorer or on your Desktop, it opens. If you double-click a template (.potx), it creates and opens a copy of itself. The original is protected from unintentional changes because it does not open. To change a template (.potx), you must open it through the Open dialog box.

CHAPTER 9

Using Masters

Masters enable you to make global settings for your slides, such as inserting your company logo or a page number on every slide. When you change a master, all slides based on that master also change.

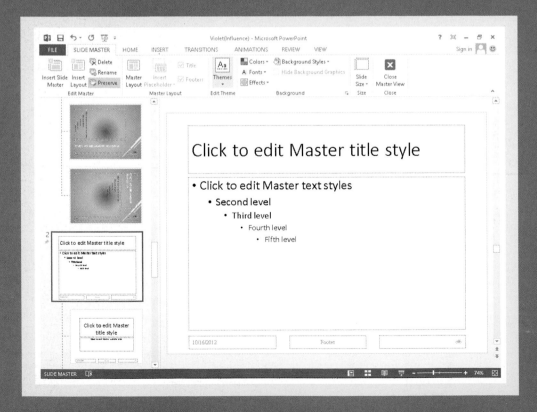

Understanding Masters

PowerPoint offers three master views: the *Slide Master*, which determines how presentation slides look; the *Handout Master*, which controls how a printed version of your presentation looks; and the *Notes Master*, which dictates how a printout of your notes looks. The three master views enable you to set up the basic structure for each slide layout, plus the notes and printed handouts. This saves time because you do not need to design each presentation slide from scratch. For example, the Title and Content slide layout is designed once in the Slide Master view, but you can use it over and over again.

Work with Three Kinds of Masters

The *Master Slides* consist of a set of slides called the *Layout Masters* — there is one Layout Master for each slide layout that you will use to build your presentation. The Master Slides also include a slide called the *Slide Master*, which controls the theme and formatting for the Layout Masters. The Handout Master controls the look and layout of the printed handouts when you print the slides of your presentation. The Notes Master controls how the printout of your presentation notes looks.

Using Masters to Make Global Changes

Any change, including formatting, that you make to a Layout Master is applied to its corresponding presentation slides. For example, if you redesign the Layout Master that controls the Title and Content layout by moving the title from the top of the page to the bottom, every slide in the presentation using the Title and Content layout reflects that change. This saves you time and gives your presentation a consistent look and feel. If you change the formatting of an element on the Slide Master, PowerPoint changes that element on all Layout Masters and all presentation slides.

How Masters Relate to the Theme

Masters are based on themes. When you apply a theme to your presentation, PowerPoint automatically creates a set of Master Slides with that theme. You can alter the theme of your Master Slides and then save it as a new theme. If you apply more than one theme to your presentation, you will have multiple sets of Master Slides — one for each theme. For example, if you have three themes, you will have three Title and Content Layout Masters, one for each theme. You can change the design of the Layout Master of the Title and Content slide in one theme without affecting the Title and Content slides in the other two themes.

Overriding Master Settings

When you make changes to individual presentation slides, those changes take precedence over settings on the corresponding Layout Master or the Slide Master. For example, if you change the font color of the title placeholder of a Title and Content presentation slide in Normal view, a change to the title placeholder font color of the Title and Content Layout Master does not affect it. The change on the individual presentation slide takes precedence. If you place a graphic on a Layout Master, you can omit it from the background of an individual presentation slide in Normal view.

Understanding Slide Master Elements

You can use the Master Slides to create global design settings for your slides. The Slide Master and Layout Masters contain placeholders where you can format text. They also contain various placeholders for footer information, slide numbers, and a date. Any change to a Layout Master is applied to any presentation slide that has its corresponding layout. When you make a formatting change to a placeholder on the Slide Master, PowerPoint applies that change to any corresponding placeholder anywhere in the presentation. One change can affect many slides, but only for the theme associated with the Master Slide you are changing.

Ⓐ Slide Master

The Slide Master is connected to its related Layout Masters with a dotted line. The Slide Thumbnails pane shows one set of Master Slides for each theme.

Ⓑ Layout Masters

Layout Masters represent the various slide layouts that you can insert into a presentation, such as the Title and Content layouts. Changes on a Layout Master affect only those presentation slides with the layout of that particular master.

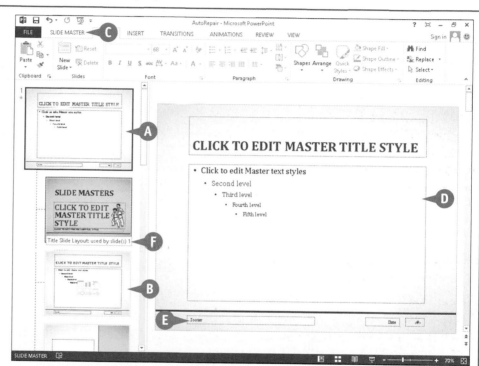

Ⓒ Slide Master Tab

Use the Slide Master tab to change Master Slides — you can design the background of masters, change or insert placeholders, and change theme colors and font schemes.

Ⓓ Placeholders

You can format an entire placeholder, some of its text, or each bullet point individually by selecting a particular bullet point before formatting.

Ⓔ Footer, Date, and Slide Numbers

The Date placeholder positions the date on slides; the Page (#) placeholder provides page numbers on slides; the Footer placeholder provides a footer on the slides.

Ⓕ Dependency on a Master Design

Position the mouse pointer (ₖ) over any slide in the Slide Master view and a ScreenTip shows you which presentation slides use that Layout Master design.

Open and Close Slide Master View

You work with the Slide Master and Layout Masters in Slide Master view. Opening Slide Master view automatically displays the Slide Master tab for working with the set of Master Slides. This tab was created to help you design the Master Slides, but you can also use the other tabs on the ribbon. After you make changes to the Master Slides and close Slide Master view, PowerPoint redisplays whatever view you had open previously — Normal view, Slide Sorter view, or Notes Page view. Global changes to presentation slides due to changes in Master Slides are reflected there.

Open and Close Slide Master View

1 Click the **View** tab.

2 Click **Slide Master**.

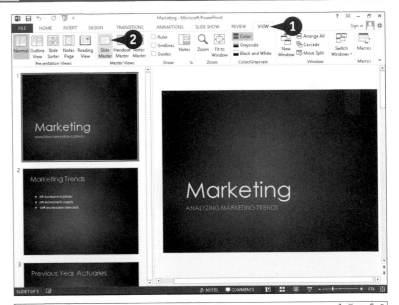

Slide Master view and the Slide Master tab appear.

3 Click the **Slide Master** tab.

4 Click **Close Master View**.

Slide Master view closes and PowerPoint restores the previous presentation design view.

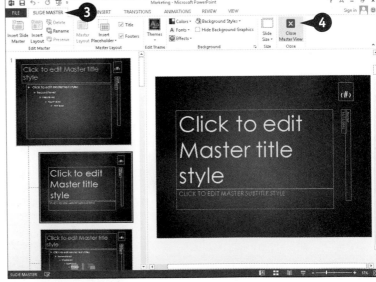

Remove a Placeholder

The Layout Masters contain placeholders for the slide title, text or graphic content, date, footer, and slide numbers. If you are not using a particular placeholder, you can remove it from the Layout Masters.

Deleting a placeholder from the Slide Master at the top of the Slides Thumbnail pane does not delete it from the Layout Masters, though formatting changes that you make to placeholders on the Slide Master do affect the formatting of associated presentation slides.

Remove a Placeholder

1. Display Slide Master view.

Note: To display Slide Master view, see the section, "Open and Close Slide Master View."

2. Click the Layout Master that contains the placeholder you want to remove.
3. Click the border of the placeholder to select it.
4. Press Delete.

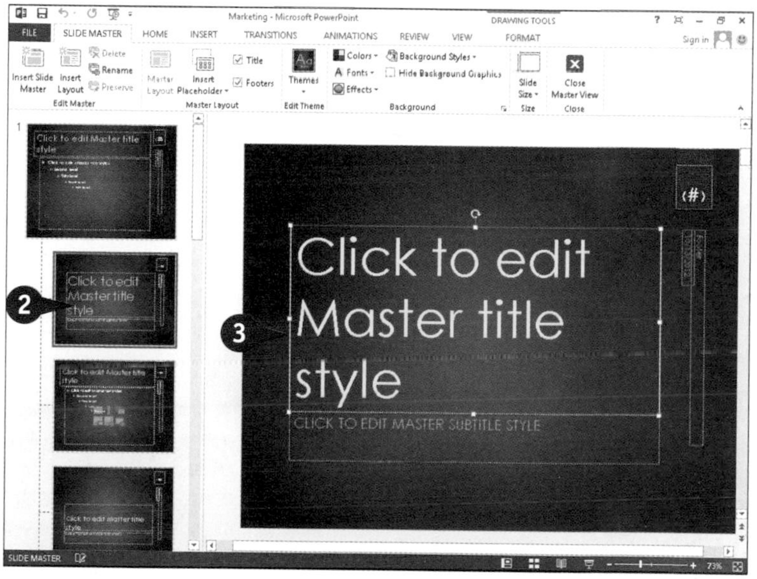

A PowerPoint deletes the placeholder.

Note: If you delete a placeholder from a Layout Master, PowerPoint does not delete the placeholder from *existing* presentation slides. Slides inserted in the presentation *after* you make this deletion from the Layout Master will not contain the placeholder.

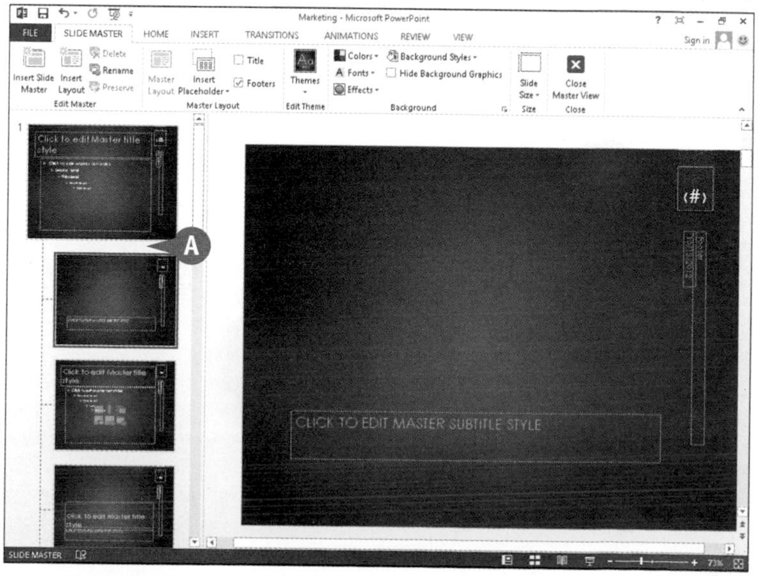

Insert a Placeholder

Sometimes the slide layouts that are available to you are not quite right. You may need to add a placeholder to a Layout Master to create a slide layout that suits your needs. You can insert a new placeholder in any Layout Master in Slide Master view. This saves time because you do not have to add the placeholder to every presentation slide that needs one. You can insert placeholders for text or content, plus other types of placeholders like picture or chart placeholders. You can also resize, reposition, or reformat any placeholder at any time.

Insert a Placeholder

1 Display Slide Master view.

Note: To display Slide Master view, see the section, "Open and Close Slide Master View."

2 Click a Layout Master.

3 Click the **Insert Placeholder** down arrow (▼).

4 Click a placeholder type.

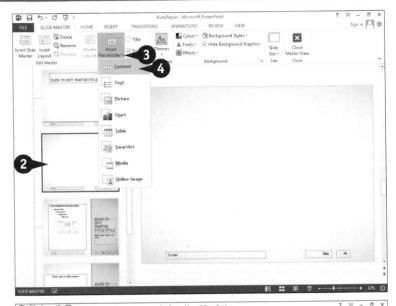

The crosshair pointer (+) appears.

5 Click where you want the upper-left corner of the placeholder and drag across the slide to where you want the lower-right corner of the placeholder.

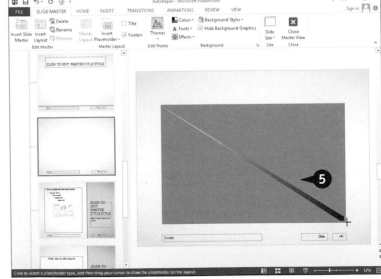

(A) When you release the mouse button, the placeholder appears.

6 With the new placeholder still selected, click the **Home** tab.

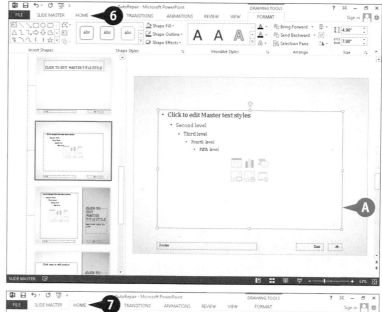

7 Use the tools on the Home tab to format the placeholder.

8 Click outside the placeholder when finished.

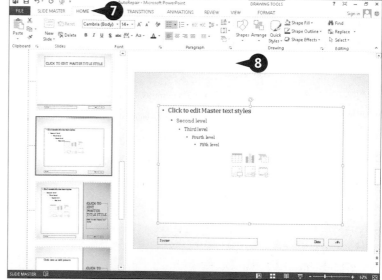

Is there an easy way to reinstate a placeholder that I deleted from the Slide Master?
Yes. Click the Slide Master thumbnail in Slide Master view. The Slide Master is the top slide in the Slide Thumbnails pane — it is the first slide in the set of Master Slides. Click the **Master Layout** button of the Master Layout group on the Slide Master tab. In the Master Layout dialog box, click the check box for the deleted placeholder (☐ changes to ☑) and then click **OK**. PowerPoint reinstates the placeholder. You may notice that you can also control the footer, date, and slide number placeholders in the dialog box.

Add a Footer

The Slide Masters have placeholders for footers that you can use to show information such as your company name on slides. You can move the footer anywhere on the Master Slide. To save time, you can add a footer to a single Master Slide instead of individual presentation slides.

If you add a footer to the Slide Master, it appears on all slides. If you add a footer to a Layout Master, it appears only on presentation slides with that layout. You can also use footers in the Handout Master and Notes Master.

Add a Footer

1 Display Slide Master view.

Note: To display Slide Master view, see the section, "Open and Close Slide Master View."

2 Click the Slide Master or one of the Layout Masters.

3 Click the **Insert** tab.

4 Click **Header & Footer**.

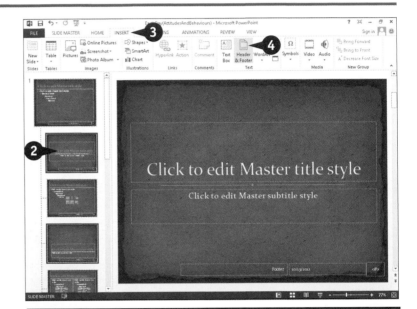

The Header and Footer dialog box appears.

5 Click **Footer** (☐ changes to ☑).

6 Type your information in the text box.

7 Click **Apply**.

Ⓐ You can click **Apply to All** to add the footer to the entire set of Master Slides.

Note: Adding the footer to the entire set of Master Slides also applies the footer to all presentation slides.

Ⓑ The footer appears on the Layout Master and any presentation slides that share its layout.

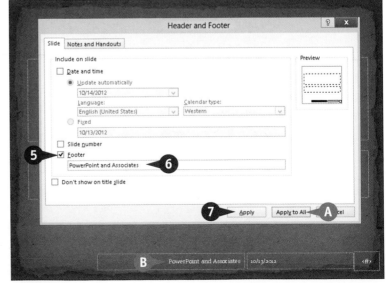

Add a Date

The set of Slide Masters includes a placeholder for a date. You can add a particular date or one that shows the computer's system date. You can move the date anywhere on the Master Slide. To save time, you can add the date to a single Master Slide instead of individual presentation slides.

If you add the date to the Slide Master, it appears on all slides. If you add the date to a Layout Master, it appears only on presentation slides with that layout. You can also use dates in the Handout Master and Notes Master.

Add a Date

1 Display Slide Master view.

Note: To display Slide Master view, see the section, "Open and Close Slide Master View."

2 Click the Slide Master or one of the Layout Masters.

3 Click the **Insert** tab.

4 Click **Header & Footer**.

The Header and Footer dialog box appears.

5 Click **Date and time** (□ changes to ☑).

6 Click the **Update automatically** option (○ changes to ◉).

Ⓐ You can change the format of the date by clicking the down arrow (☑) and selecting a format from the list.

7 Click **Apply**.

Ⓑ You can click **Apply to All** to add the date to all presentation slides.

Ⓒ The date appears on the selected slides.

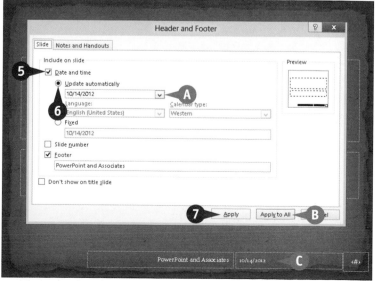

Set Up Slide Numbers

You can have PowerPoint automatically number the presentation slides with the option to not include a slide number on the title slide. You can reposition the slide number placeholder anywhere on the Slide Master or Layout Masters. To save time, you can add the slide number to a single Master Slide instead of numbering presentation slides individually.

You can set up slide numbers on the Slide Master, which affects all slides; Layout Masters, which affect only slides with corresponding layouts; or particular presentation slides in Normal view.

Set Up Slide Numbers

1 Display Slide Master view.

Note: To display Slide Master view, see the section, "Open and Close Slide Master View."

2 Click the Slide Master or one of the Layout Masters.

3 Click the **Insert** tab.

4 Click **Header & Footer**.

The Header and Footer dialog box appears.

5 Click the **Slide Number** option (☐ changes to ☑).

6 Click the **Don't show on title slide** option (☐ changes to ☑).

7 Click **Apply to All**.

Ⓐ You can click **Apply** to apply slide numbers only to selected slides.

Slide numbers appear on all presentation slides except the title slide.

Insert a Graphic in Slide Master View

You can use Slide Master view to insert a graphic or picture that appears on every slide. For example, your organization or company might want its logo on all slides for professionalism and consistency. You can place a graphic or picture on every slide of your presentation by inserting a single graphic in the Slide Master.

If you insert a graphic on the Slide Master, it appears on all slides. If you insert a graphic on a Layout Master, it appears only on presentation slides with that layout.

Insert a Graphic in Slide Master View

1 Display Slide Master view.

Note: To display Slide Master view, see the section, "Open and Close Slide Master View."

2 Click the **Slide Master.**

3 Click the **Insert** tab.

4 Click **Pictures**.

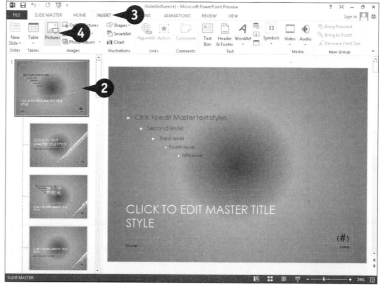

The Insert Picture dialog box appears.

5 Click the folder that contains the image file you want to insert.

6 Click the image file.

7 Click **Insert**.

A The dialog box closes and the image appears on the Slide Master, where you can move and resize it as needed. It also appears on all slides.

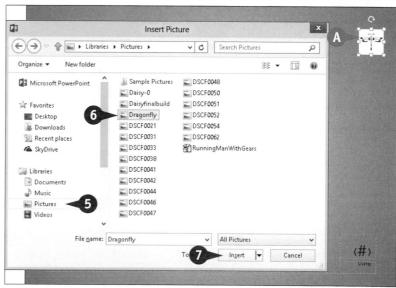

Work with Multiple Masters

You may decide to use a few different looks in your presentation. For example, you may have a theme for your morning session and one for the afternoon session of an all-day presentation. You may decide to use different themes for visual differentiation between sections, yet you want consistency for the slides within each section. When you apply a theme to your presentation, PowerPoint automatically creates a set of Master Slides with that theme. If you apply more than one theme to your presentation, you then have multiple sets of Master Slides — one for each theme.

Occurrence of Multiple Masters

When you apply more than one theme within a single presentation, PowerPoint creates a set of Master Slides for each theme. Each set of Master Slides has a Slide Master, plus one Layout Master for each slide layout that you see in the slide gallery, which you see when you insert a slide. Masters are based on themes, so you cannot switch the theme of a set of Master Slides, though you can create a new blank set of Master Slides and design it from scratch. This enables you to save the theme so you can use it later.

Themes with Multiple Masters

If you use multiple themes (and therefore multiple masters), make sure the themes are complementary. You can do this by selecting slide designs with similar color themes and fonts, plus graphics and backgrounds that work well together. Although you can, you would not typically mix and match themes throughout your presentation; you should apply a theme to a particular section. You can learn how to create sections in a presentation in Chapter 6. When you have sections in your presentation, PowerPoint applies a change in theme to the selected section, not the entire presentation.

Multiple Masters and Slides

If your presentation has multiple masters, you can apply the different master designs to presentation slides by layout and theme. When you insert a slide, you find each theme in the slide gallery. Grouped within each theme, you find the various slide layouts — one for each Layout Master in the Master Slides. For example, if you use three themes in your presentation, you have three Title and Content Layout Masters, one for each theme and all independent of each other. If you change the Title and Content Layout Master of one theme, it does not affect the Title and Content Layout Masters of the other themes.

Masters are Independent

If you change the Layout Master of one set of Master Slides, this change does not affect the same layout on another set of Master Slides. Changes to your Layout Masters are automatically applied and only appear on corresponding presentation slides — those changes only affect the presentation slides with that particular slide layout and theme combination. This means you can change a slide layout for any particular theme without affecting any other Layout Masters with the same layout, but a different theme. To make a universal change for a particular slide layout, you must change each Layout Master for that slide layout in each set of Master Slides.

Insert a New Blank Master

I f you cannot find a presentation template that you like, or you need a very specific and unique look, you can create your own set of Master Slides with its own theme. You can insert a blank set of Master Slides and customize it in Slide Master view. You can then format the text in placeholders, change the background, add graphics, and so on. Chapter 4 tells you how to format text, and Chapter 10 provides information on working with graphics. By changing various elements, you can create a unique master design.

Insert a New Blank Master

1 Display Slide Master view.

Note: To display Slide Master view, see the section, "Open and Close Slide Master View."

2 Click **Insert Slide Master**.

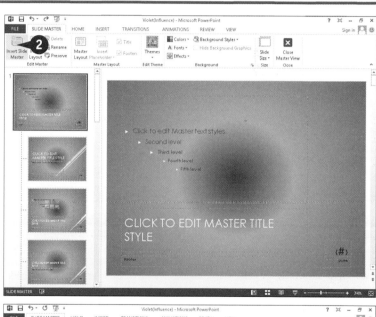

A new set of Master Slides appears.

A PowerPoint numbers each master.

B You can apply an existing theme to the new set of Master Slides by clicking the **Themes** button and selecting a theme from the gallery.

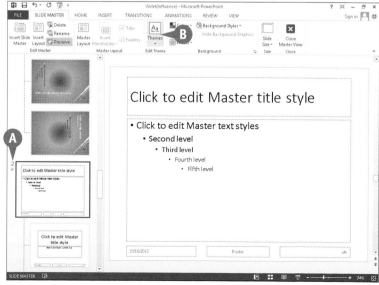

Preserve Master Slides

When you preserve a set of Master Slides, this means that it will not automatically be deleted from a presentation. If you do not preserve it, PowerPoint removes a set of Master Slides if you delete all of the presentation slides that use it. PowerPoint automatically preserves all Master Slides. If a set of Master Slides is not preserved, you can preserve it to avoid its automatic removal. That way, you can use it for future presentation slides. You can also unpreserve a set of Master Slides. You can manually delete a set of Master Slides in Slide Master view even if it is preserved.

Preserve Master Slides

1 Display Slide Master view.

Note: To display Slide Master view, see the section, "Open and Close Slide Master View."

2 Click the Slide Master you want to preserve.

Note: You must click a Slide Master, not a Layout Master.

3 Click **Preserve**.

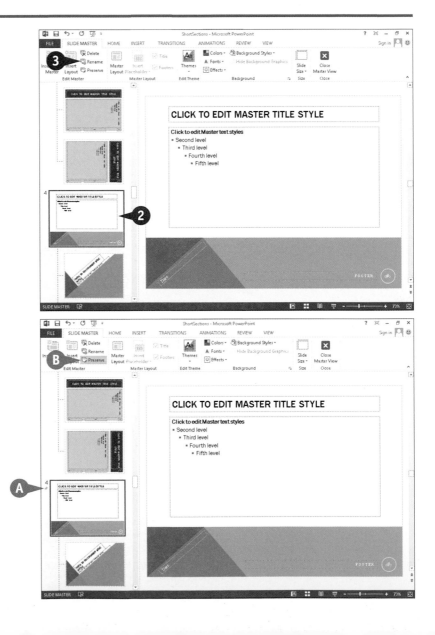

A PowerPoint preserves the master and a Preserve icon (⚹) appears on the Slide Master thumbnail.

B The Preserve toggle button becomes highlighted.

Note: To reverse the process, perform Steps **1** to **3** again so the Preserve button is no longer highlighted.

Rename Master Slides

If you insert a blank set of Master Slides, PowerPoint automatically gives it a default name, but you can apply a more descriptive name. For example, if you designed a set of Master Slides with colorful, geometric shapes, you might rename it Deco so the name is easy to remember when you want to refer to it. Giving the Master Slides your own descriptive name makes it easier to select the correct Master Slides when you apply a layout to a slide.

Rename Master Slides

① Display Slide Master view.

Note: To display Slide Master view, see the section, "Open and Close Slide Master View."

② Click the Slide Master you want to rename.

Note: You must click a Slide Master, not a Layout Master.

③ Click **Rename**.

The Rename Layout dialog box appears.

④ Type a name.

⑤ Click **Rename**.

The dialog box closes, and PowerPoint renames the Master Slides.

Ⓐ You can position the mouse pointer (🔓) over the Slide Master thumbnail to see a ScreenTip with the new name.

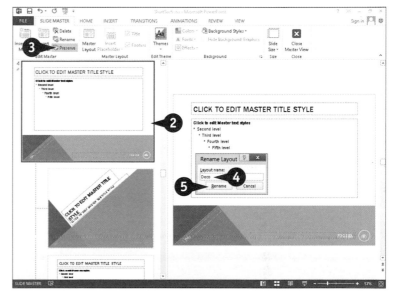

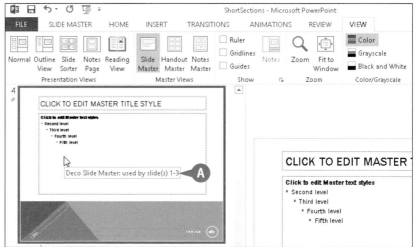

Work with the Notes Master

Changes in the Notes Master affect the Notes Page view and how the Notes Pages print. Notes Page view shows what you will see when you print Notes Pages in Backstage view. The Notes Master has a placeholder for the slide and for the Notes area, as well as placeholders for the header, footer, date, and slide number.

You can modify the format of Notes text, move placeholders around, delete placeholders, and enter headers and footers. See Chapter 14 for information about printing notes.

Work with the Notes Master

1 Click the **View** tab.

2 Click **Notes Master**.

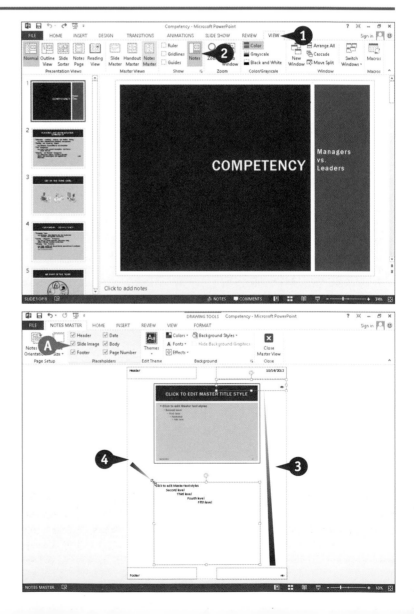

The Notes Master view appears and the Notes Master tab appears on the ribbon.

3 Click any placeholder border and then drag the placeholder to another location.

4 Click any placeholder border and resize it by clicking and dragging one of the handles.

Ⓐ You can click options to add (☑) or remove (☐) placeholders.

This example resizes the Notes text placeholder, and moves the page number placeholder to the bottom.

⑤ Click any placeholder border to select it.

⑥ Click the **Home** tab.

⑦ Click the **Italic** button (*I*).

⑧ Type **30** into the **Font Size** text box.

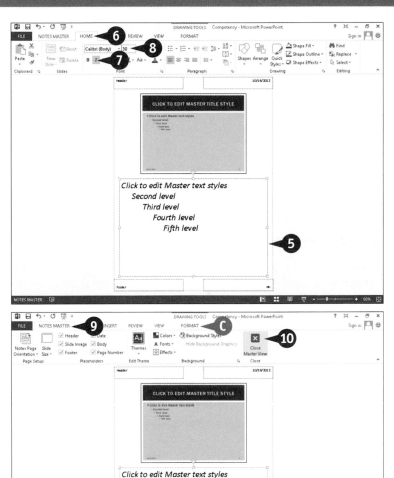

Ⓑ You can select a bullet point to format an individual bullet.

Ⓒ You can click the **Drawing Tools Format** tab to display other formatting options.

⑨ Click the **Notes Master** tab.

⑩ Click **Close Master View**.

Notes Master view closes.

TIPS

Is there a way to print just notes, and not slides?
Yes. If you remove the slide placeholder from the Notes Master, the slide images still appear on Notes Page view. You must display Notes Page view, go to each individual page, and delete the slide placeholder. Then the notes print without the slides.

Can I format the font for the header, footer, date, and page number?
Yes. You can format the header, footer, date, and page number placeholders just like any other placeholder. Click the border of the placeholder, and then use commands from the Home tab to format the text or the placeholder.

173

Work with the Handout Master

Sometimes you may not have notes to print, but you still want to give your audience a handout to take notes. *Handouts* are printouts of the slides in your presentation and they are printed in Backstage view. Handout Master view determines what is printed on the handouts. You cannot move or resize the slide placeholders, but you can move, resize, and format the font of the other placeholders to control the appearance of your printed handouts. Any formatting you do on the Handout Master appears in the Handout printout.

Work with the Handout Master

1 Click the **View** tab.

2 Click **Handout Master**.

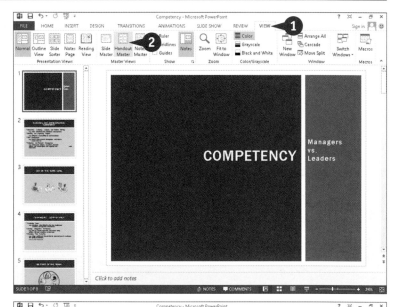

Handout Master view and the Handout Master tab appear.

A You can click options to add (☑) or remove (☐) placeholders.

B You can click **Fonts** to change the font style of all text placeholders on the page.

Note: You can click commands on the Home tab to format individual placeholders.

3 Click **Close Master View**.

Handout Master view closes.

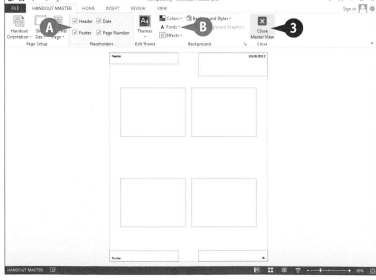

Omit Master Graphics on a Slide

Inserting a graphic on the Slide Master applies that graphic to all presentation slides; inserting a graphic on a Layout Master causes that graphic to appear on corresponding presentation slides. You can prevent a Slide Master graphic from appearing on individual presentation slides. For example, you may need to remove a graphic from a specific presentation slide because the graphic overlaps with other objects, such as a table or chart. You may also need to remove a graphic from certain slides because it simply does not apply to those slides.

Omit Master Graphics on a Slide

1 Select the slide(s) you want to change in Normal or Slide Sorter view.

Note: To select multiple slides, click the first slide, and then press Ctrl while clicking additional slides.

2 Click the **Design** tab.

3 Click **Format Background**.

The Format Background task pane appears.

4 Click **Hide Background Graphics** (☐ changes to ☑).

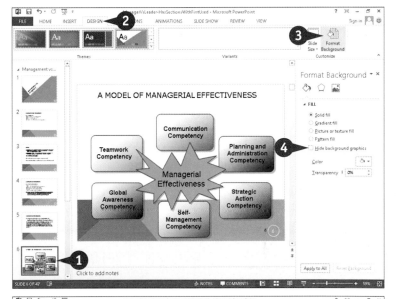

The master graphics disappear from the slide.

5 Click the **Close** button (✖) to close the Format Background task pane.

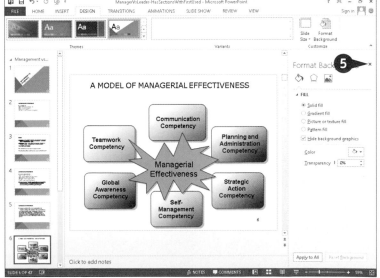

175

Create a Custom Slide Layout

There may be times when you need a slide with a unique layout. For example, you may want to compare three items, but there is no slide layout with three content placeholders. You can work in Slide Master view to add a new slide layout to the set of Master Slides. This saves time because you do not need to insert additional placeholders into individual slides. You create your custom slide layout with three content placeholders, then insert new slides with the custom layout, or apply the custom layout to existing slides in your presentation.

Create a Custom Slide Layout

1 Display Slide Master view.

Note: To display Slide Master view, see the section, "Open and Close Slide Master View."

2 Click in between the thumbnails where you want to insert the new slide layout.

3 Click **Insert Layout**.

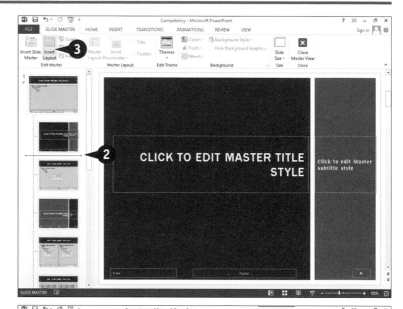

A A new Layout Master appears as a thumbnail.

4 Click **Insert Placeholder**.

5 Click and drag across the slide where you want the placeholder.

Note: See "Insert a Placeholder" earlier in this chapter.

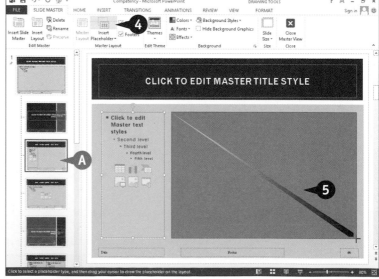

The placeholder appears.

You can move, format, and resize the placeholder as needed.

6 Click **Close Master View** when finished.

Slide Master view closes.

7 Click the **Home** tab.

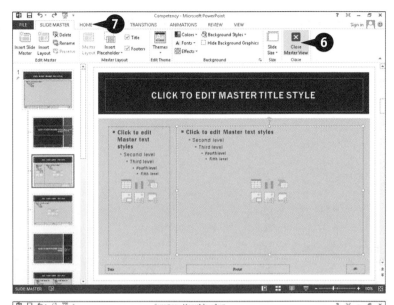

8 Click the **New Slide** down arrow (▼).

The gallery of layouts appears.

Ⓑ Your custom layout appears in the gallery.

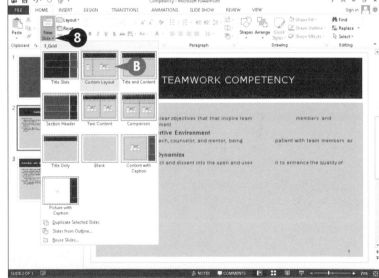

Can I assign a unique name to my custom Layout Master?

Yes. Your custom Layout Master works just like any other Layout Master. See "Rename Master Slides" earlier in this chapter to learn how to rename your custom Layout Master. Try to give it a name that uniquely identifies it so you can quickly find it when you insert a slide.

Can I change the background for my custom slide layout?

Yes. You cannot change the theme, but you can change the background. Click your custom Layout Master. You can click commands such as **Colors** and **Effects** in the Background group on the Slide Master tab to make background changes. See Chapter 8 for more on changing backgrounds of slides.

Adding Graphics and Drawings

Adding graphic elements such as photographs, clip art, and shapes to your slides can enhance the attractiveness and effectiveness of your presentation. While you can insert graphics into slide placeholders, you can place graphic elements anywhere on a slide — you are not bound by placeholders. You can also use color and various formatting options to make your presentation picture-perfect.

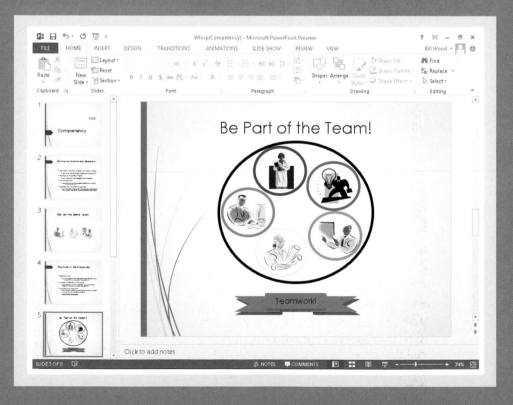

Select Objects

You will often need to format or reposition slide objects such as shapes or pictures. To change an object on a slide, you must first select it. When you click the border of an object to select the entire object, the border becomes solid; when you click the text within an object to select the text, the border becomes a dashed outline. You can also select objects in the Selection pane where you can hide objects, too.

You must select an entire object to format or reposition it. You can format specific text by selecting only that text.

Select Objects

1 Select a slide in Normal view.

Note: To learn how to select a slide, see Chapter 2.

2 Click the text within an object.

The insertion point appears within the text and the border becomes a dashed outline.

Note: You can learn how to select text in Chapter 4.

A The object's contextual tab appears on the ribbon.

3 Click the border of the object.

PowerPoint selects the entire object and the border becomes solid.

4 Press **Ctrl** while you click additional objects (⟨ changes to ⟨).

Note: You can also select multiple objects by clicking and dragging on the slide around them.

5 Click the **Home** tab.

6 Click **Select**.

7 Click **Selection Pane**.

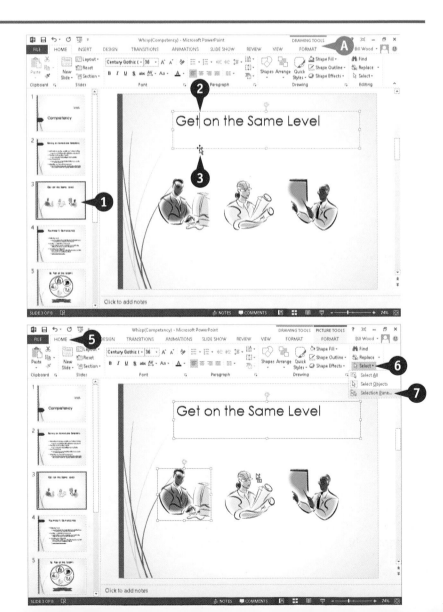

The Selection pane appears.

An item appears in the Selection pane for every shape and placeholder on the slide.

An object is selected or highlighted in the Selection pane if you select it on the slide.

8 Click the **eye** icon (👁 changes to —) to hide an object.

9 Click an item in the list.

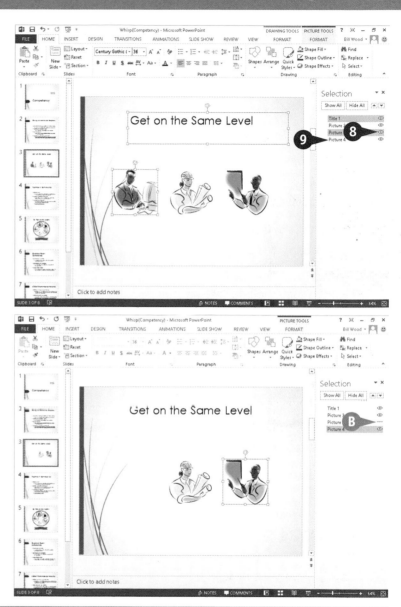

PowerPoint hides and selects the objects.

Ⓑ You can click the dash icon (—) to expose a hidden object.

Note: You can select multiple objects in the Selection pane by pressing `Ctrl` while clicking them.

Can I change the names that PowerPoint gave my shapes?

Yes. You can change their names in the Selection pane. Click the name that you want to change, then double-click it. When the insertion point appears in the text, delete the name that PowerPoint has assigned. Type the name that you want and press `Enter`.

I unintentionally clicked a shape while selecting multiple shapes. Can I deselect it without starting all over?

Yes. That can also happen when you click and drag around a group of objects on a slide — you may get one that you do not want as part of the selected group. Press `Ctrl` while clicking a shape that is part of the selected objects and it becomes deselected.

Move Objects

Details such as the position of the various objects on a slide are very important to the professional appearance of a presentation. When you insert an object, such as a picture, text box, placeholder, or shape, it usually does not appear in the location where you want it. When you insert a slide, you may prefer to position the text and content placeholders in a different location than the standard layout. You can reposition objects on a slide so that you can strategically place them. You move an object by clicking and dragging it.

Move Objects

① Click an object to select it.

② Position the mouse pointer (⬉) over the border of the object (⬉ changes to ✛).

③ Click and drag the object to a new position.

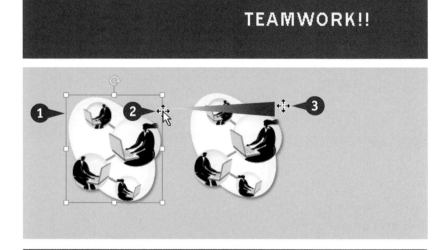

When you release the mouse button, the object appears in its new position.

④ Click anywhere outside the shape when finished.

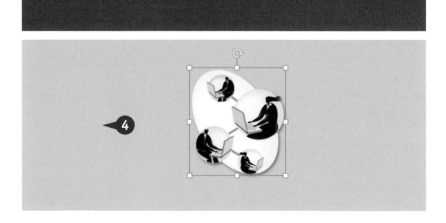

After placing an object on a slide, you will often want to resize it. For example, when you insert a picture, it may be too small for your audience to see, or it may be bigger than the slide. You can resize objects such as charts, WordArt, pictures, and shapes on your slide to optimize their visual impact.

When you select an object, handles appear on the border. You click and drag a handle to resize the object. Dragging a corner handle while pressing the Shift key retains the object's original proportions.

Resize Objects

① Click an object to select it.

Ⓐ Handles appear on the border around the object.

② Position the mouse pointer (⇱) over a handle on the border of the object (⇱ changes to ⇔).

③ Click and drag outward from the object's center to enlarge it or inward to shrink it (the double-arrow pointer ⇔ changes to a crosshair pointer +).

When you release the mouse button, the object appears at its new size.

④ Click anywhere outside the object when finished.

Change Object Order

When you work with multiple objects, you may want to stack them in layers so that they overlap as objects do in real life; or you may want to overlap them to create a special effect or make them appear three dimensional. For example, if you want to create a shadow effect for an object, the shape that you use as the shadow must be behind that object. Controlling which object appears in front of another object is called *ordering*. PowerPoint includes a feature that makes ordering objects easy and fast.

Change Object Order

1 Click the **Home** tab.

2 Click **Select**.

3 Click **Selection Pane**.

The Selection pane appears.

4 Select an object behind other objects.

5 Click the **Bring Forward** button (▲).

The object moves in front of the other objects.

Ⓐ You can click the **Send Backward** button (▼) to send an object behind the other objects.

6 Click outside the object when finished.

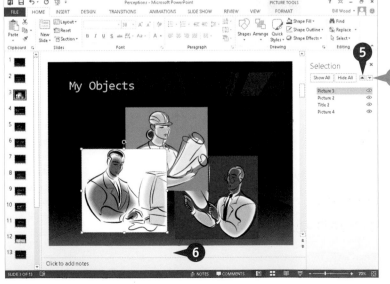

Group and Ungroup Objects

Y ou may create a set of objects that you want to move or format as a unit. For example, you may draw a car using ovals and lines. After assembling the car, you need not move its pieces individually. You can group the objects so that the collection of objects acts as a single object. After grouping objects, changes you make then apply to all the objects in the group, whether you reposition, resize, or format them. Grouping allows you to save time by applying changes to multiple objects.

Group and Ungroup Objects

1 Select multiple objects.

Note: See the section, "Select Objects," to learn how to select multiple objects.

2 Click the **Picture Tools Format** tab.

3 Click the **Group** button ( ).

4 Click **Group**.

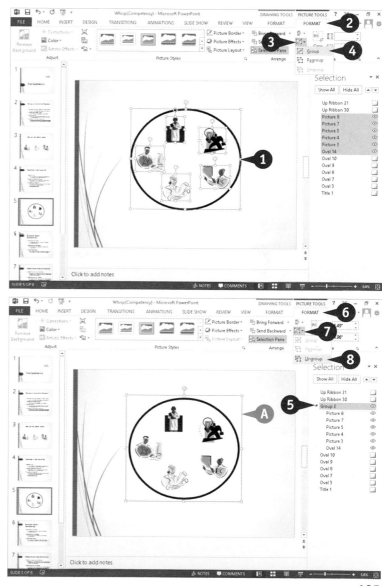

Ⓐ A single selection box appears around the grouped objects.

The group appears in the Selection pane.

5 If not selected, select the grouped objects.

6 Click the **Picture Tools Format** tab.

7 Click the **Group** button ( ).

8 Click **Ungroup**.

The objects ungroup.

Merge Shapes

You can make your presentation more interesting by creating and using your own shapes by merging two or more shapes together. For example, you may need a shape that is a circle with a star cut out of the center to frame a person's picture. You can also fragment multiple shapes for a puzzle effect. You can even merge a variety of slide objects — standard geometric shapes, pictures, and clip art. After merging shapes, the new shape works just like any other distinct shape on a slide. You need at least one geometric shape to merge shapes.

Merge Shapes

1 Insert and overlap multiple shapes similar to the example.

Note: To insert a shape, see the section, "Draw a Shape."

Note: Some shapes in the example are transparent so you can see each shape completely.

2 Click two overlapping shapes while pressing **Ctrl**.

3 Click the **Drawing Tools Format** tab.

4 Click the **Merge Shapes** button ( ).

5 Click **Subtract**.

The shapes subtract.

Note: The order in which you select the shapes is important — the first shape that you click remains.

6 Click the picture.

7 Click the shape while pressing **Ctrl**.

8 Click the **Drawing Tools Format** tab.

9 Click the **Merge Shape** button ( ).

10 Click **Intersect**.

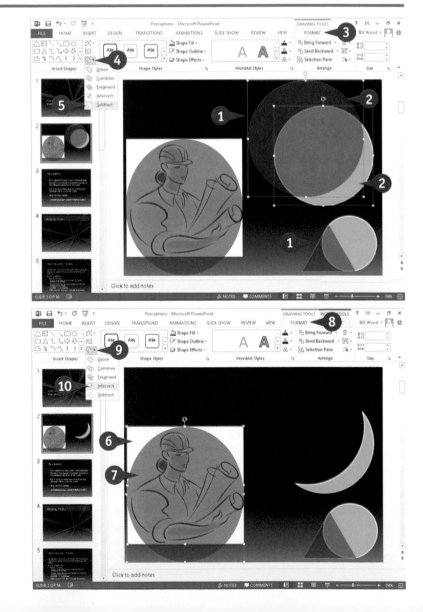

186

The area where the two shapes intersect remains.

11 Click two overlapping shapes while pressing **Ctrl**.

12 Click the **Drawing Tools Format** tab.

13 Click the **Merge Shape** button (⊘ ·).

14 Click **Union**.

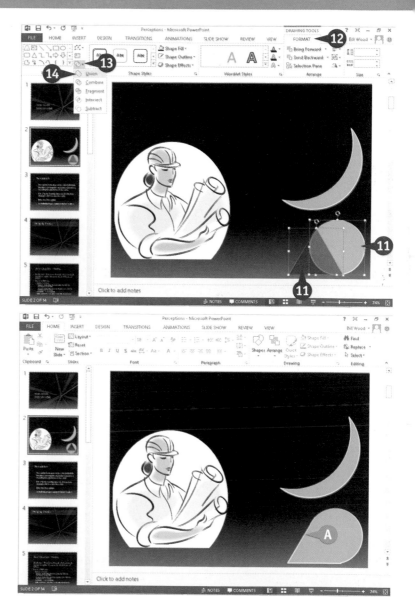

The shapes become a new shape.

Ⓐ The border extends around the entire shape.

Note: You can click and drag on the slide around multiple shapes to select them.

TIPS

I saw a nice effect where characters were made from a picture. Can I create that?

Yes. Insert your picture and type your characters into a placeholder or WordArt. Place the characters over the picture. Format the characters the way you want them — you cannot format after the merge because the characters become a shape. Click the picture first and then click the words while pressing **Ctrl**. Click the **Merge Shapes** button (⊘ ·) and then click **Intersect**.

I want everything except where my two shapes overlap. Can I do that?

Yes. You can combine the shapes. Click the **Merge Shapes** button (⊘ ·) and then click **Combine**. Combine is the opposite of intersect — it removes the intersection from the overlapping shapes.

Insert Clip Art

Clip art can be interesting drawings, silhouettes, cartoons, caricatures, and other representations. Photographs are not clip art and the clip art files are usually much smaller than photographs. You can add clip art to slides to make them interesting and engaging. Clip art is usually easier for an audience to see because it lacks the detail of a picture. You can search for clip art by keyword with the online feature in PowerPoint or you can insert your own clip art from your computer. You can insert clip art anywhere on your slide without using a content placeholder, which gives you complete flexibility with how you use it.

Insert Clip Art

1 Select a slide in Normal view.

Note: To learn how to select a slide, see Chapter 2.

2 Click the **Insert** tab.

3 Click **Online Pictures**.

The Insert Pictures dialog box appears.

4 Type a keyword or phrase in the **Office.com Clip Art** text box or the **Bing Image Search** text box.

5 Click the **Search** icon (🔎).

A You can click the **Close** button (✖) to cancel.

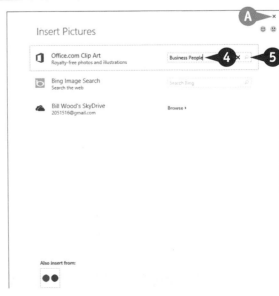

6 Click and drag the scroll bar to scroll through and view the images.

7 Click an image from the gallery.

8 Click **Insert**.

The clip art appears on the slide.

Note: See the sections, "Move Objects" and "Resize Objects," to learn how to position and size the clip art.

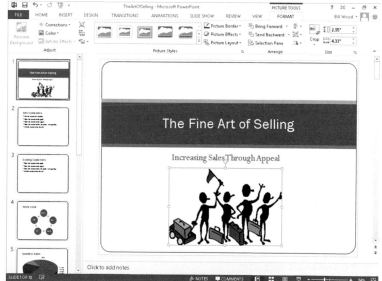

TIPS

Can I search the entire Internet for clip art?
Yes. First, try the Bing Image search feature. If unsuccessful, Search the web with your browser and save an image to your computer. Then click **Pictures** on the Insert tab and use the Insert Picture dialog box to browse to your saved clip art.

What happens if I insert a sound clip instead of clip art?
When you insert a sound clip on a slide, a small megaphone icon appears on the slide. You can set the sound clip so the sound plays automatically or only when you click the icon. See Chapter 12 for more about inserting sound and movie clips.

Draw a Shape

There are many predefined shapes that you can easily draw on a slide to add visual interest. For example, you might want to put a solid, rectangular background behind a few clip art images. There are many available shapes, from simple geometric shapes to thought bubbles and arrows. You can choose these shapes from a gallery and draw them by simply clicking and dragging. You can type text into many of the shapes, and change the formatting of the shape, the border, and the text. The shape gallery even includes action buttons that run simple actions.

Draw a Shape

1 Select a slide in Normal view.

Note: To learn how to select a slide, see Chapter 2.

2 Click the **Insert** tab.

3 Click **Shapes**.

The gallery of shapes appears.

4 Click the shape you want to draw.

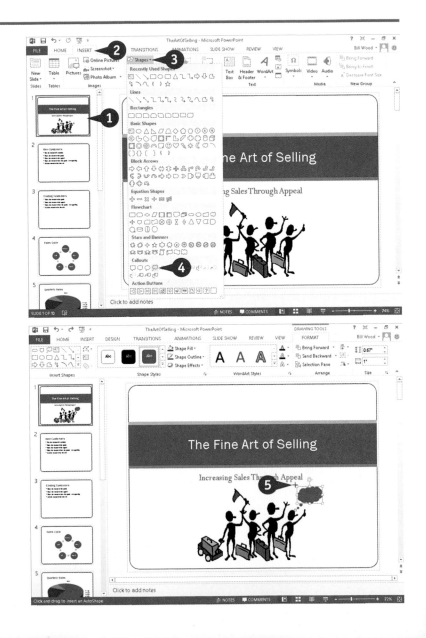

The gallery closes, and the mouse pointer (⬉) changes to the crosshair pointer (+).

5 Click the slide to insert the shape.

When you release the mouse button, the shape appears.

Note: You can also click and drag the crosshair pointer (+) to size the shape while inserting it.

Note: You can use the Rectangle or Oval shape to draw a square or circle. Press Shift as you drag to keep the shape perfect.

Add Text to a Shape

If you think that a plain text box lacks pizzazz, you can create a jazzier text box by adding text to a shape. For example, you can use an arrow with text in it to describe something on your slide. The text appears within the shape, and the shape effectively becomes a fancy text box. You lose a little versatility using shapes with text because shapes lack some of the automation that text boxes have. For example, they do not automatically enlarge or shrink based upon the amount of text you type.

Add Text to a Shape

1 Right-click the shape in which you want to add text.

2 Click **Edit Text**.

The insertion point appears inside the shape.

3 Type your text.

4 Click anywhere outside the shape when finished.

The text appears in the shape.

Note: If the text you type exceeds the width of the shape, PowerPoint continues the text on the next line automatically. You can force a new line by pressing `Enter`.

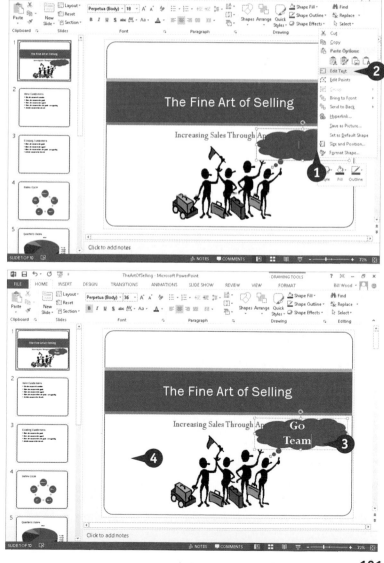

Add WordArt

The WordArt feature enables you to create special effects with text. You can distort WordArt text and apply interesting color styles. For example, if you have a picture of a product, you can use the WordArt feature to bend a phrase over and around the picture. Or, you can emphasize an important word or phrase anywhere on your slide. You can even create a simple logo! WordArt is an object that you can move, resize, or format using techniques discussed earlier in this chapter.

Add WordArt

1 Select a slide in Normal view.

Note: To learn how to select a slide, see Chapter 2.

2 Click the **Insert** tab.

3 Click **WordArt**.

The WordArt gallery appears.

4 Click a WordArt style.

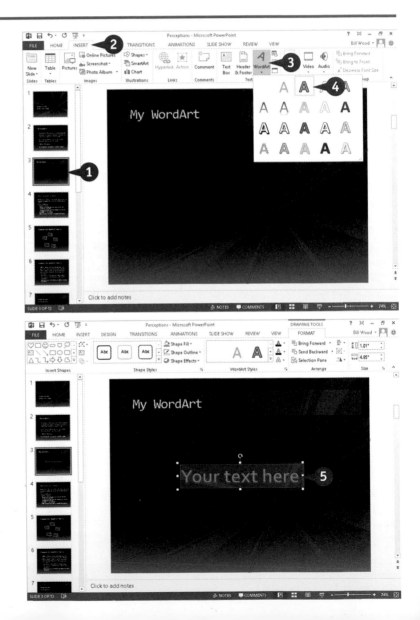

The WordArt appears on the slide ready for you to type a word or phrase.

5 Type your text.

This example creates the text, "Perception is Everything."

As you type, the WordArt automatically sizes itself.

6 Click the **Drawing Tools Format** tab.

7 Click the **Text Effects** button (A﹀).

8 Click **Transform**.

The Transform gallery appears.

9 Click a variation from the gallery.

PowerPoint applies the special effect to the WordArt.

10 Resize the WordArt as needed to distort the effect.

11 Drag the pink handles on or inside the WordArt border to change the distortion of the effect.

Note: There may be multiple pink handles.

You can use other tools on the Drawing Tools Format tab to format the WordArt.

12 Click outside the object when finished.

TIPS

I created a WordArt object, but then realized it contains a typo. Is there any way to change it?

Yes. Click the object just like any text box or placeholder. The insertion point appears within the text of the WordArt so that you can make the necessary changes.

How do I change the style and color of the WordArt?

Click the WordArt object, and then click the **Drawing Tools Format** tab when it appears. Click the **WordArt Styles** down arrow (﹀). When the WordArt gallery appears, choose a WordArt style.

Insert a Hyperlink

A hyperlink can perform a variety of actions when you click it during a PowerPoint slide show. It gives you an easy way to go to a different slide in your slide show. You can have a hyperlink open another PowerPoint presentation or open a document from another Office application. A hyperlink also provides you a way to open and create an e-mail message and gives you the convenience of opening a Web page from your slide show. Using hyperlinks to execute these actions during a slide show enables you to run a smooth presentation and impress your audience.

Insert a Hyperlink

Go to a Slide in the Current Presentation

1. Click inside a placeholder where you want to insert the hyperlink.

2. Click the **Insert** tab.

3. Click **Hyperlink**.

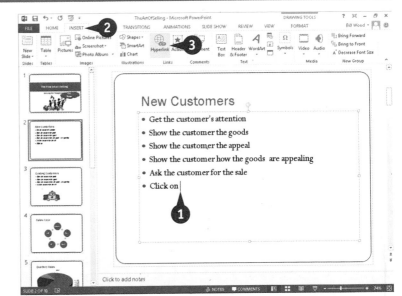

The Insert Hyperlink dialog box appears.

4. Click the **Text to display** text box.

5. Type a name for your hyperlink.

6. Click **Place in This Document**.

7. Click a slide.

8. Click **OK**.

PowerPoint inserts the link to the slide.

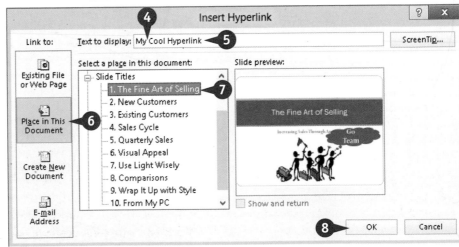

Open a File

1 Repeat Steps **1** to **4**.

2 Click **Current Folder**.

3 Click the **Look in** down arrow (⌄).

4 Navigate to and click the folder that contains the file you want to open.

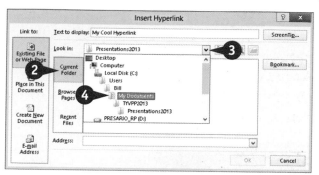

Ⓐ You can also click the **Browse** button (⌧) and find your file with the Browse dialog box.

5 Click the file to open.

6 Click **OK**.

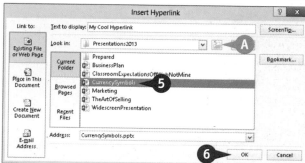

Ⓑ PowerPoint places the link on your slide.

During the slide show, click the text to follow the link.

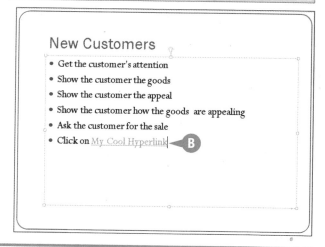

How do I remove a link to a file but leave the link text?

Right-click the hyperlink, and click **Edit Link** on the shortcut menu. When the Edit Hyperlink dialog box opens, click **Remove Link**. The link text remains, but PowerPoint removes the link.

Can I give the hyperlink a longer description?

Yes. You can do this by creating a ScreenTip. Right-click the hyperlink, and click **Edit Link** on the menu. In the Edit Hyperlink dialog box, click the **ScreenTip** button. In the ScreenTip dialog box, type the description and click **OK**. If your ScreenTip feature is enabled, the ScreenTip appears in a little box when you position the mouse pointer (Ⓚ) over the link during the slide show.

Add a Text Box

You can add a text box anywhere on a slide, which allows you to have almost unlimited versatility with text. A text box is more flexible than a placeholder because it does not automatically produce a bulleted list and it does not become part of the outline in Outline view. A text box is great for freeform text and automatically enlarges, shrinks, and wraps text, depending on the amount of text you type. Keep in mind that text box contents do not appear in Outline view.

Add a Text Box

1 Select a slide in Normal view.

Note: To learn how to select a slide, see Chapter 2.

2 Click the **Insert** tab.

3 Click **Text Box.**

The mouse pointer (⬚) changes to the Text box insertion (↓).

4 Click where you want to place the upper-left corner of the text.

The text box appears with an insertion point inside.

5 Type your text.

6 Click anywhere outside the text box when finished.

Note: You can adjust the text box width; the height adjusts automatically based on the amount of text you type. You can also move the text box anywhere. For more information, see the sections, "Resize Objects" and "Move Objects."

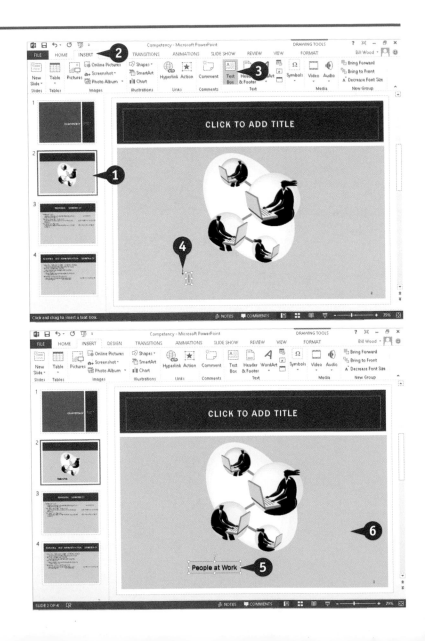

Apply a New Effect

Occasionally, you may want to give an object a special effect to make the object vivid or dramatic. You can use shape effects to add dimension and realism to the object's appearance. For example, you can apply a reflection effect that gives the appearance of the object reflecting in a lake. You can also give an object a soft, blurred border, or give it a shadow or glow. When you select an object, the contextual Format tab that appears on the ribbon provides you with many tools to apply effects and formatting to the object.

Apply a New Effect

1 Click an object to select it.

2 Click the **Picture Tools Format** tab.

3 Click **Picture Effects**.

Note: For a shape, you would click **Shape Effects**.

4 Click a Picture Effect.

This example selects the Reflection effect.

5 Click a variation of the effect.

This example selects a reflection variation.

A PowerPoint applies the special effect to the object.

6 Click anywhere outside the object when finished.

Note: You can also apply special effects from the Home tab.

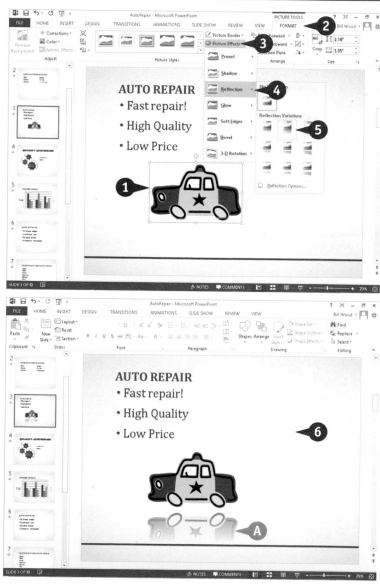

Format Objects

Y ou can adjust the formatting of an object to make it more visually appealing or easier to see against a slide background. For example, you can add a fill color, modify the font, change the thickness or color of lines, and modify arrow styles. Details and fine-tuning such as object formatting make your presentation pop — you can produce objects very specific to your needs and adjust the colors of objects to look good against the background of the slide and other objects on the slide.

Format Objects

1 Click the object to format.

The object's contextual tab appears.

Note: You can learn how to select and format text in Chapter 4.

2 Click the **Drawing Tools Format** tab.

3 Click the **Shape Styles** down arrow (⥥).

4 Click a color scheme from the gallery.

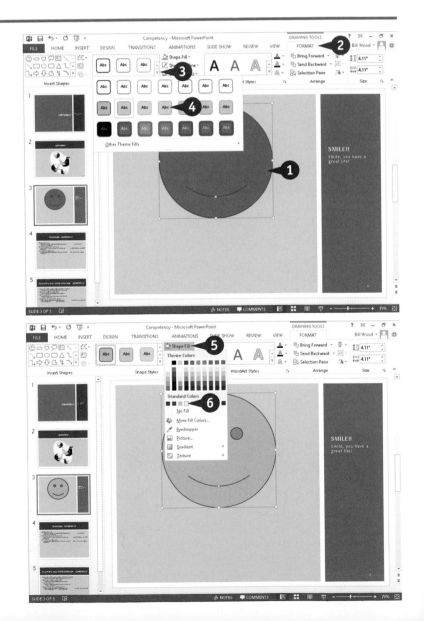

The color scheme changes.

5 Click **Shape Fill** to change the color of the object.

6 Click a color from the color palette.

The shape changes color.

7 Click **Shape Outline**.

8 Click **Weight**.

Ⓐ You can change the border color.

Ⓑ You can change the border style.

9 Click a weight from the menu.

This example changes the weight of the shape's border.

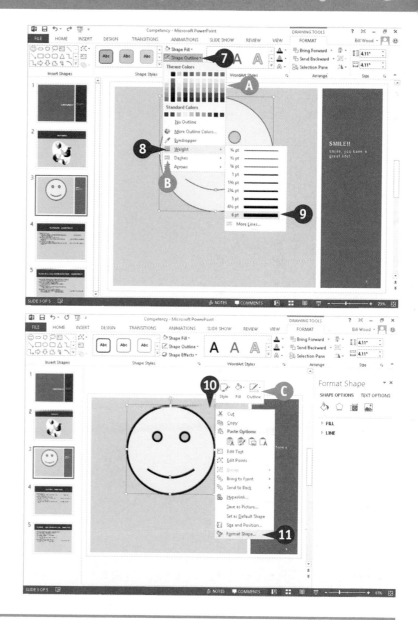

PowerPoint applies your changes.

10 Right-click the object.

The shortcut menu appears.

Ⓒ You can also use the Mini Toolbar to apply formatting.

11 Click **Format Shape**.

The Format Shape task pane appears; you can use the task pane to perform any formatting.

Color with the Eyedropper

You can match colors by sampling a color from anything on your slide and then applying it to anything on the slide that you select. Matching colors is important because color is essential to the look and feel of your presentation. Determining the color of something in PowerPoint is a cumbersome task, and if the color is not a standard color, it becomes difficult. The eyedropper allows you to match colors with a couple of clicks, saving you time. You can sample from anything on your slide such as the background, text, objects, and even pictures!

Color with the Eyedropper

1. Select the object whose color you want to change.

2. Click the **Drawing Tools Format** tab.

3. Click **Shape Fill**.

4. Click **Eyedropper**.

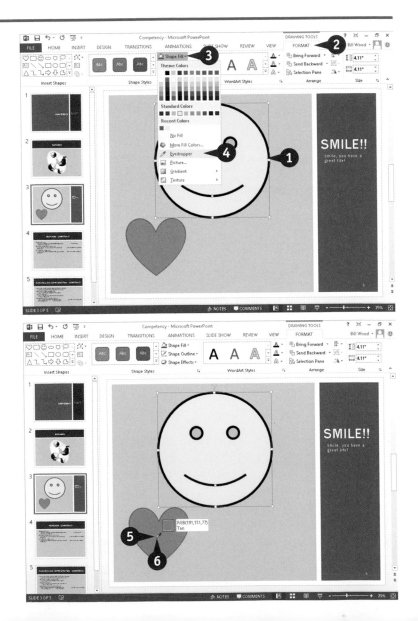

The Eyedropper pointer ( ) appears.

5. Position the Eyedropper pointer ( ) over the color you want to sample.

6. Click the object.

The object now matches the color of the sampled color.

7 Click the border of an object that contains text.

Note: Optionally, you can change the color of specific text by selecting only that text within the object.

8 Click the **Home** tab.

9 Click the **Font Color** button (A ▾).

10 Click **Eyedropper**.

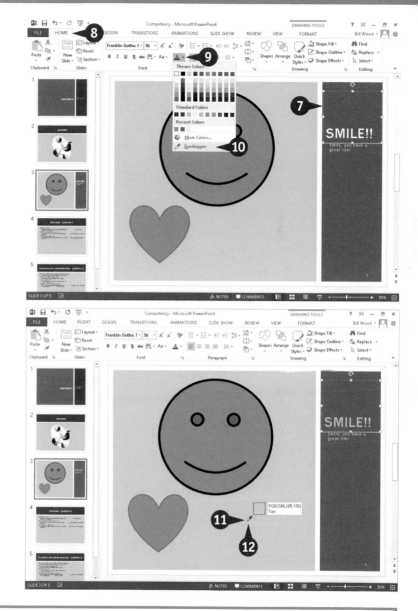

The Eyedropper pointer (✐) appears.

11 Position the Eyedropper pointer (✐) over the color you want to sample.

12 Click the object.

The text now matches the color of the sampled color.

TIPS

Can I sample a color from a different slide than the slide that holds the object whose color I want to match?

No. As soon as you click on a slide in the Slide Thumbnails pane, you lose the Eyedropper pointer (✐). You can cut and paste the object onto the slide with the sample color, match the color, and then cut and paste the object back to the original slide.

Why does the Eyedropper feature not seem to work when I click a placeholder containing text?

The insertion point is between characters. You must either click the placeholder border to select the entire placeholder or click and drag across text to select specific text.

Arrange Objects with Smart Guides

Symmetry on a slide is important for its look and is pleasant for the audience to view. For example, you may want similar objects on a slide to be proportionate to and equidistant from each other. PowerPoint 2013 introduces a new feature called Smart Guides. Smart Guides allow you to align objects, center objects, resize multiple objects to the same proportions, and arrange objects equidistant from each other — all in real time. You can use Smart Guides to save time while designing an outstanding presentation.

Arrange Objects with Smart Guides

1 Insert three similar objects, such as clip art or pictures, onto a slide that contains a placeholder.

Note: See the section, "Insert Clip Art," for more information.

2 Resize an object so it is a different size from the others.

Note: See the sections, "Move Objects" and "Resize Objects," for more information.

3 Click and drag an object until the left edge aligns with a placeholder.

A red, dashed line appears, indicating that the object is aligned with the placeholder.

4 Release the mouse button.

5 Click and drag the object until the top edge is aligned with another object.

6 Click and drag the object until it is equidistant from the other objects.

Red, dashed lines and arrows appear, indicating that the object is aligned with the other objects.

7 Release the mouse button.

8 Click and drag the resized object so the top is aligned with and equidistant from the others.

Red, dashed lines and arrows appear, indicating that the object is aligned with the other objects.

9 Release the mouse button.

10 Resize the object to be the same size as the others.

Red, dashed lines and arrows appear, indicating that the object is aligned with the other objects.

11 Release the mouse button.

PowerPoint aligns the objects.

TIP

How are Smart Guides different from gridlines and guidelines?
Smart Guides change as you move and resize objects. They are particularly helpful in making objects equidistant from each other. Smart Guides appear and disappear as you move objects around. You need to be very close to an aligned position for them to appear, and so they can be challenging to use. Gridlines and guidelines are continuously visible while they are enabled. Gridlines can help you plot objects on a slide, while guidelines are movable and are particularly useful for lining up objects with background features. All of these tools have similar uses, but some are more helpful than others with certain tasks.

Use the Grid and Guides

There are times when you may need a guide to help you line up objects on a slide. PowerPoint offers a feature that helps you position and align objects with precision. The grid looks like graph paper lines on your slide; guides run across the entire slide and can help you line objects up with details on the slide background. You can also adjust the granularity of the grid. If you need to make small, fine positioning, you can make the distance between gridline points small, or make the distance large for easier alignment. You can also have objects snap to the gridline for easy and fast alignment.

Use the Grid and Guides

1. In Normal view, click the **View** tab.

2. Click the check box to enable (☑) **Gridlines**.

3. Click the check box to enable (☑) **Guides**.

4. Position the mouse pointer (↕) over the Guide until it changes to the mouse splitter (↕).

5. Click and drag the Guide to move it in a position to align two objects.

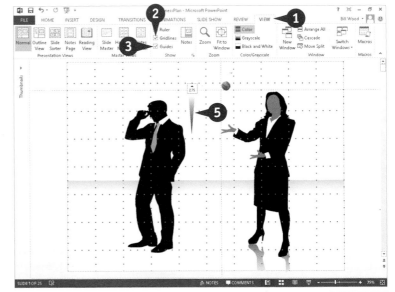

6. Click the **dialog box launcher** (⌐⌐).

   The Grid and Guides dialog box appears.

7. Click the check box to enable (☑) **Snap objects to grid**.

   Ⓐ You can change the spacing of the Gridlines.

   Ⓑ You can click the check box to disable (☐) Smart Guides.

8. Click **OK**.

   Objects will now snap to the Gridlines as you move them.

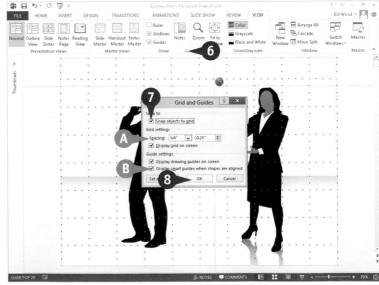

Nudge Objects

You may want to move an object by very small increments. For example, you may want two objects to touch, but not overlap. Using the mouse to perform delicate and precise movements can be tricky, yet these small details can be important to a presentation. Nudging is a feature that moves objects by small increments using keystrokes. The nudge feature enables you to move a selected object incrementally to the right, left, up, or down on the slide. You can use nudging together with the gridlines and guidelines feature to align objects perfectly.

Nudge Objects

1 In Normal view, select an object.

2 Press ⬆, ⬇, ⬅, or ➡ as many times as needed to nudge the object in the desired direction.

This example presses the Up arrow 20 times to move the object up one gridline, a distance of one-quarter inch.

3 Click outside the object to deselect it.

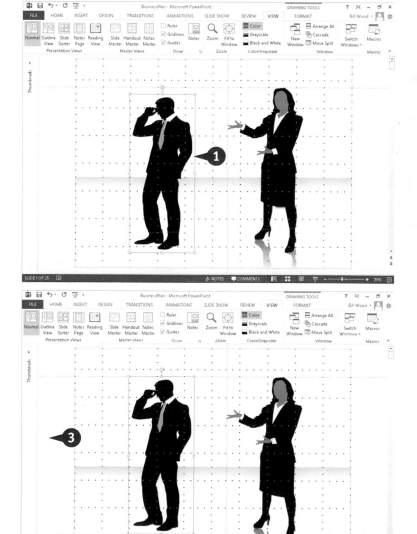

Align Objects

You can align objects relative to each other quickly and easily for a picture-perfect look. For example, you can align several objects at the same position as the leftmost object, or you can distribute objects evenly relative to one another. With the advent of Smart Guides, this feature may seem antiquated, but it is not. It allows you to align many objects perfectly with a couple of clicks, as opposed to the Smart Guides feature, which performs alignment in a very convenient way, but only one object at a time.

Align Objects

① Select multiple objects.

Note: See the section, "Select Objects," to learn how to select multiple objects.

② Click the **Picture Tools Format** tab.

③ Click the **Align** button (≣ ▾).

④ Click **Align Bottom**.

The bottoms of all the selected objects align with the bottom-most object.

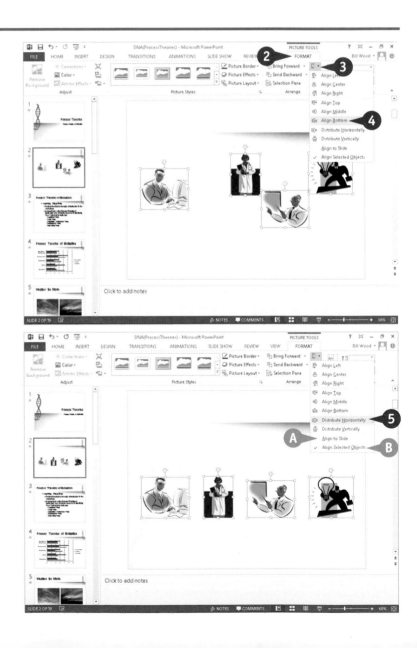

⑤ Click **Distribute Horizontally**.

The objects distribute evenly horizontally.

Ⓐ You can click **Align to Slide** (✓ appears on the menu) to make the objects align with the edges and center of the slide as a reference.

Ⓑ You can click **Align Selected Objects** (✓ appears on the menu) to make the objects align with each other.

Flip and Rotate Objects

Sometimes when you combine several shapes to create a more complex graphic or you want a picture to appear more dramatic, you can rotate it. For example, you may have a triangle shape as a hill with a clip art car going up the hill. PowerPoint enables you to rotate an object 360 degrees or quickly flip it horizontally or vertically to accomplish that dramatic effect. The Picture Tools Format tab offers all of the flip and rotation tools, but you can also click and drag to rotate the object.

Flip and Rotate Objects

Flip Objects

1 Click an object to select it.

2 Click the **Picture Tools Format** tab.

3 Click the **Rotate** button (▲▾).

Note: For SmartArt, you must first click **Arrange** after clicking the SmartArt graphic and before clicking **Rotate**.

4 Click **Flip Horizontal**.

The object flips horizontally.

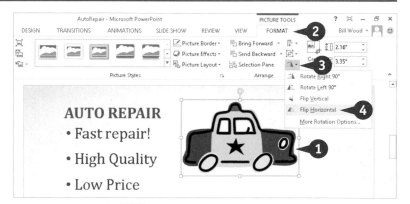

Rotate Objects

1 Click an object to select it.

2 Position the mouse pointer (⬉) over the rotation handle (⟳) (⬉ changes to ⟳).

3 Click the handle.

The rotation pointer (⟳) changes to the rotation movement arrows (⟲).

4 Drag clockwise or counterclockwise.

When you release the mouse, the object stays at the new angle.

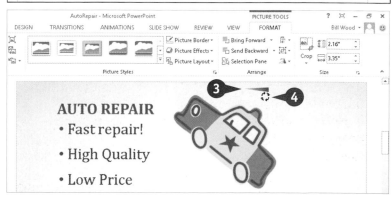

CHAPTER 11

Enhancing Slides with Action

Animations and transitions create action in your slide show presentations. Animations give movement to text and objects so a slide show does more than display static bullet points. Transitions add an interesting effect when the slide show advances from one slide to another.

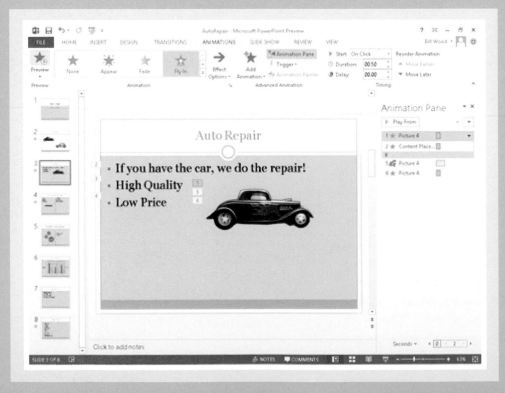

Understanding Animations and Action Buttons

Animations help you add emphasis to text or an object on a slide. Adding animation to slide objects causes them to appear on the slide at different times and with special motion. For example, you might animate a set of bullet points to move onto the screen one at a time. Animations keep your audience engaged with the presentation, but you should use them sparingly — overusing animations can make your presentation seem too busy. Action buttons perform an action when you click them during a slide show. This action might be moving to a particular slide or opening a different application or file.

What Is Animation?

In PowerPoint, *animation* refers to object motion on slides. There are many animations from which to choose and you can apply several animations to one object. For example, you can have a ball bounce onto the slide and then have it spin. There are three types of animation: An entrance animation brings an object onto the slide; an exit animation takes an object off the slide; an emphasis animation does something to an object while it is on the slide, such as rotate or spin — it does not move the object on or off the slide.

How Animations Work

You apply animations to objects one at a time and one after another. You determine when they run. You can have them run automatically when the slide advances, set them to be triggered by the previous animation, or trigger them manually by clicking the slide. You can also run the animation for a particular object by clicking that object. An animation can be set up to run after a delay, and it has a duration time that you can change. You can also arrange the sequence order of animations. This can all be controlled through the Animation pane. Let your imagination come alive with animation!

How Action Buttons Work

Action buttons provide interaction, not just action. You can draw an action button on a slide and then select the action that occurs when you click the button during the slide show. For example, clicking the action button might open a web page or an external document such as a proposal. The action button may take you to a different slide or update a chart with the most recent data. There are various standard actions that you can assign to an action button, and if you are advanced enough to use macros, action buttons can also trigger them.

Preview Animations and Action Buttons

To create a professional presentation, choose appropriate effects and always make sure they run properly. Both the Animation pane and the Animations tab on the ribbon offer a Play button so you can easily observe the animation at the click of a command. Previewing the behavior of an action button is not as easy; you must run the slide show and click the button to verify its behavior. Animations and action buttons add complexity to your slide show, so use them sparingly and always thoroughly review them before showing your slide show to an audience.

Embracing the Animation Pane

Designing and running animations can be a complicated business, and it is nice to have a central place from which to do it. PowerPoint provides you with a handy tool called the Animation pane to help you manage animations. The Animation pane allows you to reorder the animations, see what objects they move, view and set the duration of the animations, and set the trigger for each animation. You can also perform these tasks on the Animations tab of the ribbon. Click the Animation Pane button on the Animations tab to show the Animation pane.

Ⓐ Animation List

PowerPoint lists each animation in the order that it runs; each animation is attached to an object, which is also listed. Green items are entrance animations, yellow items are emphasis animations, and red items are exit animations.

Ⓑ Animation Description

Position the mouse pointer (🇰) over the animation to view its trigger and name.

Ⓒ Duration Bars

These bars show the timing and duration of each animation. Position the mouse pointer (🇰) over the bar to view the duration time.

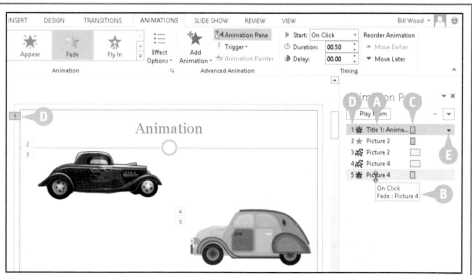

Ⓓ Sequence Numbers

These numbers correlate with the sequence numbers attached to the objects. Click either number to select the animation.

Ⓔ Animation Settings

Click the down arrow (▾) on any animation to change its settings.

Apply an Animation

A dd some excitement and creativity to your presentation by designing it with some animation! You can have your bullet points fly onto the slide point by point to keep your audience focused on one point at a time. You may decide to have SmartArt appear one piece at a time, or have a picture zoom into the slide and then do a turn! You can use the Animations tab on the ribbon to apply an animation to any slide object.

Apply an Animation

Apply to Clip Art or a Picture

1 Select an object to animate.

You can apply the same animation to multiple objects by selecting them all at the same time.

Note: See Chapter 10 to learn how to select objects.

2 Click the **Animations** tab.

3 Click the down arrow (⏷) in the Animations group.

The gallery of animations appears.

4 Click an animation.

A PowerPoint applies the animation to the object and assigns it a sequence number.

B PowerPoint places an animation icon (⭐) next to the slide thumbnail.

Note: You can apply multiple animations to one object.

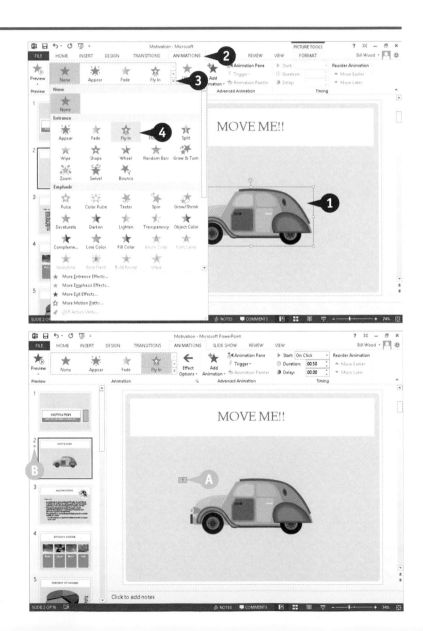

Apply to Bullets

1 Select a placeholder with bullet points, or click the border to select the entire placeholder.

Note: See Chapter 10 to learn how to select objects.

2 Click the **Animations** tab.

3 Click the down arrow (⤓) in the Animations group.

4 Click an entrance transition.

This example chooses Fly In.

C You can click these menu items to see more animations.

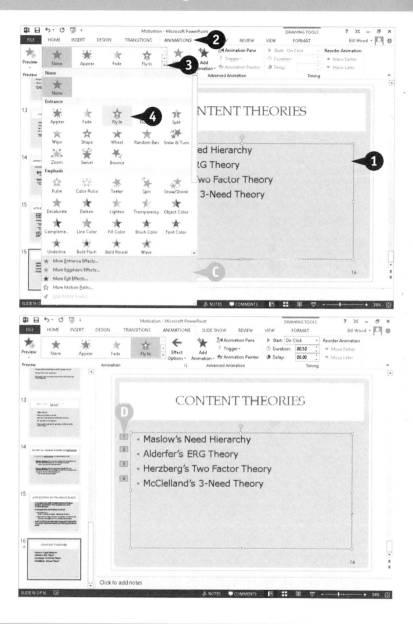

D PowerPoint applies a sequence number to each bullet on the placeholder.

During the slide show, one bullet point will fly onto the slide every time you click the mouse button.

TIP

How do I use the different types of animations?

Typically, you would not use multiple entrance or exit animations on the same object, or even a single entrance and exit on the same object. For example, if you want to substitute a new car for an old car, you would start with the old car on the slide. Maybe next, you would use some entrance animations to fly in some bullet points explaining that you are swapping cars, and drive the new car onto the slide. Then you would use emphasis animations to make the new car glow and the old car teeter. After that, an exit animation could make the old car fade off the slide.

Preview an Animation

You can see each and every animation in your presentation simply by running the slide show, but if you are working on the animation for a slide, previewing animations in Slide Show view is not very convenient. To be efficient and effective, you need a way to look at the animation while on the slide you are designing. You can see the animation on individual slides in Normal or Slide Sorter view. Previewing the animation of a slide enables you to verify that the animation works as expected and is appropriate for the slide's content.

Preview an Animation

1 Select a slide with animation in Normal view.

Note: You can also preview animations in Slide Sorter view.

2 Click the **Animations** tab.

All of the animation sequence numbers appear.

3 Click **Preview**.

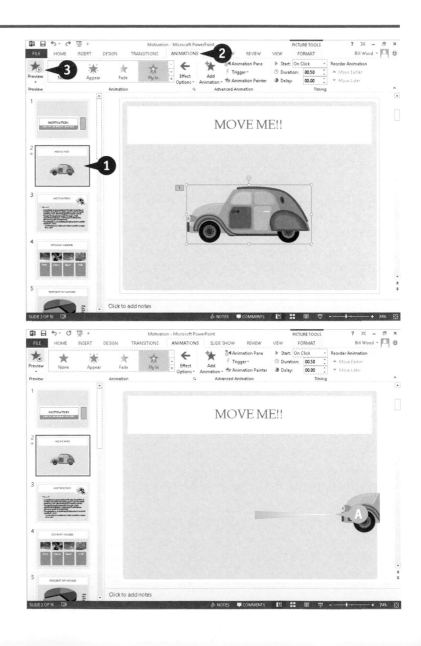

PowerPoint runs all animations on the slide.

Ⓐ In this example, the car flies in from the right.

Note: You can also preview animations by running the entire slide show. See Chapter 15 to learn how to run a slide show.

Add an Animation

You can apply different animations to different objects on a slide, and you can also apply multiple animations to one object. This enables you to make an object perform a variety of movements, creating a complex special effect. For example, you can have a ball bounce onto the slide, grow larger, do a spin, and then glow or pulse. Simple is usually best, so try not to create too much complexity. Impress your audience with your showmanship and your design abilities!

Add an Animation

1 Select an object that already has an animation.

2 Click the **Animations** tab.

3 Click **Add Animation**.

The gallery of animations appears.

A Use the scroll bar to see more animations.

4 Click an animation.

B An additional sequence number appears.

In this example, the object has two animations that will run sequentially. The Teeter animation will run second because its sequence number is 2.

Change Animation Effects

PowerPoint gives you the flexibility to choose the motion of an animation. For example, the Fly In animation can bring the object onto the screen from any direction. For complex objects made from multiple parts such as SmartArt, the animation can appear on the screen as one piece, in pieces simultaneously, or in pieces at separate times. You can move a shape and its text separately. You have complete control over the animations, which gives you almost unlimited possibilities.

Change Animation Effects

1 Select a slide with animation in Normal view.

2 Click the sequence number of the animation you want to change.

3 Click the **Animations** tab.

4 Click **Effect Options**.

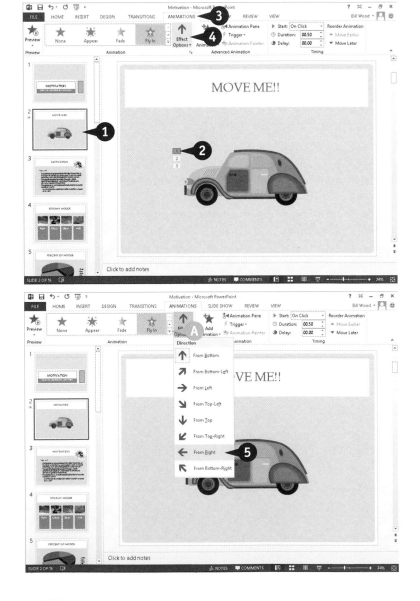

The gallery of effects appears.

5 Click an effect from the gallery.

Note: For objects with multiple pieces, there are two additional options: All at Once and By Paragraph. Click **All at Once** to have multiple pieces move independently but at the same time. Click **By Paragraph** to have multiple pieces appear separately.

PowerPoint changes the effects for the animation.

Ⓐ To change the actual animation, select a different animation from the Animation gallery.

Change the Animation Trigger

S omething must trigger an animation to run, and you can determine what that trigger is. The trigger can be the appearance of the slide on the screen, it can be you clicking anywhere on the slide, or it can be you clicking a particular object on the slide. You can also trigger the animation to run with or after another animation. The default trigger is clicking the slide, but you can change it to any of the other triggers. Clicking the slide or an object on the slide gives you complete control over when the animation runs.

Change the Animation Trigger

Standard Trigger

1 Click the **Animations** tab.

2 Click an animation.

3 Click the **Start** down arrow (▼).

4 Click a start option.

This example chooses After Previous, which means that the animation will automatically run after the previous animation ends.

A On Click runs the animation when you click the slide.

B With Previous runs the animation simultaneously with the previous animation.

Note: To run the first animation automatically when the slide first appears, set its trigger to With Previous.

C The sequence number becomes the same as the animation that triggers it.

D Note the timing change.

Trigger with Click of Object

1 Click **Trigger**.

2 Click **On Click of**.

3 Click an object name.

The animation will now run when you click that object during your slide show.

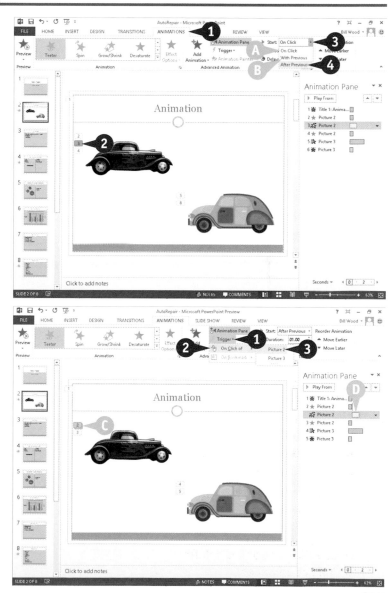

Modify Animation Timing

Sometimes you want things to happen quickly, while other times slow is better. You can modify the duration of your animation — *duration* is the amount of time the animation runs from beginning to end. You can also change the delay time between the animation's trigger and its start. For example, if you set an animation's trigger to Previous Animation and the Delay to one second, the animation will start one second after the previous animation ends. This flexibility enables you to be very exact while creating an effect that will have maximum impact on your audience.

Modify Animation Timing

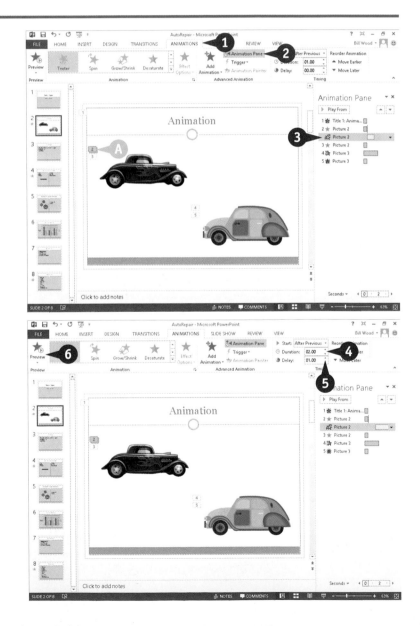

1 Click the **Animations** tab.

2 Click **Animation Pane** to open the Animation pane if it is not open.

3 Click an animation.

The trigger of the selected animation is After Previous.

Ⓐ This animation's sequence number is the same as the previous animation because its trigger is set to After Previous, which means the previous animation triggers it.

4 Click the **Duration** spinner (⬍) or type a number into the text box to adjust the length of time that the animation runs.

5 Click the **Delay** spinner (⬍) or type a number into the text box to adjust the delay between the trigger and when the animation starts.

6 Click **Preview**.

This example sets the duration to 2.00, and the delay to 1.00. The third animation will now start after a 1-second delay and last for 2 seconds.

Reorder Animations

After applying multiple animations on a slide, you can change the order in which the animations play on the slide during your presentation. You can arrange the order of the animations in many ways. You can even run an animation of one object, then an animation of another object, and then more animations of the first object. Each bullet on a placeholder can be animated, and you can treat them as a group or individually when reordering animations. When you run the slide show, each bullet appears on the slide individually.

Reorder Animations

1 Select a slide with multiple animations.

2 Click the **Animations** tab.

3 Click **Animation Pane** if it is not open.

4 Click an animation.

5 Click an order option for the animation.

This example selects Move Earlier.

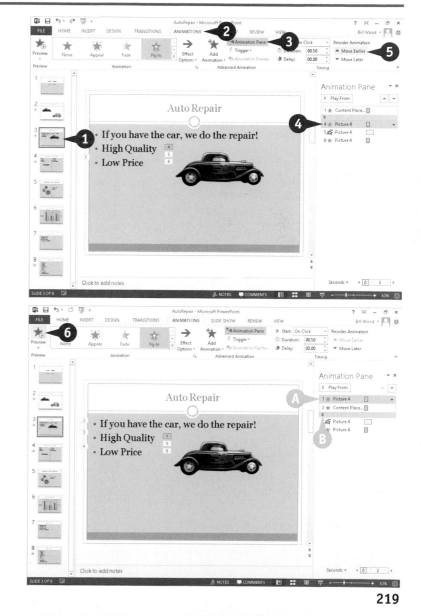

Ⓐ The animation moves in the list.

This example moves the animation earlier in the list.

Ⓑ Note that the bullets are grouped, so the animation moved ahead of the entire group. You can move the animation in between bullets by clicking the chevron (⌄) to ungroup the bullets, and then clicking the Move Earlier or Move Later buttons.

6 Click **Preview**.

Add a Motion Path

When you animate an object bouncing onto the slide, the shape and length of the bounce are determined by the animation. If you want more versatility than that, you can use a motion path, which is another kind of animation. With a motion path, you determine the object's location on the slide, the starting point of the animated movement, and the ending point of the movement. The object's location on the slide and the starting location of the motion path do not need to be the same.

Add a Motion Path

1 Click an object.

2 Click the **Animations** tab.

3 Click the **Animation** down arrow (▼).

4 Click and drag the scroll bar to the bottom to see the motion paths.

Ⓐ Click **More Motion Paths** to see all motion paths.

5 Click a motion path.

The motion path appears.

Ⓑ The green and red markers indicate the beginning and end of the motion.

6 Click the motion path if it is not selected.

7 Click **Effect Options**.

8 Click **Edit Points**.

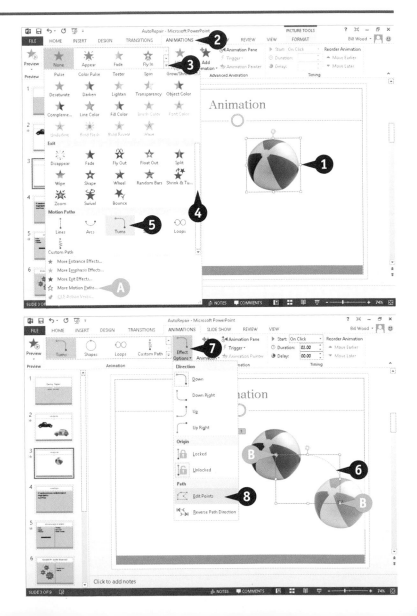

The motion path enters edit mode.

9 Click and drag anywhere on the line to change the shape of the motion path.

10 Click and drag the handle on the blue line to distort the motion path.

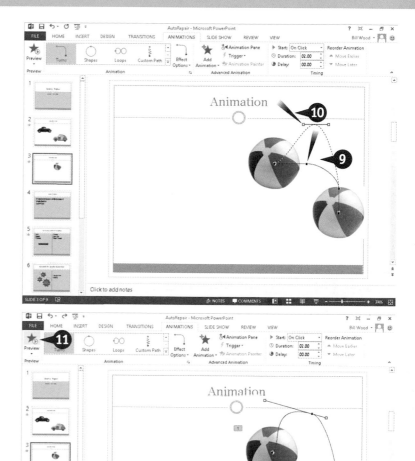

11 Click **Preview** to see the movement of the motion path.

Is there a way to change the size of the motion path without changing the shape of the line?

Yes. Click and drag a handle on the border to change the size of the motion path without changing its shape.

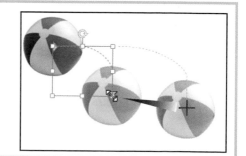

Remove an Animation

As you experiment with various animations, it is useful to know how to add them, as well as how to remove them. Too many animations on a slide can be distracting for your audience, so if you apply animations to a slide and decide they make it too complex, PowerPoint makes it quick and easy for you to remove some of them. The most convenient way to remove an animation is in the Animation pane.

Remove an Animation

1 Click the **Animations** tab.

2 Click **Animation Pane** if it is not open.

3 Click an animation.

4 Press Delete .

Ⓐ PowerPoint removes the animation from the object.

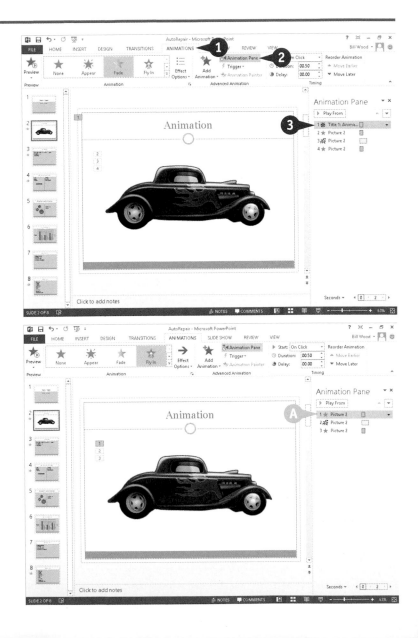

Apply a Transition

A *transition* is the act of going from one slide to another, and it offers yet another opportunity to add variety to your presentation. With transitions, you can vary the way a slide appears, such as fading from one slide to the next. You can apply a transition in Normal or Slide Sorter view to a single slide, multiple slides, or all slides. You may want to use the same transition throughout your presentation, or mix it up and use various transitions on different slides. Applying the Random transition tells PowerPoint to randomly apply a different transition to each slide in your presentation.

Apply a Transition

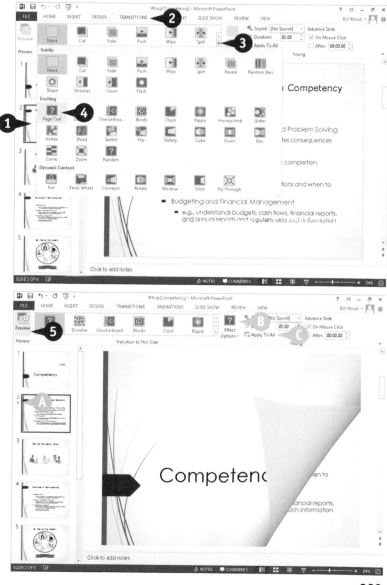

1 In Normal view, select the slides to which you want to apply a transition.

Note: See Chapter 10 to learn how to select objects.

2 Click the **Transitions** tab.

3 Click the **Transitions** down arrow (⟱).

The gallery of transitions appears.

4 Click a transition.

PowerPoint applies the transition to the selected slides.

Ⓐ The transition icon (⋆) appears beside the slide's thumbnail.

Ⓑ You can click **Effect Options** to change the direction of the transition movement.

Ⓒ You can click **Apply To All** to apply the transition to all slides.

5 Click **Preview** to see the transition.

Remove a Transition

Sometimes while designing a presentation, you may apply a transition and then decide that it just does not work. As you experiment with various transitions, you need to know how to apply them, as well as how to remove them. Using too many transitions in a presentation can be distracting for your audience, so if you decide your presentation is too complex, you may want to remove some of the transitions. PowerPoint enables you to remove any transition in your presentation easily and quickly.

Remove a Transition

① Select a slide with a transition in Normal or Slide Sorter view.

Note: See Chapter 10 to learn how to select objects.

② Click the **Transitions** tab.

③ Click the **Transitions** down arrow (⏷).

The gallery of transitions appears.

④ Click **None**.

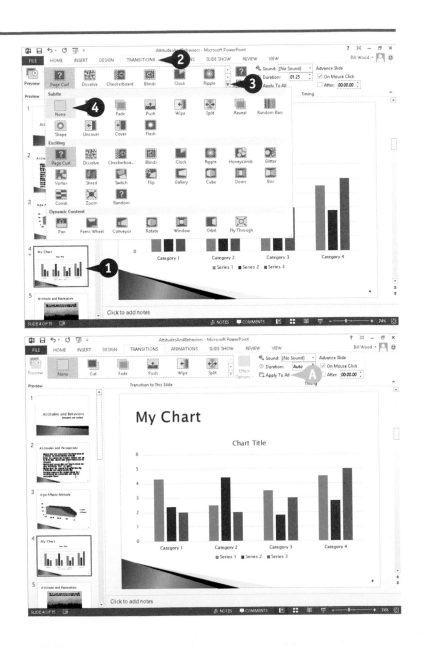

PowerPoint removes the transition and the transition icon disappears from the slide.

Ⓐ You can click **Apply To All** to remove transitions from all slides in the presentation.

Advance a Slide after a Set Time Interval

W hen you run a slide show, you can use one of two methods to advance from slide to slide. You can advance slides manually by clicking the slide, or you can set a timer that automatically advances to the next slide after a set amount of time. For example, if you are showing a presentation with pictures of a house, you may want to advance the slides automatically every ten seconds while you talk about the house. You can change these settings in Normal view, but Slide Sorter view is preferable.

Advance a Slide after a Set Time Interval

1 Select a slide with a transition in Slide Sorter view.

Note: See Chapter 10 to learn how to select objects.

2 Click the **Transitions** tab.

3 Click the **After** check box (☐ changes to ☑); this makes the slide automatically advance.

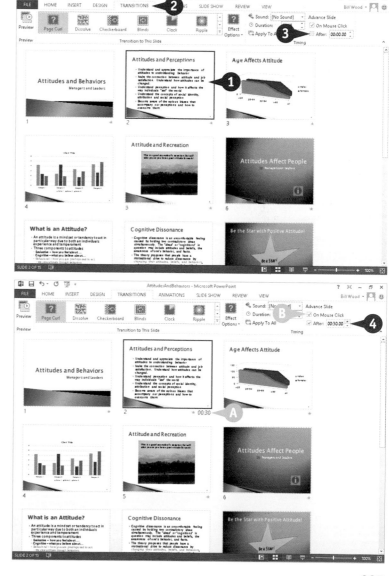

4 Click and hold the spinner (🔄) to set a time interval.

Ⓐ The time interval appears under the slide.

Ⓑ If you leave the On Mouse Click check box selected (☑), you can also advance the slide by clicking your mouse.

Add a Transition Sound

Y ou can apply a sound to one or more slides in a presentation to accent important points. When used appropriately, transition sounds highlight important information during a slide show. For example, you may want applause when the slide that shows the top three sales representatives appears. Use transition sounds sparingly because the sounds will have greater impact, drawing attention to the most important information. Using transition sounds on too many slides can ruin the impact of using sounds. Using the same sound repeatedly also reduces its impact. You can apply a sound without using a visual transition.

Add a Transition Sound

1 Select a slide with a transition in Normal or Slide Sorter view.

Note: See Chapter 10 to learn how to select objects.

2 Click the **Transitions** tab.

3 Click the **Sound** down arrow (▼).

4 Click a sound.

Note: You can select [No Sound] from the menu to remove a sound from a transition.

PowerPoint applies the sound to the transition.

5 Click **Preview** to hear the sound.

Note: Preview is available only if you apply a visual transition to the slide, not just a sound.

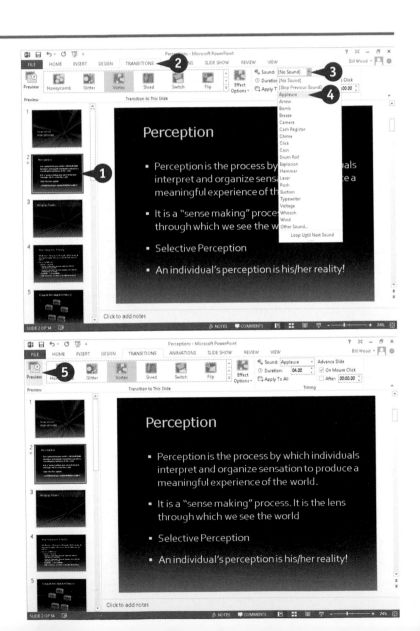

Set a Transition Speed

You can further customize a transition by changing the transition speed. The transition speed controls the rate at which the transition effect plays. Transitions are set with a default run speed that seems to be the right speed for each particular transition, but you may need a faster or slower transition speed. For fade-and-dissolve transitions, you might prefer a slow transition speed so the audience gets the full effect. For transitions such as wipes, you might prefer a faster speed that keeps the slide show moving.

Set a Transition Speed

1 Select a slide with a transition in Normal or Slide Sorter view.

Note: See Chapter 10 to learn how to select objects.

2 Click the **Transitions** tab.

3 Click the **Duration** spinner (⬍) to change the transition speed.

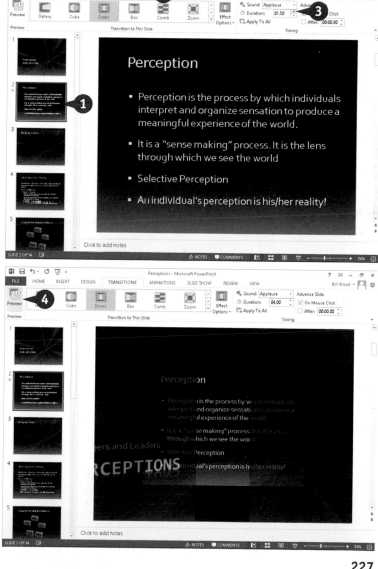

4 Click **Preview** to view the transition at the speed you specified.

The transition plays.

Insert an Action Button

Action buttons enable you to jump quickly and easily to a slide during a slide show. You can also use them to open a web page, another presentation, or a document from another application such as Excel. There are various standard actions that you can assign to an action button, and if you are advanced enough to use macros, action buttons can also trigger them.

Jumping to a web page requires an Internet connection. Any document that opens via an action button must be available on your computer.

Insert an Action Button

1 Select a slide in Normal view.

2 Click the **Insert** tab.

3 Click **Shapes**.

4 Click an action button style.

The mouse pointer (⬚) turns into a crosshair (+).

5 Click where you want the button.

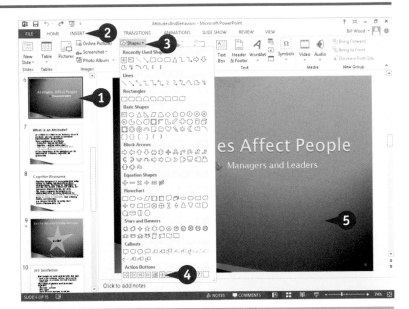

A The action button appears and the Action Settings dialog box opens.

6 Click **Hyperlink to** (○ changes to ◉).

7 Click the **Hyperlink to** down arrow (⌄).

8 Click **URL**.

The Hyperlink to URL dialog box appears.

9 Type **http://www.microsoft.com** in the text box.

10 Click **OK**.

Ⓑ You can click the **Play sound** check box and select a sound from the list. The sound will play when you click the action button during the slide show.

11 Click **OK**.

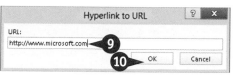

12 Click the button during the slide show.

Ⓒ The default browser opens the Microsoft web page.

TIPS

My web page address is long. Is there a better way to enter it in the text box besides typing it?
Yes. Open your web browser and browse to the web page that you want to open during the slide show. Select the URL and press Ctrl+C to copy the address. Edit the action button and then press Ctrl+V to paste the URL into the text box.

What if I want to change what an action button does?
Right-click the action button and then click **Edit Hyperlink**. This displays the Action Settings dialog box, where you can make your changes.

CHAPTER 12

Incorporating Media

PowerPoint enables you to build exciting visual and sound effects into your presentations. You can place photographs, videos, and audio clips anywhere on your slides to enhance presentations. You can add dramatic artistic effects to your photographs or remove the background from them. Finally, you can edit photos and videos directly in PowerPoint, saving time and money because you do not need an editing program.

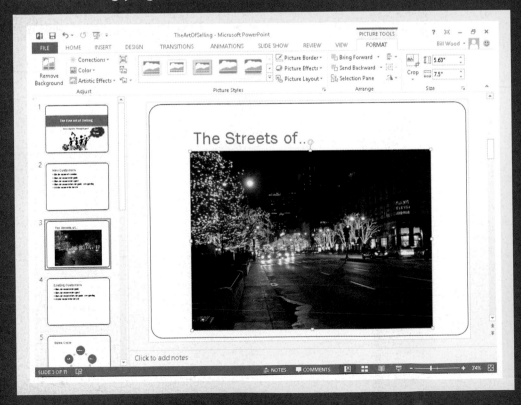

Insert a Picture

If you have an image file stored on your computer, such as your company logo or a picture of your product, you can insert the image into a PowerPoint slide. It is common for PowerPoint presentations to have pictures in them. You can insert pictures into a placeholder using the Insert Picture icon in the placeholder, or you can insert a picture directly on a slide to give you more versatility when you work with it. After you insert an image file, it becomes an object on your slide. To learn how to move, resize, and format objects, see Chapter 10.

Insert a Picture

1 Select a slide in Normal view.

2 Click the **Insert** tab.

3 Click **Pictures**.

The Insert Picture dialog box appears.

4 Select the folder containing the file you want to insert.

5 Click the file.

6 Click **Insert**.

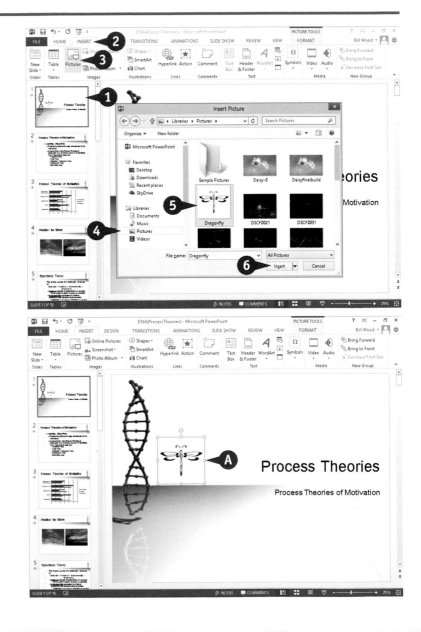

A The image appears on your slide. Size and position the image as needed.

Note: To learn how to position and resize objects, see Chapter 10.

Add a Border

Some clip art has transparent backgrounds, but sometimes the background of the picture or clip art does not blend with the background of the slide. After you insert a picture, you may want to set it apart from the rest of the slide by adding a border to it. A border makes the picture crisp, and also helps it stand out from other items on the slide and makes a clear break from the background of the slide. You can format the border by changing the thickness, making it something other than solid, or converting it to a different color.

Add a Border

1 Click a picture.

2 Click the **Picture Tools Format** tab.

3 Click **Picture Border**.

The gallery of borders appears.

4 Click a border color.

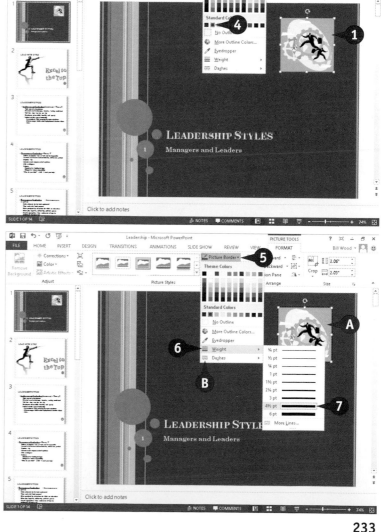

Ⓐ The border appears around your picture.

5 Click **Picture Border**.

6 Click **Weight**.

7 Click a border thickness.

The border thickness changes.

Ⓑ You can click **Dashes** to change the border to something other than solid such as dashes or dots.

Adjust Brightness and Contrast

You can adjust the brightness and contrast of a picture in PowerPoint to maximize its visual impact. Many times, a picture is not perfect when you take it, or it does not show well on a screen. Brightness indicates how bright or dark the entire picture is. Contrast indicates how well you can see shades and colors against each other in the picture. Typically you want the picture to be bright and have high contrast because then it is easy for the audience to see. Adjusting the brightness and contrast may be all the picture needs to look good.

Adjust Brightness and Contrast

① Click a picture.

② Click the **Picture Tools Format** tab.

③ Click **Corrections**.

The gallery of corrections appears.

④ Click a **Brightness/Contrast** option from the gallery.

Ⓐ You can also apply a **Sharpen/Soften** effect.

Ⓑ You can click **Picture Correction Options** for more detailed options.

PowerPoint adjusts the brightness and contrast.

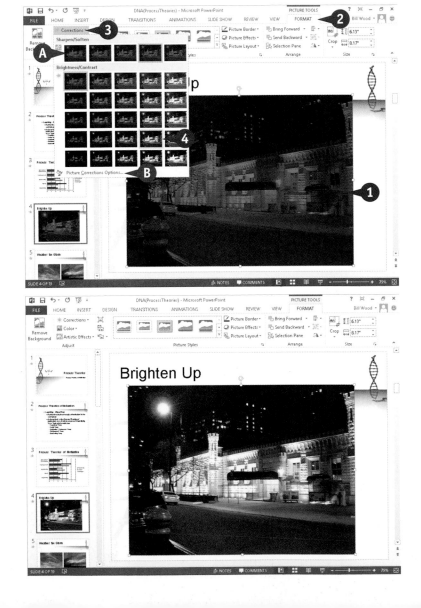

Adjust Color

Conditions outside of your control can affect a picture that you take with your camera. PowerPoint saves you the time and effort of performing color corrections in another program because you can do it right in PowerPoint! You can adjust the color of your pictures to make them pleasing to the eye, or recolor them for interesting effects. For example, you may want a picture that is monochrome in a color that matches the color scheme of your presentation. Standard color variations are determined by the theme of the presentation, but many other variations are also available.

Adjust Color

1 Click a picture.

2 Click the **Picture Tools Format** tab.

3 Click **Color**.

The gallery of colors appears.

4 Click your choice of **Color Saturation**, **Color Tone**, or **Recolor** options.

This example selects a recolor option.

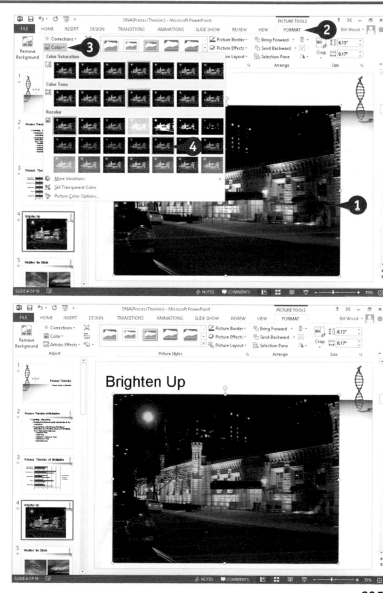

PowerPoint adjusts the color.

Note: Color Saturation determines how much color is in the picture and varies anywhere from black and white to a lot of color.

Note: Color tone affects the actual color — for example, a change in color tone may give the white items in your picture a slightly yellow hue.

Crop a Picture

A picture often contains things that you would rather not have in the image. For example, you may have a picture of a few friends, but only want the face of one particular friend in the picture. You can crop a picture so that the main subject of the picture fills the entire image. When you resize a picture, the objects in the picture change size accordingly and proportionately — you simply change the size of the picture. Cropping trims the edges from a picture in the same way as cutting them with a pair of scissors.

Crop a Picture

1. Select a picture.

2. Click the **Picture Tools Format** tab.

3. Click **Crop**.

   Black crop marks appear around the picture.

4. Position the mouse pointer (⬉) over a crop mark (⬉ changes to ⌐).

5. Click the crop mark (⌐ changes to +).

6. Drag the crop mark inward to remove a part of the picture.

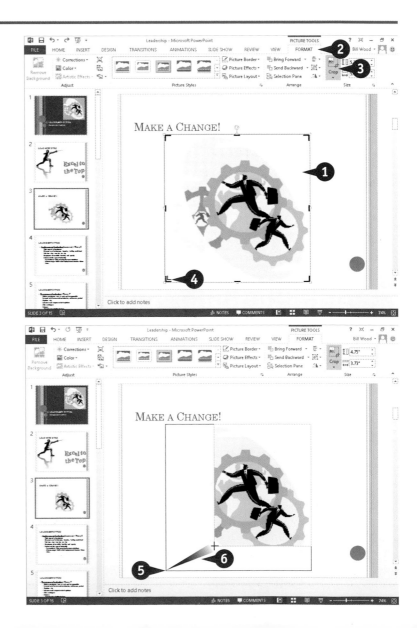

When you release the mouse button, you can see both the original picture and the cropped picture.

7 Click **Crop**.

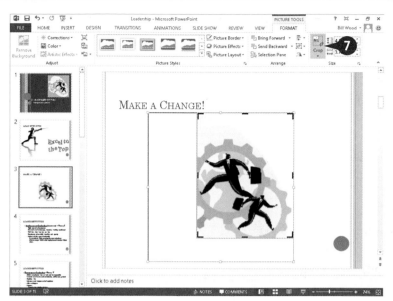

PowerPoint crops the picture.

8 Move and resize the picture if needed.

Note: See Chapter 10 to learn how to move and resize objects.

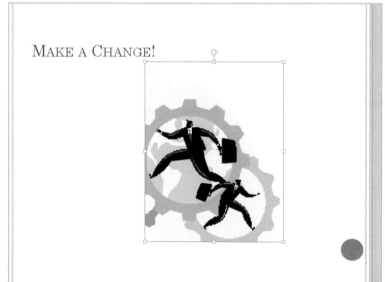

TIP

Can I crop a picture to an interesting shape?
Yes. There are two ways to crop to a shape. The first way is to click a picture and then click the **Picture Tools Format** tab. Click the **Picture Styles** drop-down arrow (⩯), and then click an option from the gallery. This method also includes a picture effect such as a picture frame. The second way is to crop to a shape without a picture effect, click the **Picture Tools Format** tab and then click the **Crop** drop-down arrow (⩯). Click **Crop to Shape** and then click one of the myriad options from the shapes gallery; the picture crops to that shape.

Remove the Background from a Picture

You may want to remove the background of a picture so you can work with just the main subject of the picture. Using the Remove Background feature in PowerPoint, you can remove the background from a picture easily and simply, and superimpose the remaining image onto a slide background or possibly another picture. This automated feature helps you avoid the inconvenience of importing the picture into PowerPoint after using a separate program to remove the background.

Remove the Background from a Picture

1 Select a picture.

2 Click the **Picture Tools Format** tab.

3 Click **Remove Background**.

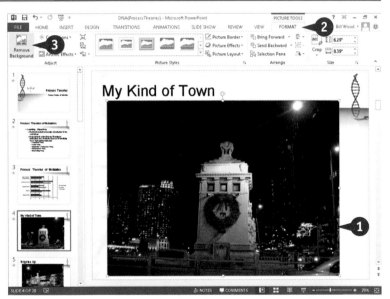

The background becomes magenta and PowerPoint automatically attempts to detect the object in the foreground. A marquee with handles appears.

4 Position the mouse pointer over a marquee handle (⟨ changes to ⟺).

5 Click and drag the marquee handle (⟺ changes to +) to resize the marquee.

6 Repeat Steps **4** and **5** with the various marquee handles until PowerPoint detects the foreground object that you want.

Note: Very small adjustments to the marquee help PowerPoint determine the object that you want in the foreground.

7 Click **Keep Changes**.

A To escape without saving changes, you can click **Discard All Changes**.

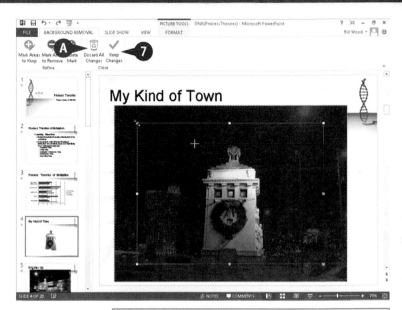

PowerPoint removes the background and only the foreground subject remains.

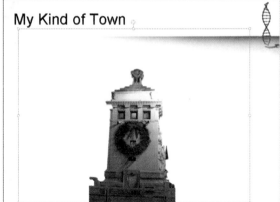

TIP

How can I include or exclude an image detail?

You can fine-tune the detected object. To add an area for inclusion:

1 Click the **Mark Areas to Keep** button in the Refine group.

2 Click and drag across the magenta area that includes your detail.

A PowerPoint includes the detail and marks it with a plus sign.

To erase the mark so that the detail is excluded, click the **Delete Mark** button, and then click the mark.

Using Artistic Effects

You may want to apply an interesting effect to a photo to add spice to your slide show. For example, you can make a picture look as if an artist sketched it. Many of these common special effects are available at the click of a button in graphics programs. Several artistic effects are also available in PowerPoint, so there is no need to use a separate program to give your picture a special effect. You can apply effects such as pixelation, blurring, and pencil sketch without leaving PowerPoint.

Using Artistic Effects

1 Select a picture.

2 Click the **Picture Tools Format** tab.

3 Click **Artistic Effects**.

The gallery of artistic effects appears.

4 Click an artistic effect.

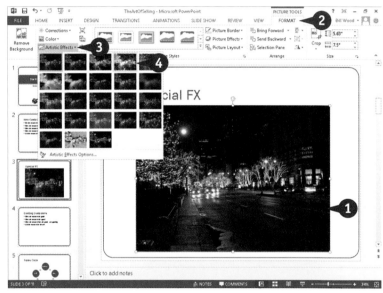

PowerPoint applies the artistic effect.

Compress Pictures

Image and picture files can be very large. When you insert them into your presentation, your PowerPoint file also becomes large. This can slow the performance of your slide show presentation as well as performance while designing your presentation. You can improve performance by compressing image files, which has little impact on their quality. PowerPoint gives you the ability to determine how much compression occurs, thereby determining how much the compression affects the quality of the image. Compressing pictures permanently changes the images — you cannot reverse those changes.

Compress Pictures

1 Select a picture.

2 Click the **Picture Tools Format** tab.

3 Click the **Compress Pictures** icon (⌑).

The Compress Pictures dialog box appears.

4 Click to disable (☐) **Apply only to this picture** so all pictures in your presentation are compressed.

5 Click **Screen** (○ changes to ◉) for a resolution you can show to an audience with a projector.

6 Click **OK**.

PowerPoint compresses the pictures.

Using Layout Effects

You may want to organize and compare several pictures on one slide. You can make pictures look sharp by combining them with SmartArt Graphics, which is much more attractive than arranging the pictures on the slide with a list of bullet points. SmartArt Graphics enable you to combine pictures in many interesting groupings, and then apply text to the individual pictures or the entire group. You can also apply a workflow or hierarchy to pictures using SmartArt Graphics — using pictures in this way can give the audience an immediate impression without you saying a word.

Using Layout Effects

Apply a Layout

1 Select pictures in Normal view.

Note: To select multiple pictures, click the first picture, and then press **Ctrl** while clicking additional pictures.

2 Click the **Picture Tools Format** tab.

3 Click **Picture Layout**.

The gallery of picture layouts appears.

4 Click a picture layout.

PowerPoint applies the SmartArt Graphics picture layout to the pictures.

Note: See Chapter 5 to learn how to edit and change SmartArt Graphics and how to enter text into SmartArt Graphics.

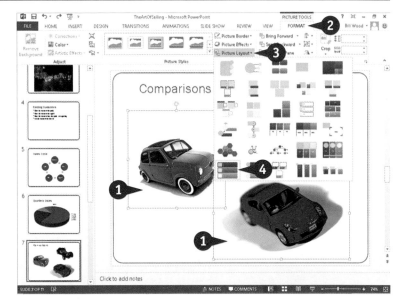

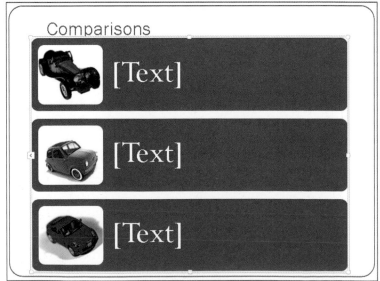

Change a Picture

1 Click a picture.

2 Click the **Picture Tools Format** tab.

3 Click the **Change Pictures** icon (🖼).

The Insert Pictures dialog box appears.

4 Click **From a file**.

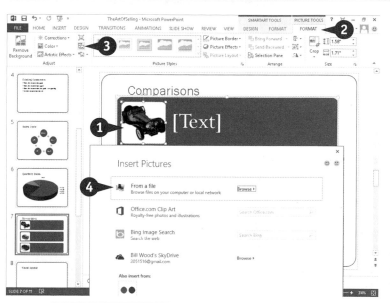

The Insert Picture dialog box appears.

5 Click the folder containing the picture file.

6 Click the picture.

7 Click **Open**.

A PowerPoint changes the picture to the image you selected.

TIPS

Can I change the order of the pictures?
Yes. Click a picture in the SmartArt layout, and then click the **SmartArt Tools Design** tab. Click either **Move Up** or **Move Down** and the order of the picture changes accordingly.

Can I add another picture holder?
Yes. Click the SmartArt layout, click the **SmartArt Tools Design** tab, and then click **Add Shape**. You can also move a picture from one side of SmartArt to the other; click the SmartArt, click the **SmartArt Tools Design** tab, and then click **Right to Left**.

Insert Media from the Internet

When you try to use only your own resources to design a presentation, you severely limit yourself while designing it. The Internet has an unlimited amount of clip art, pictures, video clips, and audio clips. Much of this media is royalty-free, as is the case with the media from the Microsoft Office.com website. Searching the Internet for this type of content can be cumbersome, but PowerPoint has a search feature for just this purpose so you can save time and effort. You can insert the perfect video or picture directly into your presentation with just one or two keywords.

Insert Media from the Internet

1 Select a slide in Normal view.

2 Click the **Insert** tab.

3 Click **Online Picture**.

The Insert Pictures dialog box appears.

4 Click the **Office.com Clip Art** text box and type a keyword.

5 Click the **Search** icon (🔍).

The Office.com results appear.

Ⓐ You can click the **Close** button (✖) to cancel.

Ⓑ Note the picture description and picture size.

6 Click **Back to Sites**.

7 Repeat Steps **4** and **5** using the Bing Image Search.

The Bing Image Search results appear.

C Note the picture description, picture size, and the hyperlink to the website where the picture originates.

D Some of these pictures are not royalty-free.

8 Click **Show all web results** for even more results.

9 Click an image.

10 Click **Insert**.

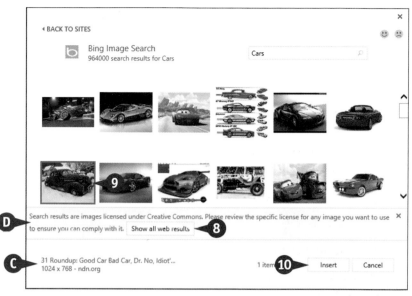

The image you selected appears on the slide.

Note: PowerPoint filters its search to the choice you make. For example, if you click the **Video** button on the Insert tab, PowerPoint only searches for videos.

TIPS

What is the SkyDrive search option in the Insert Pictures dialog box?

Microsoft has a convenient, free service called SkyDrive where you can store and share files in your own space. For example, you can load pictures to SkyDrive and give your friends access to it so they can download your pictures to their computer. PowerPoint accesses your SkyDrive directly to search and download pictures into your presentation.

Can I also download video and sound clips from the Internet?

Yes. This procedure also works for downloading video and audio clips from the Internet. Instead of clicking **Online Pictures** on the Insert tab, you click **Video** or **Audio**, and PowerPoint looks for only video or audio clips depending on your choice.

Insert Video and Audio Clips

You can enhance your slide show by inserting video or audio on a slide. A video clip can provide endorsements, testimonials, or instructional pieces that can be helpful during a presentation, or you may want to include something interesting or funny. An audio clip can play interesting sounds, such as applause, during a slide, or you can play an audio clip as background audio during several slides or even the entire slide show.

Both audio and video clips use this same procedure, except when you insert audio, a megaphone icon appears on the slide instead of a video.

Insert Video and Audio Clips

① Select a slide in Normal view.

② Click the **Insert** tab.

③ Click **Video** or **Audio**.

④ Click an option in the drop-down menu.

This example chooses **Video on My PC**.

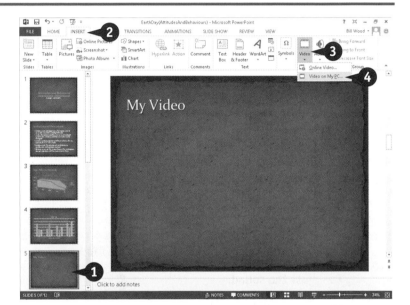

The Insert Video or Insert Audio dialog box appears.

⑤ Select the folder containing the file.

⑥ Click the file.

⑦ Click **Insert**.

The video or audio appears on your slide.

Note: You can size and position a video as needed. To learn how to position and resize objects, see Chapter 10.

Ⓐ The Control bar appears when you position the mouse pointer (⌖) over the clip.

⑧ Click the **Playback** tab.

⑨ Click **Play** (⯈ changes to ▮▮).

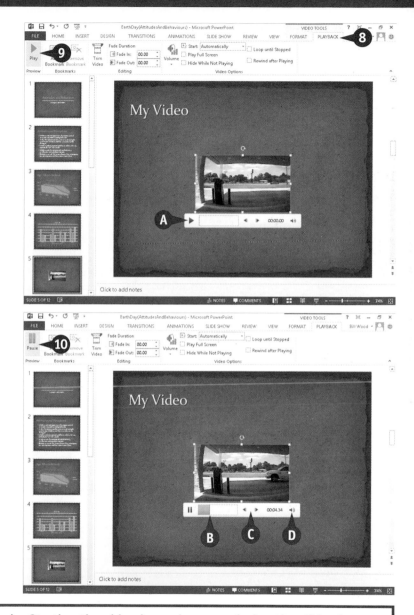

Ⓑ You can click anywhere on the slide to jump to any part of the clip.

Ⓒ You can click the **Forward** (⏵) and **Back** (⏴) buttons to jump forward or backward 0.25 seconds.

Ⓓ You can use the **Volume** button (🔊) to adjust the sound.

⑩ Click **Pause** (▮▮ changes to ⯈).

The video or audio stops playing.

TIPS

Can I play the video in full screen during the slide show?

Yes. To make the video play full screen, click the video, click the **Video Tools Playback** tab, and then click the **Play Full Screen** check box (☐ changes to ☑) in the Video Options group.

Starting the video is cumbersome during the slide show. Can I make it smoother?

Yes. On the Video Tools Playback tab, click to enable (☑) **Hide While Not Playing**, click to enable (☑) **Play Full Screen**, and then click the **Start** down arrow (▾) and select **Automatically**. Now the video plays full screen and starts automatically when the slide appears, plus you do not see it when it is not playing.

Record an Audio Clip

Y ou can bring interesting sound effects into your presentation with audio clips. You can draw your audience into your slide show by playing audio at just the right time during the show. For example, you may want applause when a slide with sales figures appears. You can also use a longer audio to play sound for several slides, or maybe background music for the entire slide show. You can record an audio clip in PowerPoint and insert it directly to a slide without using different software to record it first. Bring excitement to your slide show by recording your own audio directly to a slide.

Record an Audio Clip

1 Select a slide in Normal view.

2 Click the **Insert** tab.

3 Click **Audio**.

4 Click **Record Audio**.

Note: You need a microphone attached to your computer to perform this task.

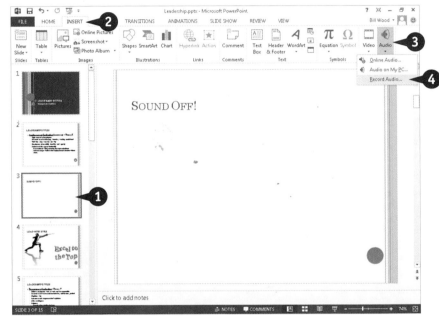

The Record Sound dialog box appears.

Ⓐ Click **Cancel** to abort the recording and discontinue insertion of the audio.

5 Click the **Name** text box.

6 Type a name for your recording.

7 Click the **Record** button (⬤).

8 Record your audio into the microphone.

9 When you are finished, click the **Stop** button (■).

10 Click the **Play** button (▶) to listen to your recording.

B You can click the **Record** button (●) to continue recording additional audio.

11 Click **OK** when you complete your recording.

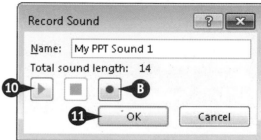

12 Click the **Audio Tools Playback** tab.

13 Click **Play** (⏯ changes to ⏸).

The audio plays.

C You can use the **Volume** button (🔊) to adjust the sound.

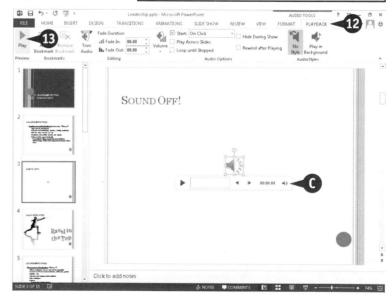

TIPS

Can I change the megaphone icon to something else?
Yes. Click the megaphone icon and then click the **Audio Tools Format** tab. Click the **Change Pictures** button (🖼) in the Adjust group and use the Insert Pictures dialog box to insert a picture as described in this chapter.

What is the Play in Background button?
The Play in Background button enables the audio clip to start automatically when the slide appears. The audio does not stop — it plays across multiple slides, looping until you stop it or the show ends. These settings appear as check boxes on the Audio Tools Format tab.

Trim Video Clips

Videos are usually not the length you want for your presentation, and so you will probably want to trim them. You may want to only play a snippet of a video during a slide show to show a little information about something, or you may have a leader or trailer in the video that you do not need your audience to see. PowerPoint gives you the convenience to trim the video right on the slide so you need not leave PowerPoint to use other software to do it.

Trim Video Clips

① Click a video clip.

② Click the **Video Tools Playback** tab.

③ Click **Trim Video**.

The Trim Video dialog box appears.

④ Click and drag the green marker where you want the video to begin.

The video frame that plays at that time appears in the window.

5 Click and drag the red marker where you want the video to end.

The video frame that plays at that time appears in the window.

6 Click **OK**.

The dialog box closes and PowerPoint trims the video to your specifications.

7 Click the **Video Tools Playback** tab.

8 Click **Play** (changes to) to view the trimmed video.

TIPS

What is the Fade Duration?

The Fade Duration fades the beginning or end of the video; you can use it only when you trim the video. The length of time the fade effect lasts is determined by the time you set in the **Fade In** and **Fade Out** text boxes. The effect gives your video a soft feel.

What is the Hide While Not Playing feature?

The Hide While Not Playing feature hides the video if it is not playing. You need to start the video automatically, because you cannot manually start the video when it is hidden. This feature is convenient because the video clip hides after it is done playing, so you can show the rest of the slide.

Trim Audio Clips

You may have an interesting part of a song to play for your audience, or a clip from an interview to share with them, but you do not want to play an entire audio clip for them. You might have an audio clip that you recorded and inserted directly onto a PowerPoint slide, but it needs to be shorter. In any of these cases, you can trim an audio clip directly in PowerPoint to make it the perfect length for your purpose. This handy feature saves you the inconvenience of trimming the audio clip in a different program and then importing it into PowerPoint.

Trim Audio Clips

1 Click an audio clip.

2 Click the **Audio Tools Playback** tab.

3 Click **Trim Audio**.

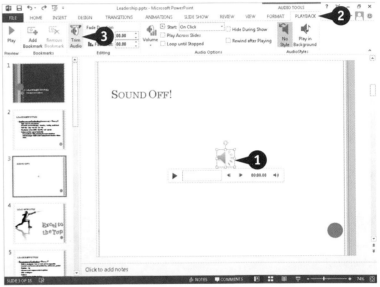

The Trim Audio dialog box appears.

4 Click the slide where you want to listen to the audio.

Note: Do not click the slide if you want to start listening from the beginning.

5 Click the **Play** button (▶ changes to ❚❚).

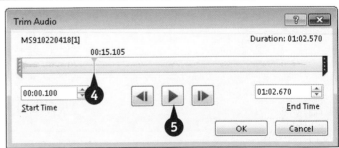

6 Listen and find where you want to trim the beginning and end of your audio.

7 Click the **Pause** button (⏸ changes to ▶) to stop the audio.

8 Click and drag the green marker where you want to trim the beginning of the audio.

9 Click and drag the red marker where you want to trim the end of the audio.

10 Click **OK**.

The dialog box closes and PowerPoint trims the audio to the length that you specified.

11 Click **Play** (▲ changes to ▼) to listen to the trimmed audio.

Note: Trimming an audio clip is reversible. Repeat this process to reverse it.

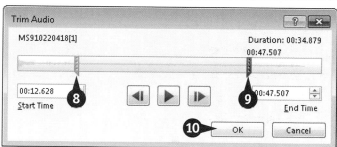

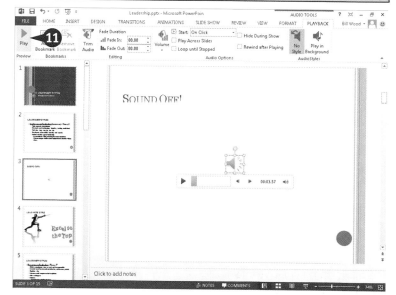

What happens when I set the Start setting to Automatically?

You can start both audio and video clips in two ways. You can start them when you click them, or they can start automatically when the slide appears when you set **Start** to **Automatically**.

How does the Play across Slides option work?

When you enable (☑) **Play across Slides**, an audio clip plays until it ends, even if you advance to other slides. If you do not want the audio to end, enable (☑) **Loop until Stopped**.

Insert a Screenshot

You may want to show something from your computer in a slide show. For example, you may want to take a screenshot of an SAP data entry screen to show why users are having difficulty entering information into a data entry form. You can take a screenshot of an open window or a section of the computer display and insert it onto a slide without leaving PowerPoint. The screenshot feature is a fast and convenient way to take a snapshot of something on your computer and put it into a presentation.

Insert a Screenshot

Choose an Open Window

1 Select a slide in Normal view.

2 Click the **Insert** tab.

3 Click **Screenshot**.

The Available Windows gallery appears. Windows that are open, but not minimized, appear in this gallery.

4 Click a window in the gallery.

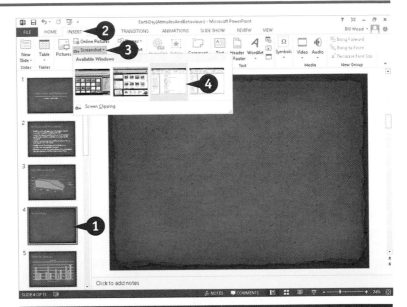

PowerPoint inserts the window screenshot onto the slide.

Note: Only windows that are not minimized appear in the Available Windows gallery. If you want to take a screenshot of a window, it must be restored or maximized.

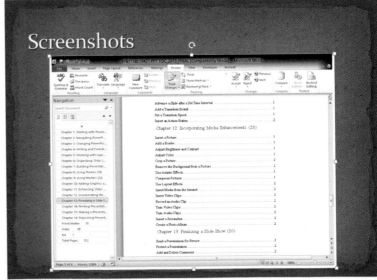

Choose a Section of the Screen

1 Repeat Steps **1** to **3** in the previous steps.

The Available Windows gallery appears.

2 Click **Screen Clipping**.

The PowerPoint window disappears, showing whatever is under it. The mouse pointer (⟨⟩) changes to the crosshair pointer (+).

3 Click and drag across the section of screen that you want in your screenshot.

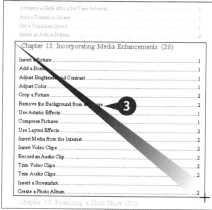

The PowerPoint window reappears and the screenshot appears on the slide. You can size and position the screenshot as needed.

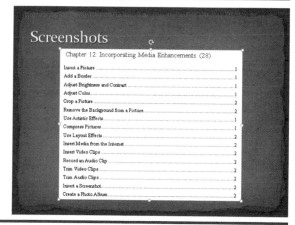

Note: To learn how to position and resize objects, see Chapter 10.

When I use the Screen Clipping option, how do I get the correct screen?

PowerPoint shows you what is directly under it when it minimizes. Minimize all active windows on your computer and then use the Windows taskbar to restore the window of interest — if you want your Desktop, restore nothing. Now restore PowerPoint and perform the Screen Clipping process.

How do I take a screenshot of two or more windows?

Minimize all windows. Restore and arrange the windows you want in the screenshot. Restore the PowerPoint window and click the **Insert** tab. Click **Screenshot**, and then click **Screen Clipping**. Click and drag across the windows with the crosshair pointer (+).

Create a Photo Album

You can set up slides so that they advance automatically, and you can also play an audio clip across slides and have it loop indefinitely. This is a perfect scenario to show a photo album. You can create a photo album and then show it like any other slide show or set it up to flip through the pictures automatically, complete with background music! You can create an especially nice photo album to share pictures with family and friends with the professionalism that PowerPoint affords you. The procedure described here creates a new presentation.

Create a Photo Album

1 Click **Insert**.

2 Click the **Photo Album** drop-down arrow (▼).

3 Click **New Photo Album**.

The Photo Album dialog box appears.

4 Click **File/Disk**.

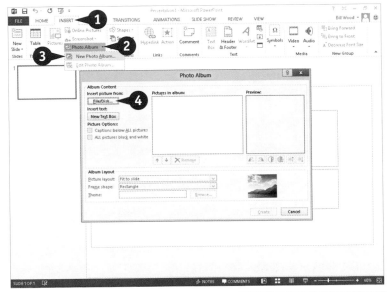

The Insert New Pictures dialog box appears.

5 Click the folder that holds your picture files.

6 Click pictures that you want in your photo album while pressing Ctrl to select multiple files. All selected pictures appear in the photo album.

7 Click **Insert**.

The Insert New Pictures dialog box closes.

The Photo Album dialog box reappears.

8 Click a picture to view it.

9 Click the **Picture layout** drop-down arrow (⌄) and select a layout.

Ⓐ You can use these picture correction features if you select only one picture.

Ⓑ You can click to select one or more pictures to move or remove them.

Ⓒ This option is available only when the layout has multiple pictures.

10 Click **Create**.

PowerPoint creates the photo album.

Note: You can design a photo album like any other presentation.

Note: Click **Edit Photo Album** from the Photo Album drop-down menu on the Insert tab to change the pictures in the slide show.

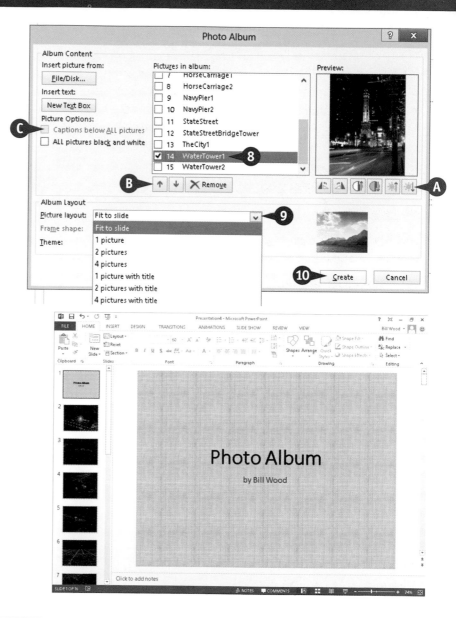

TIP

What is the New Text Box button in the Photo Album dialog box?

You may want to include an explanation or comments about your photographs on a slide. You can click the New Text Box button and PowerPoint inserts a text box in the Pictures in album list. You can move the text box or a photograph within the list by clicking it and then clicking the **Move Up** (⬆) or **Move Down** (⬇) buttons. After you create the photo album, you can click the text box on the slide and type your text. You can insert multiple text boxes into your photo album or even into a slide.

CHAPTER 13

Finalizing a Slide Show

After you add all of your slide content, tweak your slide design, and add graphics, animations, and transitions, you are almost done. Now, you perform the final tasks to complete your presentation. You review it, comment on it, set the show parameters, rehearse, and possibly record a narration. Finally, you can run your slide show!

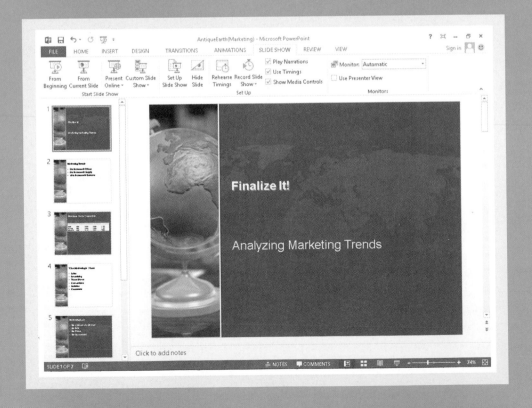

Send a Presentation for Review

You may want to seek feedback on your presentation before you give a slide show. A second opinion helps because another viewer can spot errors you missed or suggest improvements. You may want another person to check your facts, validate technical advice, or verify procedures. You can e-mail your presentation to others for review and the reviewers can add comments to the presentation and then e-mail it back to you. You then have the information you need to make your presentation as good as it can possibly get.

Send a Presentation for Review

Send the e-mail

Note: These steps assume that your e-mail program is properly configured to work with other applications.

1 Click the **File** tab to show Backstage view.

2 Click **Share**.

3 Click **Email**.

4 Click **Send as Attachment**.

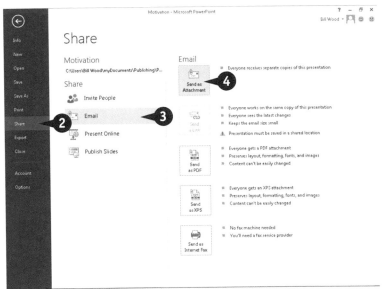

An e-mail message window appears.

5 Click the **To** text box and type the recipient's e-mail address.

6 Click the message pane and type text for the message.

7 Click **Send**.

The application sends the e-mail with the presentation attached.

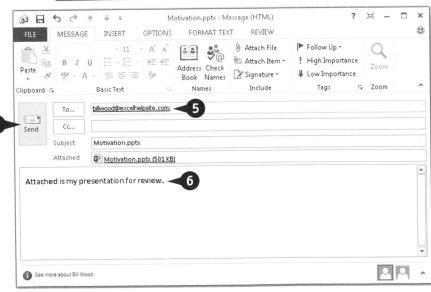

Receive the e-mail

1 After you receive a file back from a reviewer, open the e-mail.

2 Right-click the PowerPoint attachment.

3 Click **Save As**.

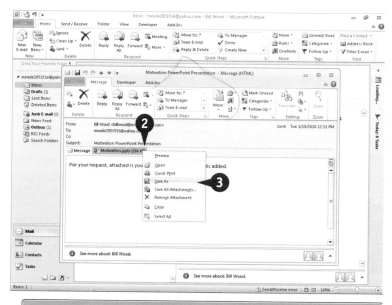

The Save Attachment dialog box appears.

4 Click the folder that you want to contain the file.

5 Click the **File Name** text box.

6 Type a name.

7 Click **Save**.

The e-mail application saves the PowerPoint presentation. You can now open and review the presentation.

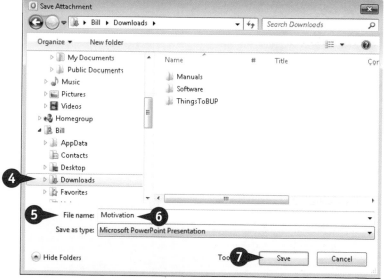

TIPS

When I e-mail a presentation for review, what does the recipient need to do?

The recipient needs to open the presentation in PowerPoint in order to review it. That person can click the **Review** tab, and then click the **New Comment** command to add comments. PowerPoint adds the reviewer's initials and a number to each comment.

What can I do if my recipient cannot open my PowerPoint 2013 file?

Try saving the file in a compatible format with older PowerPoint versions. To save in a compatible format, click the **File** tab, and then click **Export**. Click **Change File Type**, and then click **PowerPoint 97-2003 Presentation** in the Presentation File Types list. Continue to save the file as you normally would.

Protect a Presentation

You may not want anybody else to present your slide show, or you may not want others to see how you designed it. Your presentation may have sensitive information that you want to protect in case it falls into the wrong hands. PowerPoint allows you to protect your presentation. You can password-protect your presentation so that only those with the proper credentials can open it. Remember to record the password, though — you will want to open it yourself!

Protect a Presentation

1 Click the **File** tab to show Backstage view.

2 Click **Info**.

3 Click **Protect Presentation**.

4 Click **Encrypt with Password**.

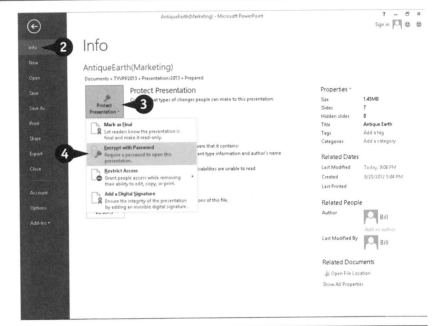

The Encrypt Document dialog box appears.

5 Click the **Password** text box.

6 Type a password.

7 Click **OK**.

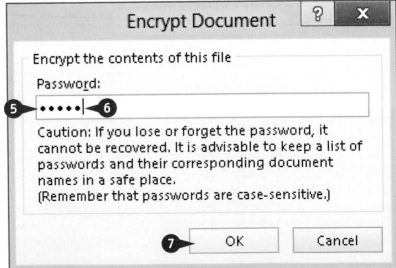

The Confirm Password dialog box appears.

8 Click the **Reenter password** text box.

9 Type the password.

10 Click **OK**.

Confirm Password

Encrypt the contents of this file

Reenter password:

Caution: If you lose or forget the password, it cannot be recovered. It is advisable to keep a list of passwords and their corresponding document names in a safe place.
(Remember that passwords are case-sensitive.)

OK   Cancel

A PowerPoint protects the presentation.

11 Click **Close**.

12 Open the presentation.

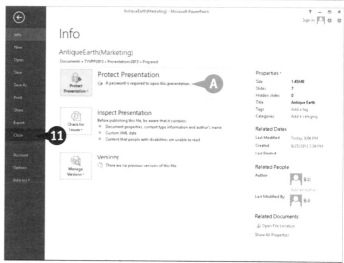

PowerPoint asks for the password.

Password

Enter password to open file
AntiqueEarth(Marketing).pptx

Password:

OK   Cancel

TIPS

How can I remove the password?
You go through the same process as when you add a password. However, when the Encrypt Document dialog box appears, it displays an encoded password. Delete the encoded password and click **OK**. The presentation then becomes unprotected.

What is the Mark as Final item on the Protect Presentation menu?
The Marked as Final feature shows you and others that the presentation is finished and ready for presenting. The Save command is no longer available and PowerPoint places an icon in the status bar indicating the final status. When you open a presentation with this status, a message appears, informing you of the status. You are given the option to edit and save the presentation.

Add and Delete Comments

If you have been asked to review a presentation or you want to mark up your own presentation, you can use the comments feature to document your notations. PowerPoint identifies each comment with a marker, making it easy for the presentation designer to find and consider each comment. Each comment contains the name of the person making the comment and the date, and the comment can be attached to a slide or an object on the slide. After you add your comments, save the file and the presentation comments are ready for review.

Add and Delete Comments

1 Select a slide in Normal view.

2 Click the **Review** tab.

3 Click **New Comment**.

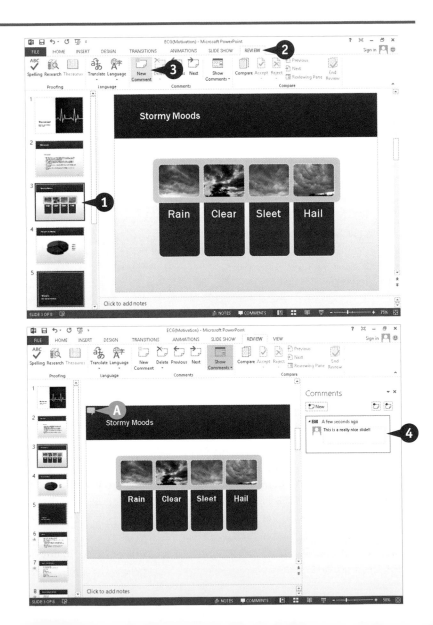

The Comments task pane appears.

Ⓐ A comment marker appears on the slide.

4 Type the comment text.

5 Press **Enter**.

Note: You can click and drag the comments marker to move it.

6 Click an object on the slide.

7 Click **New**.

8 Type the comment text.

9 Press Enter.

B A comment marker appears on the object.

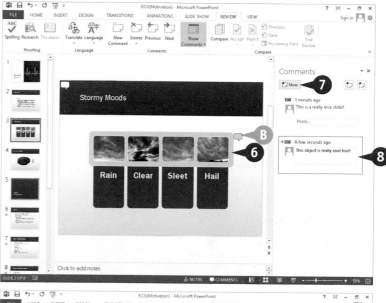

10 Position the mouse pointer (🡢) over a comment.

The Delete icon (✖) appears.

11 Click the **Delete** icon (✖).

PowerPoint deletes the comment.

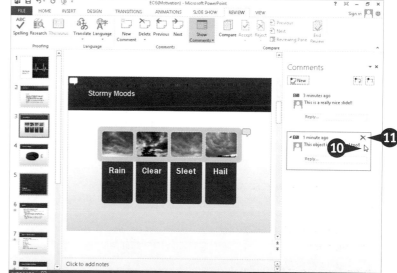

TIPS

I noticed some misspellings in the comments. How do I change them?

Select a comment by clicking either the comment marker or the comment in the Comments pane. Click the text once to select all of the text, and click again to insert the insertion point in the text. Edit the text and press Enter.

Why do some comment markers overlap a little and others overlap almost completely?

Comment markers that overlap almost completely are comments and their replies, which are grouped tightly, and when you click these markers, they are all selected. Comment markers that are grouped loosely and barely overlap are different comments on the same slide or object — you can select them individually.

Review Comments

A presentation with comments in it is like a printout with sticky notes on it. You can page through the presentation file, read the individual notes, and decide whether to make any changes based on them. You can then delete (throw away) individual comments as you review them or delete all comments on a slide or in the presentation. You can also show or hide comments — that way, you can design your presentation without distractions, but come back to comments at a later time if needed.

Review Comments

1 Select a slide with a comment in Normal view.

2 Click the **Review** tab.

3 Click **Show Comments**.

4 Click **Show Markup**.

5 Click **Show Comments**.

6 Click **Comments Pane**.

The Comments pane and all comments appear.

7 Click a comment marker.

The comment appears selected in the Comments pane.

8 Click a **Reply** text box.

9 Type a reply.

10 Press **Enter**.

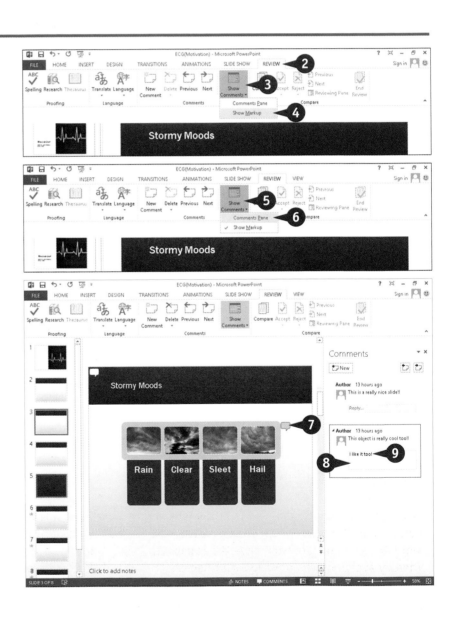

Ⓐ Note that the comment and its reply are grouped together.

⑪ Click the **Next Comment** button (🗗).

Note: You can use the Next Comment (🗗) and Previous Comment (🗗) buttons to move from one comment to another, as well as from slide to slide.

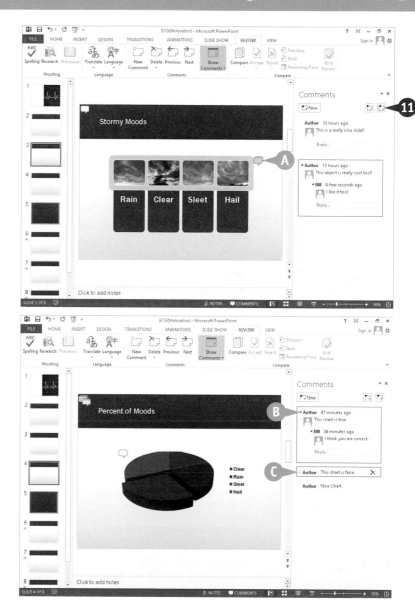

PowerPoint moves to the next comment on the next slide.

Ⓑ You can click the **Collapse** icon (◢) to collapse a comment.

Ⓒ You can click the **Expand** icon (▷) to see a collapsed comment.

I noticed that some of my comments say Author on them. Why is that?
If you view comments on the same computer where you created the comments, PowerPoint uses the word *Author* to denote who made the comment, thereby avoiding any confusion with names.

Can I print comments along with my handouts?
Yes. Comments and comment markers print by default when you print slides. However, there is an option to hide them during printing if you do not want to print them. This option is in the drop-down list where you select the slide layout for the printout in Backstage view.

Select a Show Type and Show Options

You should have no surprises during your slide show, so before you run it for an audience, you should check the settings so you know exactly what will happen when you run it. These settings include the type of slide show, whether the slide show repeats continuously, whether you want to use narration and animations, and the pen color for annotations made on the screen during the slide show. These settings allow you to configure the slide show to your particular needs so you are as comfortable as possible during the slide show.

Select a Show Type and Show Options

1. In Normal view, click the **Slide Show** tab.

2. Click **Set Up Slide Show**.

   The Set Up Show dialog box appears.

3. Click an option to select whether you want a speaker to present your slide show, a person to view it on a computer, or many people to view it at a kiosk (○ changes to ◉).

4. Click either the **Manually** option (slides advance with a mouse click) or click the **Using timings, if present** option (○ changes to ◉).

Note: This setting only has an effect if you set any slide timings. Timings, such as setting a slide to advance automatically or after you rehearse timing the show, do not work if you set this option to Manually.

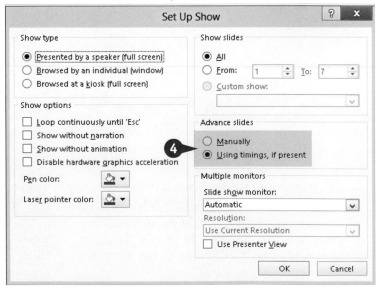

5 Click one or more options to select whether you want your show to loop continuously, run without narration, or run without animation (☐ changes to ☑).

6 Click the **Pen color** button (🎨▾) and select a color from the palette.

7 Click the **Laser pointer color** button (🎨▾) and select a color from the palette.

Note: See Chapter 15 to learn about Pen annotations and the Laser Pointer.

8 Click **OK**.

PowerPoint applies your new settings and closes the dialog box.

9 Click the **Save** icon (💾) to save the settings.

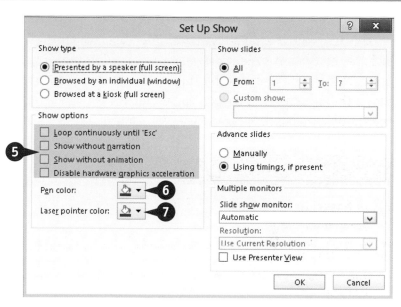

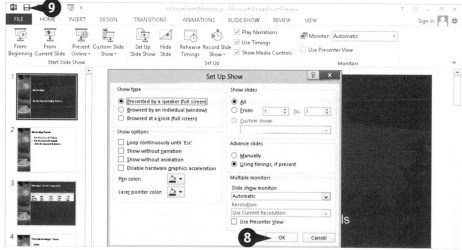

TIPS

Why would I want to show my presentation without animation?

Animations are fun, but on computers lacking adequate resources, they may run slowly and delay your show. If you are using an older computer to present your show, preview it to be sure that animations run smoothly. If they do not, change this setting to avoid any problems.

What is a loop and why would I use it?

Looping is a term for running media, such as songs or videos, over and over again from beginning to end. If you plan to show your presentation at an informational booth or kiosk, where people may stop, watch a bit, and then move on, you probably want the presentation to loop.

Specify Slides to Include

You may create a larger presentation, but decide that you want to show only some of the slides to a particular audience. For example, you may want to show the beginning, summary, and conclusion of a slide show to executives, but present the entire slide show to an audience that needs to see details, such as middle management. To limit the slides that display, you can create a custom slide show that you can quickly and easily access and play. When it is time to present your slide show, you can find and begin the custom show with a few clicks of your mouse.

Specify Slides to Include

1 In Normal view, click the **Slide Show** tab.

2 Click **Custom Slide Show**.

3 Click **Custom Shows**.

The Custom Shows dialog box appears.

4 Click **New**.

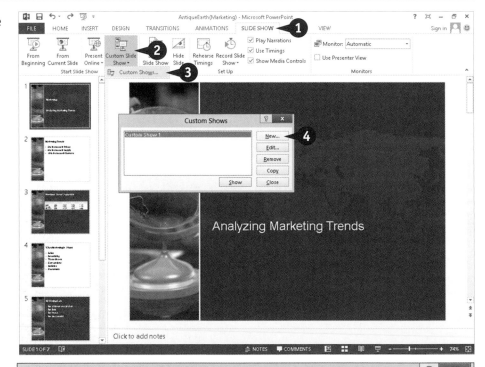

The Define Custom Show dialog box appears.

5 Click the **Slide show name** text box.

6 Type a name.

7 Click the slides that you want in your custom slide show (☐ changes to ☑).

8 Click **Add**.

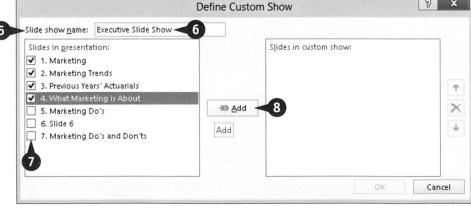

Ⓐ PowerPoint adds the slides to the Slides in custom show list.

9 Click **OK**.

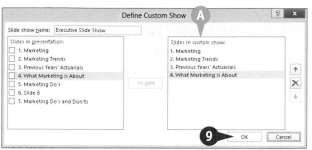

Ⓑ PowerPoint adds the custom show to the list.

10 Click **Close**.

11 Click **Custom Slide Show**.

The menu lists all custom slide shows for this particular presentation.

12 Click the custom show you want to present.

PowerPoint starts your custom slide show.

TIPS

Can I show a range of slides quickly without creating a custom slide show?

Yes. Click **Set Up Slide Show** on the Slide Show tab. Under the Show Slides heading of the dialog box, click the **From** option. Type the beginning and ending slide numbers and then click **OK**. When you present the slide show, only that range of slides are shown.

What if I do not want to show a slide located in the middle of my presentation?

With a large presentation, it may be inconvenient to build a custom show that excludes only one slide. In this case, just hide the slide. Change to Slide Sorter view, right-click the slide, and then click **Hide Slide** on the shortcut menu.

Rehearse Timing

Completing your presentation in the allotted time is considered courteous. You can use the Rehearse Timings feature to time a practice run of your slide show to ensure that it takes the proper amount of time to deliver. This helps you arrange your presentation so it fits into the time allotted for it. You can also use the Rehearse Timings feature to time slides when you set up slides to advance automatically during your slide show and when the slide show is programmed to play continuously.

Rehearse Timing

1 Click the **Slide Show** tab.

2 Click **Rehearse Timings**.

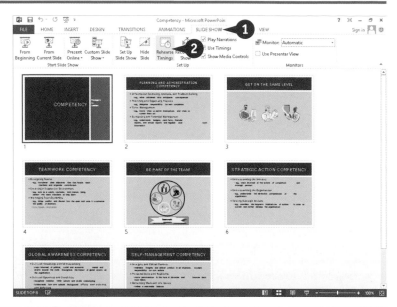

The slide show begins and the Recording toolbar appears.

3 Rehearse the slide narrative, clicking the **Next** button (➡) to advance the slide.

A This shows the elapsed time of the current slide.

B This shows the elapsed time of the entire show.

C Click **Repeat** (↺) to start the timing over for the current slide.

D Click the **Close** button (✖) to exit the slide show early.

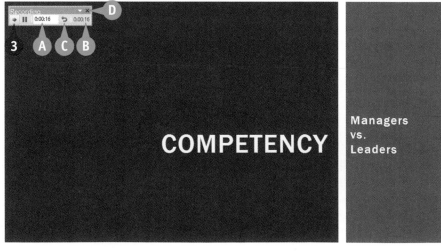

4 Click the **Pause** button (❚❚) to suspend the timing.

The Recording Paused dialog box appears.

5 Click **Resume Recording**.

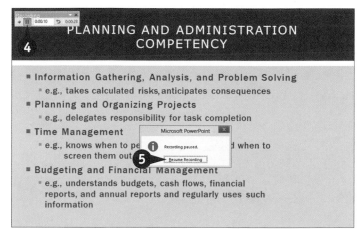

After the last slide, a message box asks if you want to save the timings.

6 Click **Yes** to save the timings, or click **No** to exit the rehearsal without saving the timings.

The presentation appears in Design view.

E The timing applied to each slide appears below its thumbnail.

7 Click the **Save** icon (💾) to save the timings.

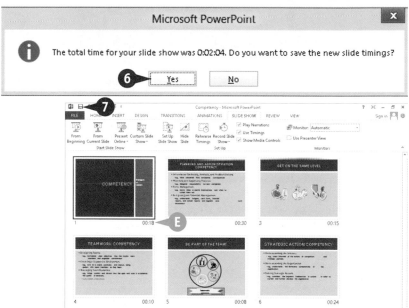

TIP

Rehearsing timings and recording a slide show seem to be the same thing. Are they?

They are very similar. You can have slides advance automatically through a slide show if you either rehearse timing or record a show. The significant difference is that you can record a narrative and the movements of the laser pointer when you record the show. Considering you usually record a show because you are absent when the slide show is running, this is a pretty important difference. If the slide show runs on a kiosk or on someone's computer, you probably want to record a narration and the movements of the laser pointer.

Record a Narration

If you do not intend to present your PowerPoint show live — for example, if you are showing your presentation at a kiosk — you can record a narration that talks the viewer through your key points. Recording a slide show also sets up your presentation to advance automatically at the end of each slide's narration. This nice feature gives you the option to give the presentation in person, or to personalize a presentation where you are not physically present. You do not necessarily need to record the entire presentation; you can record just a few slides if you choose.

Record a Narration

1 Plug a microphone into your computer.

2 Click the **Slide Show** tab.

3 Click **Record Slide Show**.

The Record Slide Show dialog box appears.

4 Click to enable (☑) both options.

5 Click **Start Recording**.

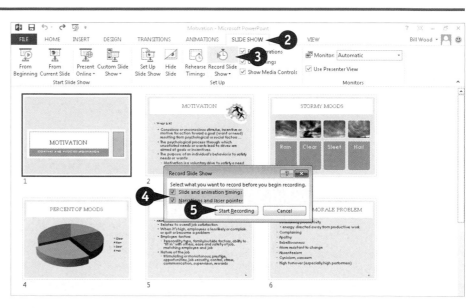

The slide show begins and the Recording toolbar appears.

6 Narrate the slide, speaking clearly into the microphone.

7 Click the **Next** button (➡) to advance the slide.

Note: See the section, "Rehearse Timing," to learn more about the Recording toolbar.

8 Press **Ctrl** while clicking the primary mouse button to display the laser pointer, and then drag it across the screen to show items of interest.

When the slide show ends, Design view reappears.

A The timing applied to each slide appears below its thumbnail.

B Slides with narration display a speaker icon.

9 Click to enable (☑) both **Play Narrations** and **Use Timings**.

10 Click the **Save** icon (💾) to save the narration.

11 Click **From Beginning**, sit back, and watch the automated slide show.

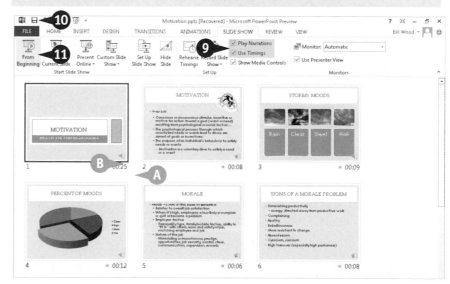

TIP

Can I clear timings and narrations?
Yes. Follow these steps:

1 Click the **Slide Show** tab.

2 Click the **Record Slide Show** down arrow (▼).

3 Click **Clear**.

4 Click an item from the menu.

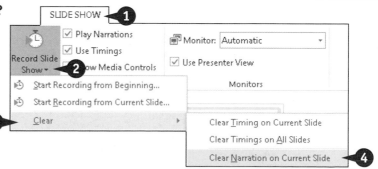

Package a Presentation

You can save a presentation in a format that includes a PowerPoint viewer, plus any files needed to view your presentation. This viewer enables the presentation to be viewed on a computer that does not have PowerPoint installed on it, thereby allowing anyone to view your presentation. This may also be a good time to personalize your presentation by recording a narrative. If any media is linked to the presentation instead of embedded in it, the package includes those files, as well as embedding fonts into the presentation.

Package a Presentation

1 Click the **File** tab to show Backstage view.

2 Click **Export**.

3 Click **Package Presentation for CD**.

4 Click **Package for CD**.

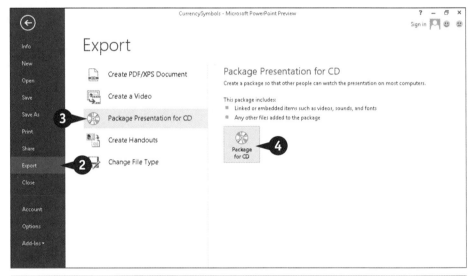

The Package for CD dialog box appears.

5 Click **Copy to Folder**.

Ⓐ You can also insert a CD in your CD drive and then click **Copy to CD** — PowerPoint burns the presentation files directly to the CD.

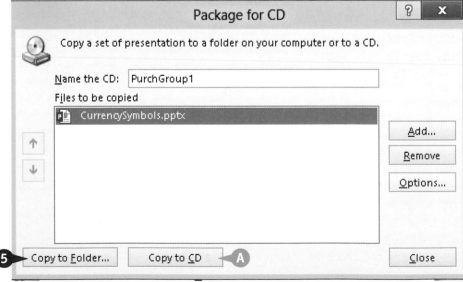

The Copy to Folder dialog box appears.

6 Click in the **Folder name** text box, and then type a name.

B Note the folder location where the presentation package will be saved. You can click **Browse** to change the location.

7 Click **OK**.

8 Click **Yes** in reply to the message that asks, "Do you want to include linked files in your package?"

C PowerPoint creates a presentation package and saves it in the folder location that you specified.

9 Send the entire folder to your intended viewers. In this example, the PurchGroup1 folder is sent to intended viewers.

D To view the slide show, double-click the presentation.

Note: If the computer does not have PowerPoint, this action opens a web page to download the PowerPoint viewer.

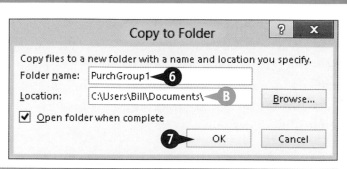

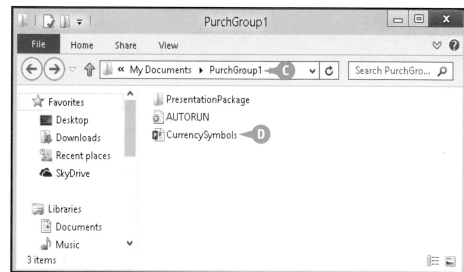

TIPS

What is the purpose of the Options button?
You can click the **Options** button to open the Options dialog box. This displays the options Linked files and Embedded TrueType Fonts — always keep these enabled (☑). This ensures that your presentation looks the way you intended. You can also set a password to open the presentation and check for personal data that may be in the presentation.

What is the Add button for?
You can include more than one presentation in a package. Click the **Add** button and the Add File dialog box appears — use it to browse to another presentation. When you find the presentation file you want to add, click it and then click **OK**. PowerPoint adds it to the list.

CHAPTER 14

Printing Presentations

There are several reasons to print a presentation. You may want a hard copy of your slides to review away from your computer, or you might want to print slide handouts for your audience to follow during your live presentation. You might also want to print a copy of your outline or notes to give to your audience.

Using Print Preview

It is a good practice to see what your slides look like before you use resources for printing. Slides with colorful or dark backgrounds can use a lot of printer ink, and color printers are expensive to operate. You can use the Print Preview feature to see what your printout looks like before printing so you do not waste these resources. Print Preview has options that allow you to see what your printout will look like: slides, black-and-white slides, notes, outline, and so on. You can preview any of these options before printing.

Using Print Preview

1 Click the **File** tab to show Backstage view.

2 Click **Print**.

PowerPoint displays the slide show in the Print Preview view.

Ⓐ You can navigate through the pages.

Ⓑ You can zoom in and out.

3 Click **Edit Header & Footer**.

The Header and Footer dialog box appears.

4 Click the **Date and time**, **Slide number,** and **Footer** options to enable settings (☐ changes to ☑).

Note: See Chapter 9 to learn more about header and footer settings.

5 Click **Apply to All**.

Ⓒ Alternatively, you can click **Apply** to apply the setting to only the currently visible page.

PowerPoint applies your
new settings and closes the
Header and Footer dialog box.

D The date and slide number
appear in the Print Preview.

6 To change printers, click the
Printer down arrow (▾).

7 Click a printer.

PowerPoint changes the printer.

8 Click the **Copies** spinner (⬍)
or type a number into the text
box to change the number of
copies to print.

9 Click **Print**.

PowerPoint prints the
presentation.

TIPS

**Why is my Print Preview black and white when I
have it set up for color?**
PowerPoint knows if a black-and-white printer is
selected for printing, so it automatically shows the
Print Preview in black and white. Select your color
printer from the Printer list, and the Print Preview
changes to color.

**How can I quickly tell how many pages will print
if I choose to print multiple slides per page?**
Look at the lower-left corner of the Print Preview
screen. The status area indicates the total number
of pages that will print and which page you
currently have displayed in Print Preview. For
example, if you have 11 slides and you want to print
two slides per page, it will say 2 of 6.

Print Slides

You can create a printout of your slides if you want to review them on paper or if you want to give your audience a handout. You can print a single slide, your entire presentation, or selected slides. You can print slides in black and white, grayscale, or in color if you have a color printer available. There are other options, too. You can print multiple slides per page, print your notes with slides, or even frame slides so you can see white slides against the white, printed pages.

Print Slides

1 Click the **File** tab to show Backstage view.

2 Click **Print**.

PowerPoint displays the slide show in Print Preview view.

3 Click the **Slides** down arrow (▼).

4 Click **Custom Range**.

A You can click **Print Current Slide** to print the visible slide.

B You can click **Print Selection** to print the slides currently selected in Normal view.

C You can print custom shows by selecting them here.

5 Type the slide numbers you want to print in the **Slides** text box, separated by commas.

D Click the **Information** icon (ⓘ) for more information.

This example types 1, 3-5, which will print slide numbers 1, 3, 4, and 5.

6 Click **Print**.

PowerPoint prints your selection of slides.

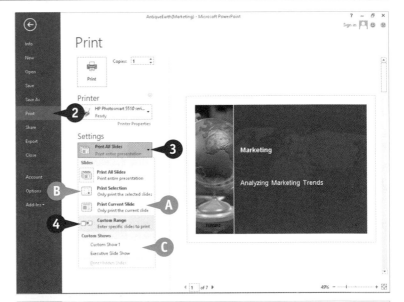

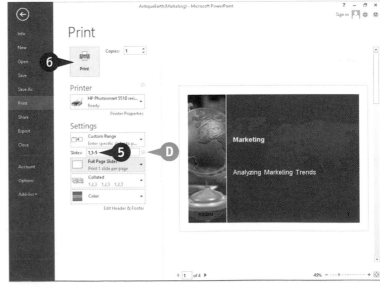

Print Hidden Slides

You may decide not to show every slide in a presentation, but you want to print the entire presentation for someone to review. For example, you may want to hide information concerning managers while presenting a slide show to workers, but you want Human Resources to review a hard copy of the presentation. You can quickly switch between printing or not printing hidden slides with a few clicks of the mouse button. By default, PowerPoint prints hidden slides, but you can easily adjust print settings to exclude hidden slides from printing.

Print Hidden Slides

1 Click the **File** tab to show Backstage view.

2 Click **Print**.

The Print Preview appears.

A In this example, 26 pages are scheduled to print.

3 Click the **Slides** down arrow (▼).

4 Click **Print Hidden Slides** (✓ disappears from the menu).

B You can also click to print a presentation section.

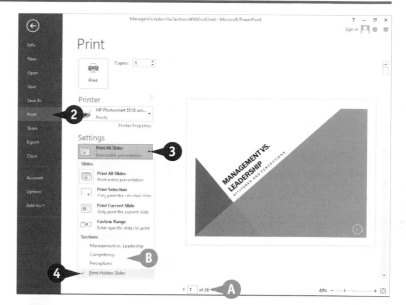

C PowerPoint changes the number of pages now scheduled to print.

5 Click **Print**.

PowerPoint prints the presentation without the hidden slides.

Note: The Print Hidden Slides option is disabled if there are no hidden slides in the presentation.

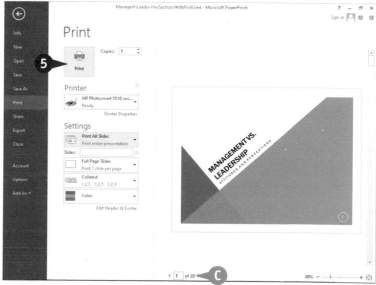

Print Handouts

A presentation handout helps audience members follow along and gives them a place where they can write notes for future reference. You can view presentation handouts in Print Preview and easily print them from that view. You can print anywhere from one to nine slides on a handout page, in landscape or portrait orientation. Printing several slides per page can save paper when you want to print handouts for a lengthy presentation, but make sure your audience can read the slides when there are several per page.

Print Handouts

① Click the **File** tab to show Backstage view.

② Click **Print**.

PowerPoint displays the slide show in Print Preview view.

③ Click the **Print Layout** down arrow (▼).

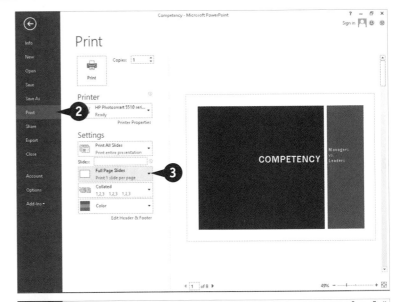

The gallery of print layouts appears.

④ Click a layout under the Handouts heading.

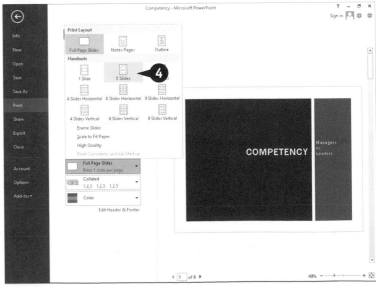

The slide layout changes in Print Preview, and the orientation drop-down list appears under the Settings heading.

5 Click the **Orientation** down arrow (▼).

6 Click an orientation.

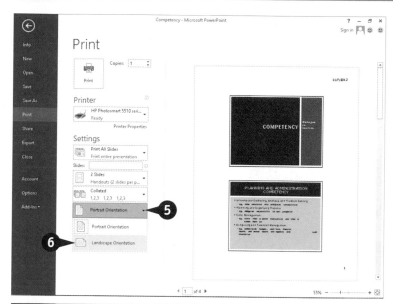

The page orientation changes in Print Preview.

7 Click **Print**.

PowerPoint prints the presentation in the layout you specified.

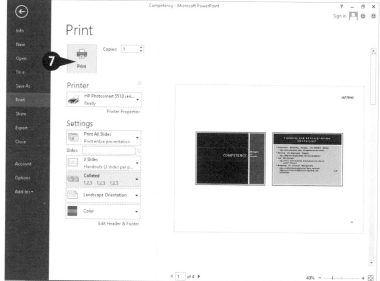

TIPS

Can I add a background color to the actual handout page, or hide information like the page number?

Yes. Click the **View** tab and then click **Handout Master** (see Chapter 9). You can enable (☑) or disable (☐) page information by clicking the check boxes in the Placeholders group on the Handout Master tab. Click **Background Styles** and click a background from the gallery. Click **Close Master View** when you finish.

How many slides should I include per page in a handout?

Two slides per page ensures that your audience can read the handout and leaves plenty of space for notes. If you have only a few bullet points per slide, you may be able to read the handout with four slides per page.

Print Handouts with Microsoft Word

Handouts in PowerPoint are structured and somewhat limited. For example, you cannot change the size of slides on the handout printout and you cannot edit notes in Print Preview. PowerPoint gives you more versatility by letting you export printouts to Microsoft Word. After exporting to Word, you can do anything to your handouts. For example, you can build a report from your presentation. Exporting to Word gives you versatility because you can now take advantage of all the capabilities of Word. Keep in mind that the Word document is not automatically saved. Remember to save it.

Print Handouts with Microsoft Word

1 Click the **File** tab to show Backstage view.

2 Click **Export**.

3 Click **Create Handouts**.

4 Click **Create Handouts**.

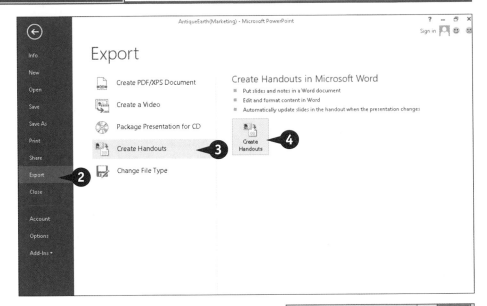

The Send to Microsoft Word dialog box appears.

5 Click an option under the Page layout in Microsoft Word heading (○ changes to ◉).

6 Click an option to paste or link the slide images in Word (○ changes to ◉).

7 Click **OK**.

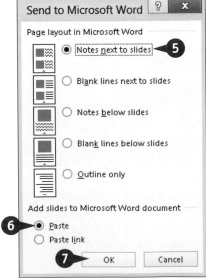

A document with the layout you chose appears in Microsoft Word.

Note: The Word document may appear only as a blinking task on the Windows taskbar. Click the icon to see the Word document.

Note: Word does not save the document automatically. If you are keeping the handouts, save it now.

⑧ Edit the Word document just like any other Word document.

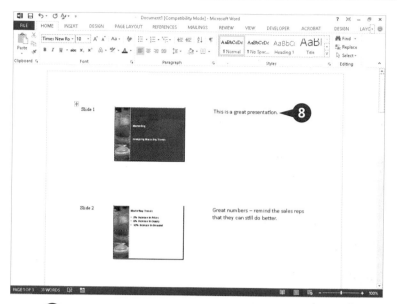

Ⓐ You can add, edit, and format any text.

Ⓑ You can delete slides and add graphics.

⑨ Click the **Save** icon (🖫) to save the Word document.

⑩ Click the **Close** button (✖) to close the Word document.

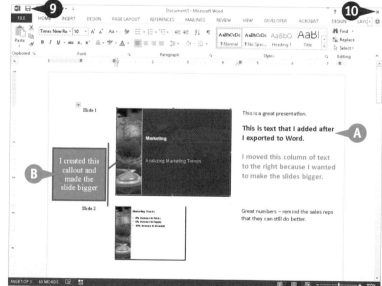

TIPS

Why does my computer seem to lock up when I create handouts with Microsoft Word?
The process takes a while, so you must be patient. The Word document may open minimized, which means it only appears on the Windows taskbar. Go to the Windows taskbar and click the Word document (it should be blinking) to make it appear.

What is the difference between Paste and Paste link?
If you choose **Paste**, PowerPoint pastes images into the Word document. If you select **Paste link**, the images in Word are linked to the presentation, and you can double-click the images to edit the presentation slides. Choosing **Paste link** creates a smaller Word document, but the presentation must accompany it. Choosing **Paste** makes the Word document independent, but bigger.

Print the Outline Only

Sometimes you want to focus only on the presentation text and not the graphics. For example, you may want to give a copy of the outline to audience members as a reference. It may also be convenient for you to have only the bullet points on paper so you can look down at the podium instead of looking at the projector screen during the slide show. You can print the presentation outline to do just that. The printed outline includes titles, subtitles, and bullet points, but does not include any text entered in footers or inserted text boxes.

Print the Outline Only

1 Click the **File** tab to show Backstage view.

2 Click **Print**.

PowerPoint displays the slide show in Print Preview view.

3 Click the **Print Layout** down arrow (▼).

The gallery of print layouts appears.

4 Click **Outline**.

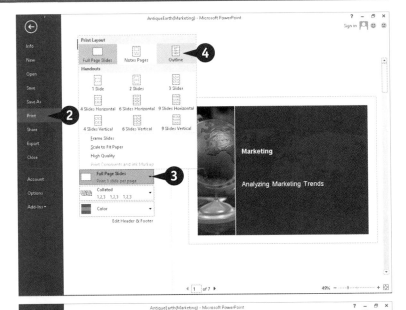

Print Preview changes to Outline view, and the orientation drop-down list appears under the Settings heading.

Ⓐ You can click here to change the orientation of the page.

5 Click **Print**.

PowerPoint prints the outline.

Print Notes

If you are presenting a slide show, you may want a cheat sheet with additional facts or answers to possible audience questions. You can print each slide with its associated notes — the notes that were typed in the Notes pane of Normal view. The Notes printout shows one slide per page and includes the notes under the slide. You can resize and move the slide and format the notes font in the Notes Master view. You can refer to the Notes pages during the presentation, or give them to audience members as a reference.

Print Notes

① Click the **File** tab to show Backstage view.

② Click **Print**.

PowerPoint displays the slide show in Print Preview view.

③ Click the **Print Layout** down arrow (⏷).

The gallery of print layouts appears.

④ Click **Notes Pages**.

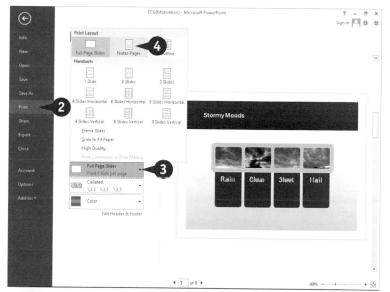

Print Preview changes to Notes Pages view, and the orientation drop-down list appears under the Settings heading.

Ⓐ You can click here to change the orientation of the page.

⑤ Click **Print**.

PowerPoint prints the Notes pages.

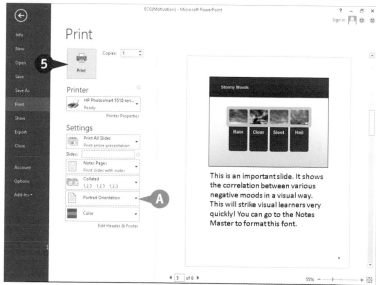

Print in Black and White or Grayscale

You can print a presentation in color, black and white, or grayscale. Grayscale provides some shading to help you see graphics and background elements. Black and white removes all shading, and this can significantly reduce your ability to see background and graphics details. Printing in color is expensive compared to black-and-white printing and it can also be slower, depending on the printer. Many times your audience does not need color printouts and printout drafts need not be in color, so you can save resources and money by printing on a black-and-white printer.

Print in Black and White or Grayscale

1 Click the **File** tab to show Backstage view.

2 Click **Print**.

PowerPoint displays the slide show in Print Preview view.

3 Click the **Color** down arrow ( ).

4 Click **Grayscale**.

A You can click **Pure Black and White** to print in black and white with no shading.

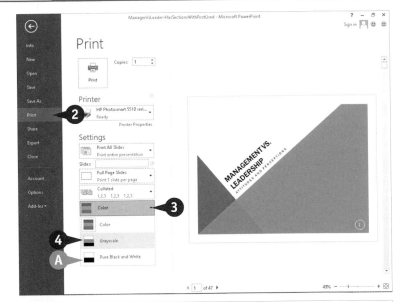

Print Preview appears in grayscale.

5 Click **Print**.

PowerPoint prints the presentation in grayscale.

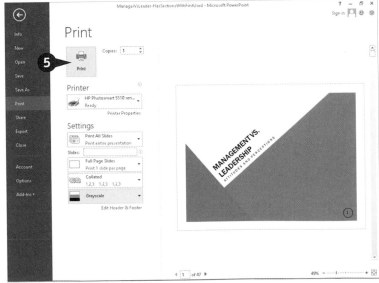

Frame Slides

You can make your presentation handouts really sharp by framing the slides. When you print slides with a frame, PowerPoint places a neat borderline around the edge of the slides and defines them on the printed page. Having a frame around slides in a printout is particularly nice when the slides of your presentation are white or a light color. The frame sets the slides apart from the white, printed page, and improves the appearance of the printout by defining the edge of the slides.

Frame Slides

1 Click the **File** tab to show Backstage view.

2 Click **Print**.

PowerPoint displays the slide show in Print Preview view.

3 Click the **Slide Layout** down arrow (▾).

The gallery of print layouts appears.

4 Click **Frame Slides**.

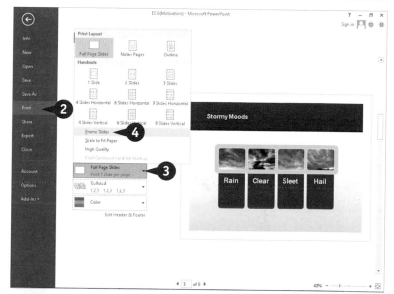

A Print Preview shows a border around the slides.

5 Click **Print**.

PowerPoint prints the presentation.

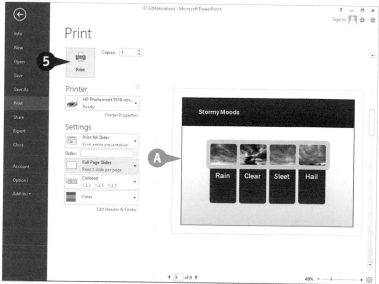

CHAPTER 15

Presenting a Slide Show

Before you present your PowerPoint slide show, be sure you understand the tools that are available to you during the show. These tools were designed to help you give a flawless presentation. Familiarity with them will enable you to present the slide show smoothly.

Game Day!

Get Ready to Present

Asuccessful live presentation requires solid content, good design, and a prepared presenter. Preparing to make a presentation involves double-checking your presentation for problems and getting comfortable with your material and presentation environment. Many times, the person presenting a slide show is not only assessed on the quality of the ideas that they are trying to convey, but also on the professionalism of the presentation, the quality of the slide show, and salesmanship. Become familiar with your presentation, the tools, and your surroundings so you can give the best show possible.

Check Your Presentation for Errors

Checking your slides for details such as spelling, grammar, and typos can save you a lot of embarrassment at show time. Use the presentation outline to review the text so you are not distracted by design elements. A person should not proofread his or her own work. Have a third party review the presentation. That person may catch errors that you miss. Use the PowerPoint tools that are available to help you; PowerPoint contains a spelling and grammar checker, a thesaurus, a research tool, and a word counter. Use these valuable tools to your fullest advantage to build the best presentation possible.

Rehearse the Slide Show

Practice your presentation several times before you present it to an audience. Rehearse in front of a mirror or with a friend, or record yourself. You may discover undesirable mannerisms or expressions that you want to avoid. Know your material so you can anticipate each slide and each bullet point — know what comes next. Avoid looking at and reading from the slide show. Finishing your presentation in the allotted time is considered courteous. Use the Rehearse Timings feature in PowerPoint to check your timing, and then change your presentation accordingly. You want the slide show to move along, but not be rushed.

Know Your Presentation Space

To avoid problems during your presentation, visit the site before the presentation if you can. Knowing the size of the room, the acoustics, and the layout of the stage and audience seating can help you prepare. If the space is large, you may need a microphone. Close the blinds if the space is too bright. Try to meet your audience before the slide show. This makes you more comfortable with them, gives them a chance to ask preliminary questions, and allows you to identify people who need extra attention. Too many questions and comments during a presentation can bog it down.

Set Up Your Show

Be sure to check those all-important slide show settings. (For more information, see Chapter 13.) Before the slide show, you should set up the format for the presentation, such as a live presentation versus one shown at a kiosk, which slides to include, monitors and resolution, and how you will control the advancement of the slides. Even if you are using your own laptop, it could crash, so bring a backup of your presentation. Package it with the PowerPoint viewer in case you find yourself on a computer without PowerPoint. Package any files that are linked to the presentation as well.

Start and End a Show

You typed a lot of text, inserted graphics, and worked with design settings. Finally, your hard work pays off and you get to present your slide show. All you need is to start the slide show and navigate through it. You can end the show at any time or view all of the slides. For the most professional presentation possible, you probably want to start the show and have the first slide or a black screen visible before the audience arrives. You can start the show from any view.

Start and End a Show

① Click the **Slide Show** tab.

② Click **From Beginning**.

Note: You can also press F5 to begin the show.

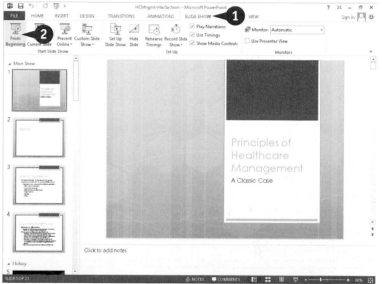

The slide show begins.

When you move the mouse pointer (⬚), the on-screen toolbar appears faintly in the lower-left corner.

③ To end the show before you reach the last slide, click the **Options** icon (◯) on the on-screen toolbar.

④ Click **End Show**.

Note: You can also end the slide show by pressing Esc.

The slide show closes.

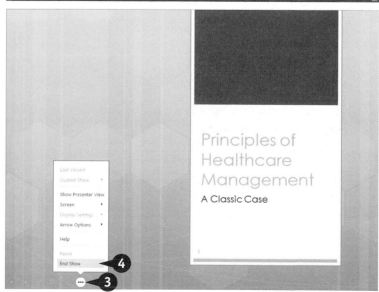

Navigate Among Slides

No slide show would be any good without the ability to move through the slides. You can use the shortcut menu or the Slide Show on-screen toolbar, or click the screen to move through a slide show. You can move back or forward one slide at a time or you can pick a specific slide to show. You can also press the keyboard arrows to move forward and backward through the slide show. All of these options are also available in Presenter view, which is covered later in this chapter.

Navigate Among Slides

1 With your presentation in Slide Show view, click the **Next** icon (⊙) to advance the slide.

Note: You can also click the slide or press ⬇ to advance the slide. Keep in mind clicking the slide also runs animations.

2 Click the **Previous** icon (⊙) to move to the previous slide.

Note: You can also press ⬆ to move to the previous slide.

The slides advance.

3 Click the **All Slides** icon (⊞).

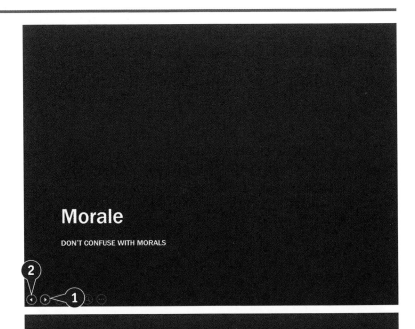

All slides appear.

4 Click the slide you want to show.

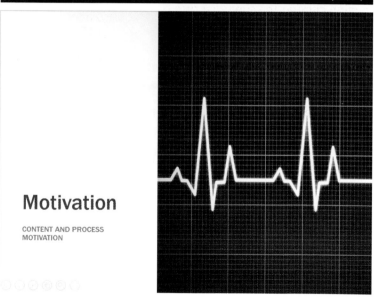

The selected slide appears.

I clicked the All Slides icon and I am now in All Slides view. Can I return to the slide show without switching slides?

Yes. In the upper-left corner of the screen is a back button (⊖). Click that button and the slide show returns to the current slide.

The slide thumbnails in the All Slides view are too small. Can I make them bigger?

Yes. In the lower-right corner of the All Slides view is a zoom slider. You can click and drag the slider or click anywhere on the zoom slider to zoom in or zoom out, which resizes the slide thumbnails. You can also use the plus and minus signs at either end of the zoom slider to zoom in and out.

Zoom In

Ideally, you want all the text and objects on a slide to be easily visible to your audience without them straining to see. You may have something on your screen, though, that is unavoidably hard to see. If your audience has trouble seeing something on a slide, you can zoom in on the slide with a click of the on-screen toolbar during the slide show. After zooming, you can move the zoom area to any region of the slide with a simple click and drag of the mouse.

Zoom In

1 With your presentation in Slide Show view, click the **Zoom** icon (⊚) on the on-screen toolbar.

A A marquee appears, showing the zoom area. The mouse pointer (⇖) changes to a zoom magnifying glass (⊕).

2 Drag the marquee with the zoom magnifying glass (⊕) to the area of interest.

3 Click the screen.

B PowerPoint zooms in on the marquee area. The zoom magnifying glass (🔍) changes to the zoom hand (🖐).

4 Click and drag the zoom hand (🖐) to any area of the slide, and the zoom area moves.

Press **Esc** to return to the full screen view.

TIPS

The slides seem to advance properly when I use the Forward icon on the on-screen toolbar, but not when I click the slide. Why not?
You may have some animations on the slide that run when you click the slide instead of advancing the slide. Also make sure that you enable (☑) **On Mouse Click** on the Transitions tab.

I set up the slide show to advance slides automatically, but sometimes I want to advance faster. Can I?
Yes. Enable (☑) the **On Mouse Click** option on the Transitions tab. The slide will advance automatically and also when you click either the slide or the **Next** icon (◉) on the on-screen toolbar.

Use the Pointer

You have options regarding how you use the mouse pointer during the slide show, such as showing or hiding it. The laser pointer is also a great way to draw your audience's attention to a particular spot on a slide. The laser pointer is an on-screen tool that gives the illusion that you are pointing at the screen with a hand-held laser pointer. You can quickly and easily enable and use the laser pointer during your slide show to point something out with flair and style, or you can stick with the faithful standard mouse pointer.

Use the Pointer

1 With your presentation in Slide Show view, click the **Options** icon (⊖) on the on-screen toolbar.

2 Click **Arrow Options**.

3 Click a setting from the menu.

Automatic shows the mouse pointer (⬉), but hides it when inactive; **Visible** shows the mouse pointer continuously; **Hidden** hides the mouse pointer continuously.

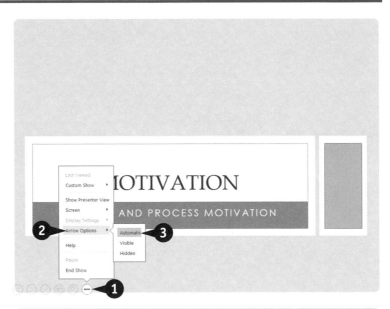

4 Click the **Pen** icon (⬛) on the on-screen toolbar.

5 Click **Laser Pointer**.

The mouse pointer (⟍) changes to the laser pointer (●), and the laser pointer appears continuously.

6 Drag the mouse around the area you want to identify on-screen.

7 Position the pointer over the on-screen toolbar.

The pointer temporarily changes back to the mouse pointer (⟍).

8 Click the **Next** icon (⊙).

A The slide advances and the pointer changes back to the laser pointer (●).

9 Press Esc.

The laser pointer (●) changes to the mouse pointer (⟍).

TIPS

Is there an easier way to turn on the laser pointer?
Yes. Constantly going to the on-screen toolbar is inconvenient and strains the audience. To use the laser pointer briefly, press Ctrl then press the primary mouse button, and then drag the mouse to move it. When you release the mouse button or the Ctrl key, the mouse pointer (⟍) comes back.

Can I change the color of the laser pointer?
No, but the laser pointer is designed in such a way that it is clearly visible, even on a red slide background, or a red graphic or table. It actually shows well on any color because it is red with a white corona.

Mark Up with Pen and Highlighter

Powerpoint enables you to draw freehand on your screen during a slide show with a pen tool. You can use it to highlight or annotate important points in the slide show. You can choose Pen for a thin, opaque line, or Highlighter, which gives you a much thicker, translucent line. You can also choose a color for both. You can save annotations so they appear the next time you present your slide show — PowerPoint asks if you want to save annotations when you exit the show, but only if that option is enabled in PowerPoint Options (see Chapter 3).

Mark Up with Pen and Highlighter

① With your presentation in Slide Show view, click the **Pen** icon (⊘) on the on-screen toolbar.

② Click **Pen**.

The pointer changes to a point of color on the screen.

Ⓐ You can click to change the color of the Pen or Highlighter.

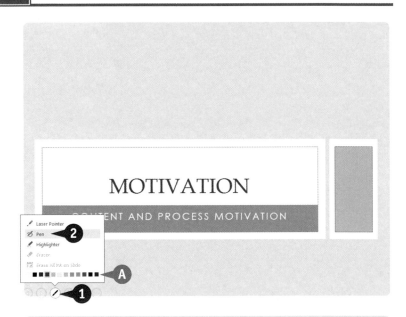

③ Click and drag on the screen around the area you want to identify.

A line appears where you dragged the mouse.

④ Press Esc to turn off the Pen.

5 Click the **Pen** icon (⊘) on the on-screen toolbar.

6 Click **Highlighter**.

The pointer changes to a rectangular patch of color on the screen.

7 Click and drag on the screen over the area you want to highlight.

A thick, translucent line appears where you dragged the mouse.

8 Press **Esc** to turn off the Highlighter.

9 Press **Esc** to exit the slide show.

PowerPoint asks if you want to save your annotations.

10 Click **Keep** or **Discard**.

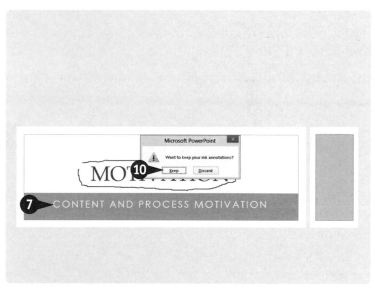

TIPS

Why can I not seem to erase my annotations?

You can only erase annotations during the current session of your slide show. If you exited the slide show and saved the annotations when prompted, they are permanent and you cannot erase them the next time you view the slide show.

Why does PowerPoint exit the slide show when I press the Escape key to clear the Pen?

You may have pressed **Esc** a second time, which exits the slide show. Be patient, it sometimes takes a few seconds for the Pen or Highlighter to change back to the mouse pointer (⇖). You may need to move the mouse to see the pointer if your on-screen arrow option is set to Automatic, which hides the pointer when inactive.

Erase Annotations

When you work with the Pen and Highlighter tools to mark up a slide, in essence, the slide becomes a whiteboard or blackboard. These tools allow you to circle or highlight many things in your slide show. However, you may want to remove some markings from a slide if you marked the wrong thing or if you need more room on a slide where there are too many markings. You can remove annotations from the slide using a tool in the on-screen toolbar.

Erase Annotations

1 With your presentation in Slide Show view, click the **Pen** icon (⬚) on the on-screen toolbar.

2 Click **Eraser**.

The mouse pointer (⬚) changes to an eraser (⬚).

A You can click **Erase All Ink on Slide** to remove all annotations from the current slide.

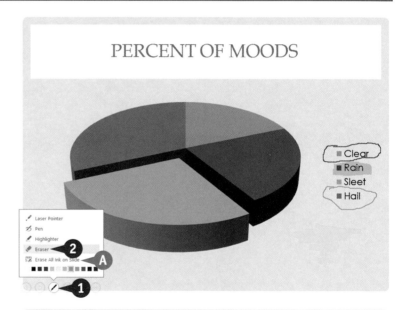

3 Position the eraser (⬚) over an annotation and click the annotation.

The annotation disappears.

4 Press Esc to clear the eraser.

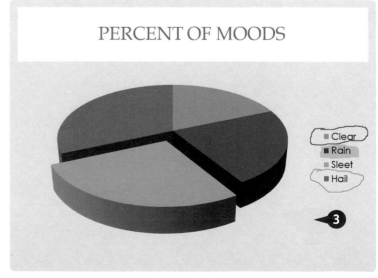

Display Slide Show Help

You probably do not know everything about PowerPoint, so you may need help during the slide show. If you need help running your show after starting it, you do not need to stop the show to open PowerPoint Help. The slide show on-screen help shows shortcuts for running the show and managing presentation features such as pointer options. If you are using Presenter view, you can open the on-screen help for the slide show without the audience seeing it because it opens on the Presenter view screen on your laptop.

Display Slide Show Help

1 With your presentation in Slide Show view, click the **Options** icon (⊙) on the toolbar.

Note: You can also right-click the screen to display the shortcut menu.

2 Click **Help**.

Note: You can also press **F1** during the slide show to see Help.

The Slide Show Help window appears.

A PowerPoint categorizes the shortcuts with a tab for each category.

3 Look up the shortcut to perform the procedure you want.

The shortcut is in the left column and the description is in the right column.

4 When you finish, click **OK**.

The Help window closes.

Enable Presenter View

You can give a smooth presentation by using Presenter view. You can view your presentation complete with speaker notes on your computer, while the audience views only the slide show on the main screen. With Presenter view, you can see your notes, the slide show controls are continuously visible and accessible, and PowerPoint Help shows only on your monitor. If you need to go to the All Slides view to go to a particular slide, only you see it. A timer shows the elapsed time, and you can see both the current and the next slide.

Enable Presenter View

1. Click the **Slide Show** tab.

2. Click **Use Presenter View** (☐ changes to ☑).

3. Begin the slide show.

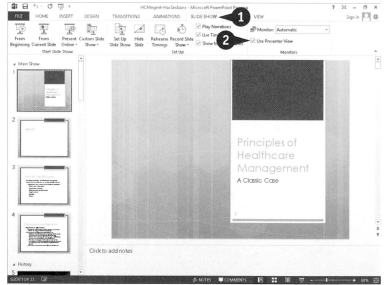

Your laptop shows Presenter view.

Ⓐ You can click **Display Settings** to specify which screen shows the main show and which screen shows Presenter view.

Ⓑ You can click **Show Taskbar** to switch to a different program.

Ⓒ You can click **Black Screen** (▨) to display a black screen.

4. Click **End Slide Show**.

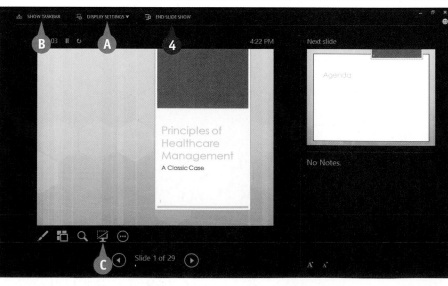

Use Presenter View

During a live presentation, you want to give the audience your full attention, which means not looking at the projector screen. If you are presenting on a projector screen or monitor, you can use Presenter view on your laptop. With Presenter view, you see the slide currently being viewed by the audience, the next slide, any notes you made, and a suite of tools specifically designed to help you give a professional presentation. There is no need to search for tools on the main screen or have the audience watch you search for another slide. Everything is visible and available in Presenter view.

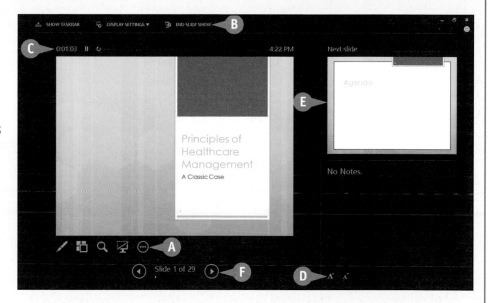

Ⓐ Toolbar

The toolbar is nearly identical to the on-screen toolbar and is always visible in Presenter view.

Ⓑ Command Buttons

These commands are conveniently visible in Presenter view, but hidden on the main screen.

Ⓒ Timer

The timer shows the elapsed time of the show, and you can pause and restart it.

Ⓓ Notes

Notes are visible and you can change their font size.

Ⓔ Slide Preview

You can see the next slide and collect your thoughts in preparation.

Ⓕ Advance Slides

You can advance slides with confidence by clicking buttons instead of slides.

Switch to a Different Program

You can switch to a different program and work with it during a slide show. For example, if you are giving a presentation on Microsoft Word, you may need to go to Word to demonstrate a feature that you are showing in your slide show. Perhaps someone asks to see the data for a chart and you want to show it during the slide show. You can quickly and easily switch to that other program, work with it, and then return to your slide show. To return to your slide show, you can minimize or close the other program.

Switch to a Different Program

1. With your presentation in Slide Show view, click the **Options** icon (⊝).

2. Click **Screen**.

3. Click **Show Taskbar**.

The Windows taskbar appears.

4. Click an open program on the taskbar.

This example clicks Excel.

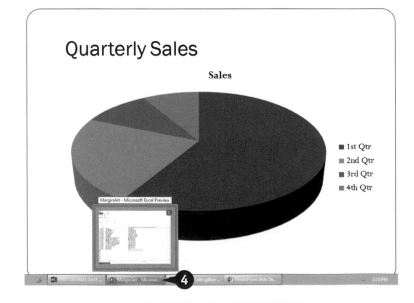

The program you clicked appears on the screen.

5 To return to your slide show, find the slide show on the taskbar and click it.

A You can also click the **Close** button (✖) to close the program, Excel in this example, or the **Minimize** button (➖) to minimize the program.

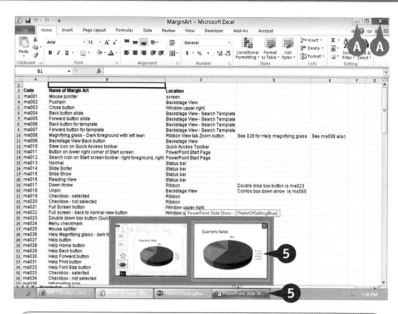

The slide show reappears.

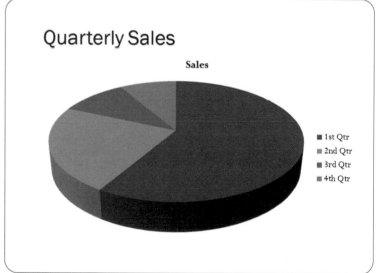

TIPS

Can I open a program during a slide show?
Yes. When the taskbar appears, you can use it in any way that you normally would, including to go to the Windows 8 Start screen to open a program. You can also press ⊞ to switch between the Windows 8 Start screen and the slide show.

Is there another way to switch to a different program?
Yes. If you are using a laptop and the audience is watching on a projector screen or monitor, you can use Presenter view. Presenter view has a command button for this very purpose. You can switch to another program with one click of the mouse.

CHAPTER 16

Publishing a Presentation

PowerPoint enables you to share your presentation in many different ways. You can save your slide show in different file formats, such as a PDF, Word document, or video file. You can also publish slides as JPEG or TIFF graphics.

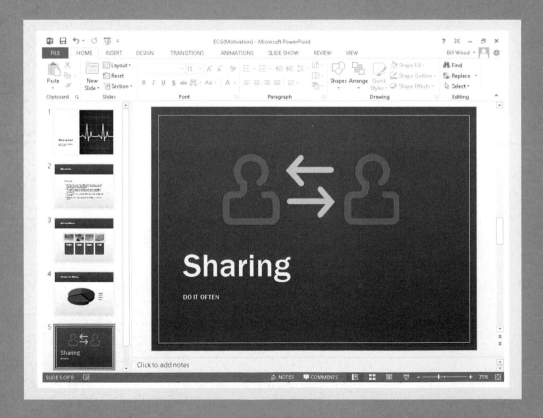

Compare Presentations

I f you have someone review your presentation and make changes, PowerPoint enables you to
compare the presentation with the original. You can send a copy of your presentation to peers,
possibly through e-mail, and allow them to review and edit it — no need to do anything special, just
send it. After everyone makes changes, you can compare them all to the original. This feature makes it
unnecessary to read the entire presentation thoroughly in order to check for changes that others have
made — PowerPoint points out the changes for you. Then, you can accept or reject their changes.

Compare Presentations

1 Open the original presentation
that you sent to others for
review.

Note: In this example, the
username of the presentation
copy was changed to Art in
PowerPoint Options.

2 Click the **Review** tab while
in Normal view.

3 Click **Compare**.

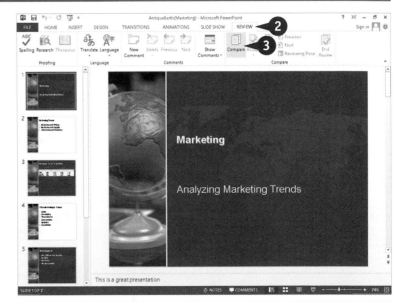

The Choose File to Merge
with Current Presentation
dialog box appears.

4 Click the folder that contains
the edited presentation.

5 Click the presentation that
others have edited.

Note: The name of the edited
presentation does not need to
be the same as the original.

6 Click **Merge**.

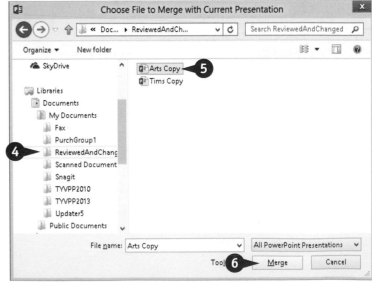

The Reviewing pane (also called the Revisions pane) appears.

7 Click a slide with changes, or click **Next** to go to the first change.

Ⓐ Changes are marked with an icon (📝).

Ⓑ Changes to slides appear in the Slide Changes box.

Ⓒ Changes to the presentation, such as slide deletions, appear in the Presentation Changes box.

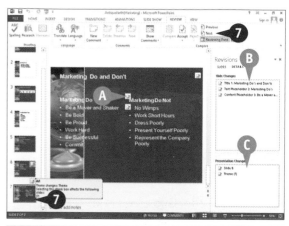

8 Click a marker (📝).

When you position the mouse pointer (🖑) over a marker, the details of the change appear.

9 Click **Accept**.

Ⓓ Accepted changes display check marks.

10 Click **Previous** or **Next** to go to other changes.

11 Click **End Review**.

A dialog box appears, asking if you want to end the review.

12 Click **Yes**.

Note: PowerPoint rejects any unaccepted changes.

Microsoft PowerPoint

Are you sure you want to end the review for 'AntiqueEarth(Marketing).pptx'? This will end the review, and any unapplied changes will be discarded.

12 Yes   No

Was this information helpful?

TIPS

Can I see the slides from the edited presentation?

Yes. The Reviewing pane automatically appears with the Details tab displayed. Click the **Slides** tab in the Reviewing pane, and PowerPoint shows you the slide from the edited presentation that correlates to the slide that you have selected in your presentation.

Can I reverse accepting a change?

Yes. Accepted changes display check marks. Click an accepted change and then click the **Reject** command button on the Review tab. Any changes that are not accepted are automatically rejected when you end the review; however, you can always run the comparison again.

Make a PDF Document from a Presentation

You can make a PDF (portable document format) file from your presentation so that anyone with a PDF reader can view your presentation. A PDF file can be viewed on virtually any computer because PDF readers are free. This feature allows you the convenience of creating a PDF file without the expense of buying a PDF writer! Another benefit of a PDF file is that you can view it on a computer monitor or print it on paper. By saving a presentation as a PDF file, you preserve your presentation's fonts, formatting, and images.

Make a PDF Document from a Presentation

1 Click the **File** tab to show Backstage view.

2 Click **Export**.

3 Click **Create PDF/XPS Document**.

4 Click **Create PDF/XPS**.

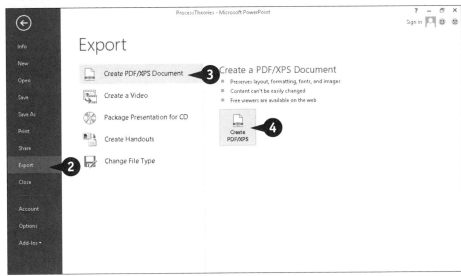

The Publish as PDF or XPS dialog box appears.

5 Click the folder where you want to save your file.

6 Click the **File Name** text box.

7 Type a name.

8 Click **Options**.

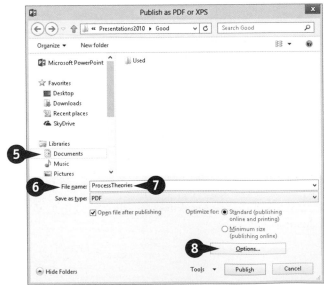

Ⓐ You can output any of the four types of printouts (see Chapter 14).

Ⓑ If you choose **Handouts**, you can specify the number of slides per page.

Ⓒ You can select a range of slides to print.

⑨ Click **OK**.

⑩ Click **Publish**.

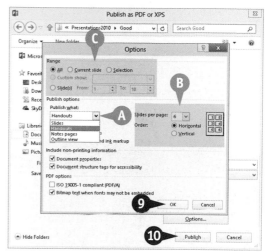

PowerPoint creates the PDF file in the specified folder and shows the status.

PowerPoint opens the file with your PDF reader.

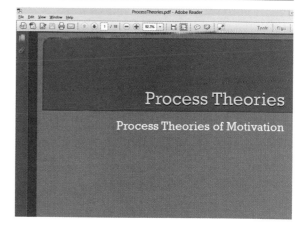

TIPS

I do not have a PDF reader on my computer. Where can I find one?

PDF viewers are free, and most computers already have a PDF reader installed at the time of purchase. However, if you do not have one, you can go to the Adobe website, www.adobe.com, and download their Acrobat Reader.

What is the advantage to preserving the fonts, formatting, and images of my presentation?

Computers can have different sets of fonts loaded with their software. It is possible that a computer viewing your presentation does not have the font you used. Preserving the fonts, formatting, and images carries that information along with the presentation so it looks the same on any computer.

Create a Video of a Presentation

You can create a video of your presentation, which gives you complete control over how people can show and distribute it. Almost anybody can view it because PowerPoint saves it in either a Windows Media Video (WMV) or MPEG-4 format, which can be viewed on most computers. A video that you make from a presentation is secure because no one can change it once it is a video — nobody can see hidden chart data or your design secrets. A video is a great way to present a slide show from a kiosk — start it, let it continually loop, and forget it!

Create a Video of a Presentation

1 Click the **File** tab to show Backstage view.

2 Click **Export**.

3 Click **Create a Video**.

4 Click the **Resolution** down arrow (▾).

5 Click a resolution suited to your needs.

6 Click the **Timings and Narrations** down arrow (▾):

Ⓐ You can click **Don't Use Recorded Timings and Narrations** if you recorded them, but do not want to use them.

Ⓑ You can click **Use Recorded Timings and Narrations** if you recorded them and want to use them.

Ⓒ You can click **Record Timings and Narrations** if you want to record them at this time.

Note: See Chapter 13 to learn about recording timings and narrations.

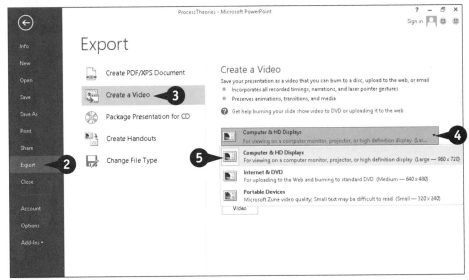

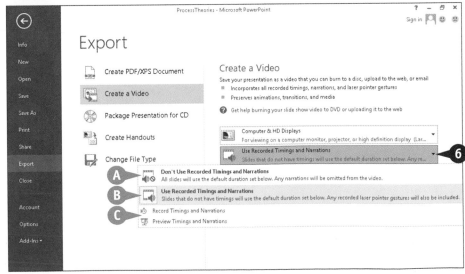

7 Click the text box and type a default time.

The default time refers to how long a slide appears if it has no timings associated with it or you chose not to use timings.

D You can click **Help** for online help.

8 Click **Create Video**.

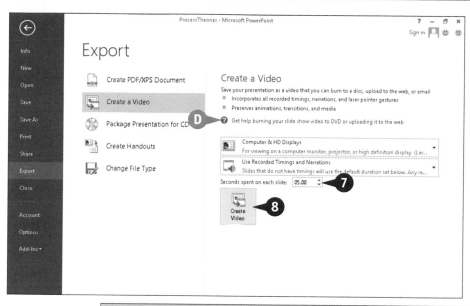

The Save As dialog box appears.

9 Click the folder where you want to save the video.

10 Click the **File name** text box to select it, and then type a filename.

E You can click here to change the file type.

11 Click **Save**.

The dialog box closes and PowerPoint creates the video in the specified folder.

TIPS

Why does nothing seem to happen when I click Save?

It takes a long time for PowerPoint to make the video. Curiously enough, it does not notify you when it is done. However, while it is working, you see a status meter and Cancel button at the bottom in the status bar. When the status meter disappears, the video is done.

Why would I want to change the resolution?

The higher the resolution of your video, the bigger the file, and the more memory it takes to run it. This affects load times and sometimes the quality of playback if computer resources are limited. The Resolution drop-down list has settings for the Internet and for portable devices. You can change the resolution for your target audience.

Save a Presentation as a Slide Show

You can make it easy on your audience and yourself by viewing your presentation through a PowerPoint Show. You can save the presentation so that it opens automatically in Slide Show view. To open it, you navigate to it with Windows Explorer, double-click it, and it opens as a slide show. This is particularly convenient if you are not familiar with PowerPoint but want to do a slide show. Not having to open the file through the PowerPoint program also prevents your audience from seeing your design copy.

Save a Presentation as a Slide Show

1 Click the **File** tab to show Backstage view.

2 Click **Export**.

3 Click **Change File Type**.

4 Click **PowerPoint Show**.

5 Click and drag the scroll bar to scroll to the bottom of the screen to show the Save As button.

6 Click **Save As**.

The Save As dialog box appears.

7 Click the folder where you want to save your file.

8 Click the **File name** text box.

9 Type a filename.

10 Click **Save**.

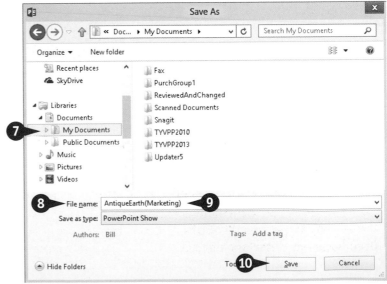

The dialog box closes and PowerPoint creates the PowerPoint Show file in the specified folder.

11 Open Windows Explorer, find the file in the specified folder, and then double-click it.

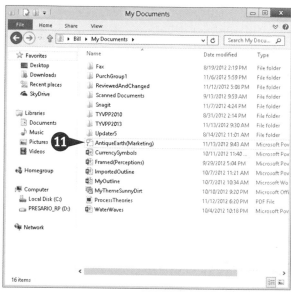

The file opens as a slide show.

TIPS

What do the different PowerPoint extensions mean?
PPSX is the extension for a PowerPoint Show file. PPTX is the extension for a PowerPoint presentation. PPTM is the extension for a presentation that contains macros, and POTX is the extension for a PowerPoint Template. PPT is the extension for a presentation in the 97-2003 format, and ODP is the extension for the Open Document Presentation format.

Are there other advantages to sending a PowerPoint Show (PPSX) to someone instead of a standard presentation (PPTX)?
Yes. If you send this format to others instead of the standard presentation format, they will not be able to see or change the details of your design. They will also not be able to copy any part of your presentation.

Publish Slides as Graphics

You can create a graphic of each slide in your presentation so that you can use them for different purposes. You may want to post them on a website, make high-quality prints, or make them part of a database. You can create either PNG images or JPEG images. PNG are print quality and JPEG are Internet or database quality. There is no need to create a new folder to hold the graphic files, because PowerPoint creates a new folder during this process.

Publish Slides as Graphics

1 Click the **File** tab to show Backstage view.

2 Click **Export**.

3 Click **Change File Type**.

4 Click an image file type.

This example selects **PNG Portable Network Graphics**.

5 Click and drag the scroll bar to scroll to the bottom of the screen so you can see the Save As button.

6 Click **Save As**.

The Save As dialog box appears.

7 Click the folder where you want to save your file.

8 Click the **File name** text box.

9 Type a filename.

This example uses the filename, ECG(Motivation).

10 Click **Save**.

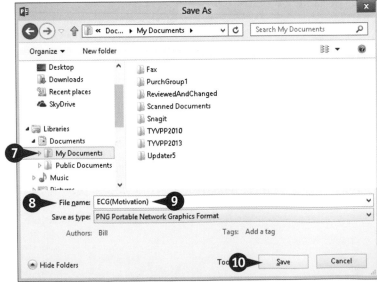

320

A dialog box appears.

11 Click **All Slides**, or click **Just This One** to save only the current slide.

A dialog box appears.

12 Click **OK**.

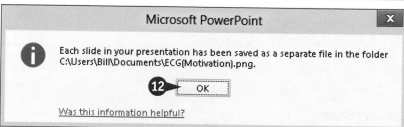

PowerPoint creates the graphics for each slide in the folder you specified.

In this example, PowerPoint created a folder called ECG(Motivation) in the specified folder, and it contains the PNG graphics.

13 Navigate to the folder with Windows Explorer.

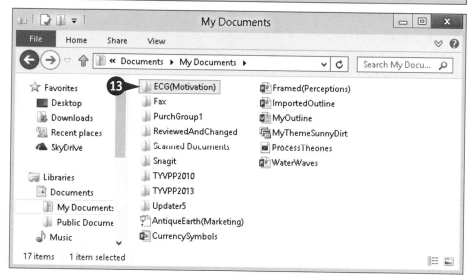

TIPS

How does the Image File Type PNG differ from JPEG?

A JPEG is a picture type that is compressed and trades image quality for smaller file size. The PNG format uses a compression format that does not trade image quality for file size. PNG produces better results for certain applications such as printing.

I saved the graphics to the My Documents folder, but I cannot find them. Where are the files?

PowerPoint creates a folder for you, and places all the graphics in it. You will find this folder in the folder you specified (My Documents, in this case) and it is named whatever you typed into the File name text box.

Broadcast a Presentation

In today's business world, it is common for people to communicate using the Internet. Many business people now join a meeting remotely instead of flying or driving to the meeting. You can broadcast your slide show so anyone who has an Internet connection can watch the show live, and without the expense of a webcast service! PowerPoint creates a link to the broadcast to share with audience members. All your audience needs is a web browser and the link to join the slide show! You must have a Microsoft account, which is free, to broadcast a slide show.

Broadcast a Presentation

1 Click the **File** tab to show Backstage view.

2 Click **Share**.

3 Click **Present Online**.

4 Click **Present Online**.

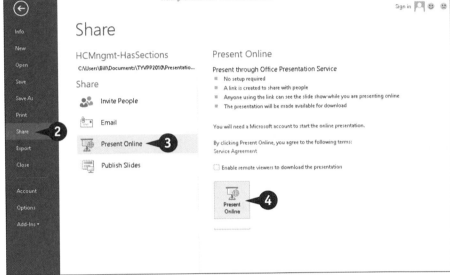

The Sign in dialog box appears. If you are already signed into your Microsoft Live account, you do not receive this dialog box.

5 Type your username.

6 Type your password.

7 Click **Sign in**.

8 Click this link if you do not have a Microsoft account.

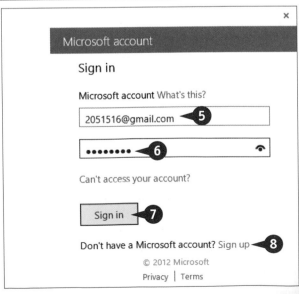

The Present Online dialog box appears. You are connected and can start presenting at any time.

9 Click **Copy Link**.

10 Paste the link into an e-mail and send it to your audience.

Audience members can copy and paste the link from their e-mail into a web browser.

11 Click **Start Presentation**.

Note: You may need to wait for all audience members to join the slide show. If the slide show has begun when they join the web session, it appears in their web browser. If the slide show has not yet started, a message appears, telling them to wait for it to begin.

12 Present the slide show.

13 When the slide show ends, click **End Online Presentation**.

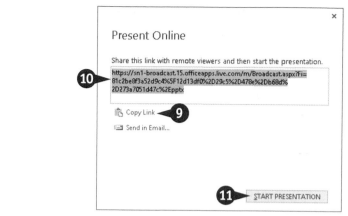

14 In the dialog box that appears, click **End Online Presentation**.

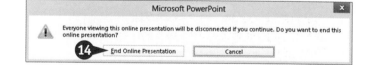

TIPS

What is the Send in Email link in the Present Online dialog box?

If you use Microsoft Outlook as your e-mail program, you can click **Send in Email**. Outlook then composes a new message and automatically pastes the link into the e-mail, so all you need to do is to add e-mail addresses to the e-mail.

Can I send more invitations after closing the Present Online dialog box or after starting the show?

Yes. If you started the slide show, press Esc to stop it and display Normal view. Click the **Present Online** tab, and then click **Send Invitations**. The Present Online dialog box appears and you can send more invitations to join the show. Click **From Beginning** to restart the show.

Save the Presentation to SkyDrive

You can post a presentation to SkyDrive and give permission to people to access it and work with it. SkyDrive is a storage location that is available to anybody who has a Microsoft Live account, and most computers with an Internet connection can access the account. SkyDrive is a service provided by Microsoft free. Storing files to SkyDrive is convenient for two reasons: it gives you an off-site place to back up important files, and you can give permission to people to access your presentation on SkyDrive.

Save the Presentation to SkyDrive

Create a SkyDrive

1 Click the **File** tab to show Backstage view.

2 Click **Save As**.

3 Click **Add a place**.

4 Click **SkyDrive**.

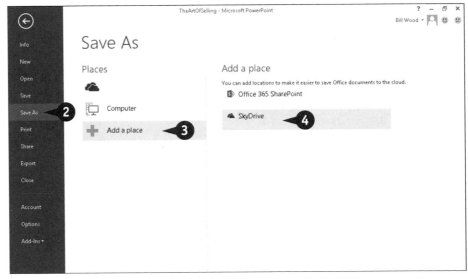

The Microsoft account Sign in dialog box appears.

Ⓐ If you do not have a Microsoft account, click the **Sign up** link.

5 Click the text box and type your username.

6 Click the text box and type your password.

7 Click **Sign in**.

Microsoft creates a SkyDrive for you.

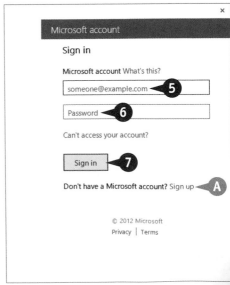

Save to SkyDrive

1 Click the **File** tab to show Backstage view.

2 Click **Save As**.

3 Click your **SkyDrive**.

4 Click **Browse**.

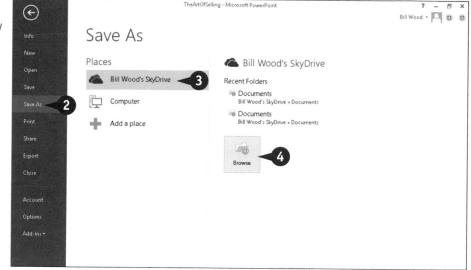

B The Save As dialog box appears with the Documents folder in SkyDrive selected.

5 Click the **File name** text box.

6 Type a name.

7 Click **Save**.

PowerPoint saves your presentation to SkyDrive.

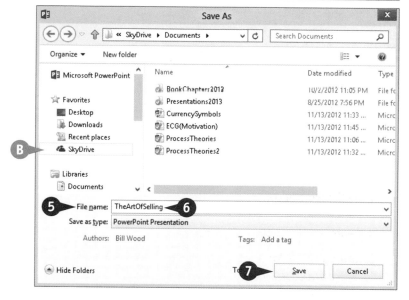

TIPS

I previously saved my presentation to my computer. Where is it now?

Just like any other Save As operation, you now have a presentation in both the original save location on your computer and SkyDrive. If you want people to see changes that you make, you need to make the changes to the presentation in the SkyDrive location.

Now that I saved the presentation to SkyDrive, how do I get to it?

Double-click your user folder icon on your Desktop, and then look in your user folder (the user folder in the example in this section is named Bill Wood). The folder is named SkyDrive and the icon looks like two clouds. You can also click **SkyDrive** on your Windows 8 Start screen.

Share the Presentation with SkyDrive

People with permission to access your presentation on SkyDrive can edit or view the presentation with the PowerPoint application on their computer. They can also access the presentation with the PowerPoint Web App if they do not have Office 2013 on their computer. Sharing a presentation with SkyDrive sends an e-mail and link to people, and enables permission in SkyDrive for those people to access the file. You can also create a link to the presentation manually so you can copy and paste the link.

Share the Presentation with SkyDrive

Share via E-mail

Note: You must save the presentation to SkyDrive before sharing it.

1. Click the **File** tab to show Backstage view.

2. Click **Share**.

3. Click **Invite People**.

4. Click the text box and type recipients' e-mail addresses.

5. Click the **Permissions** down arrow (▼).

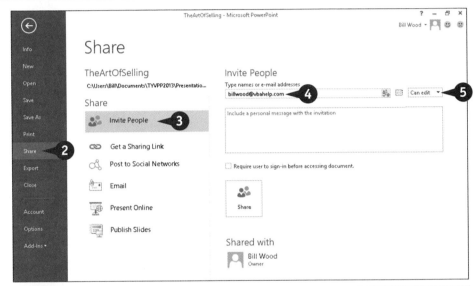

6. Click **Can edit** or **Can view**.

7. Click the text box and type a message to the recipients.

8. Click **Share**.

A. PowerPoint adds the recipients to the Shared list and sends them an e-mail with a link to SkyDrive.

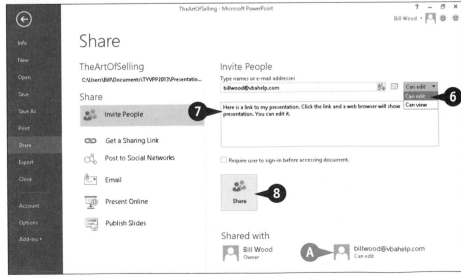

Share via a Link

Note: You must save the presentation to SkyDrive before creating a link.

1 Click the **File** tab to show Backstage view.

2 Click **Share**.

3 Click **Get a Sharing Link**.

4 Click **Create Link**.

B PowerPoint creates a link to the presentation on SkyDrive. You can copy and paste this link into a web browser to access the presentation. Note that there is a link for editing and a link for viewing.

Note: You can paste this link to a Word or Notepad document and put it on a network drive for people to access, or you can send it to someone in an instant message.

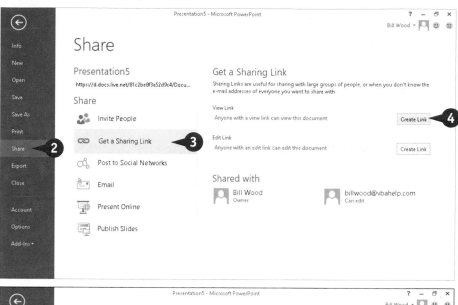

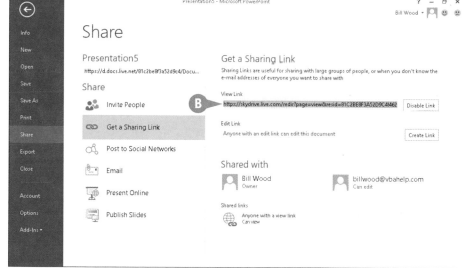

TIPS

When I click Invite People, a button appears that says Save to Cloud. What does this mean?

You have not yet saved the presentation to SkyDrive. Click **Save to Cloud** and the Save As screen appears. Then save the presentation to SkyDrive (for more information, see the section, "Save the Presentation to SkyDrive").

I want to give permission to edit to some people, and permission to view to others. Can I do that?

You can repeat Steps **2** to **8** for each person; in this case, you would need to do it twice. Repeat the process, but change the recipients, the message, and the choice in Step **6** from *Can edit* to **Can view**. Click **Share**, and PowerPoint adds those people with viewing permission.

Index

Index

N

O

Index